Register for Free Membership to

solutions@syngress.com

W9-ABX-926

Over the last few years, Syngress has published many best-selling and critically acclaimed books, including Tom Shinder's *Configuring ISA Server 2004*, Brian Caswell and Jay Beale's *Snort 2.1 Intrusion Detection*, and Angela Orebaugh and Gilbert Ramirez's *Ethereal Packet Sniffing*. One of the reasons for the success of these books has been our unique **solutions@syngress.com** program. Through this site, we've been able to provide readers a real time extension to the printed book.

As a registered owner of this book, you will qualify for free access to our members-only solutions@syngress.com program. Once you have registered, you will enjoy several benefits, including:

- Four downloadable e-booklets on topics related to the book. Each booklet is approximately 20-30 pages in Adobe PDF format. They have been selected by our editors from other best-selling Syngress books as providing topic coverage that is directly related to the coverage in this book.

- A comprehensive FAQ page that consolidates all of the key points of this book into an easy-to-search web page, providing you with the concise, easy-to-access data you need to perform your job.

- A "From the Author" Forum that allows the authors of this book to post timely updates and links to related sites, or additional topic coverage that may have been requested by readers.

Just visit us at **www.syngress.com/solutions** and follow the simple registration process. You will need to have this book with you when you register.

Thank you for giving us the opportunity to serve your needs. And be sure to let us know if there is anything else we can do to make your job easier.

SYNGRESS®

Security Log Management

Identifying Patterns in the Chaos

Jacob Babbin

Dave Kleiman

Dr. Everett F. (Skip) Carter, Jr.

Jeremy Faircloth

Mark Burnett

Esteban Gutierrez   Technical Editor

FOREWORD BY
GABRIELE GIUSEPPINI
DEVELOPER OF MICROSOFT LOG PARSER

KEY	SERIAL NUMBER
001	HJIRTCV764
002	PO9873D5FG
003	829KM8NJH2
004	HJL9823B6F
005	CVPLQ6WQ23
006	VBP965T5T5
007	HJJJ863WD3E
008	2987GVTWMK
009	629MP5SDJT
010	IMWQ295T6T

PUBLISHED BY
Syngress Publishing, Inc.
800 Hingham Street
Rockland, MA 02370

Security Log Management: Identifying Patterns in the Chaos

Printed in Canada
1 2 3 4 5 6 7 8 9 0
ISBN: 1-59749-042-3

Publisher: Andrew Williams
Acquisitions Editor: Gary Byrne
Technical Editor: Esteban Gutierrez
Cover Designer: Michael Kavish
Page Layout and Art: Patricia Lupien
Copy Editor: Beth Roberts
Indexer: Odessa&Cie

Distributed by O'Reilly Media, Inc. in the United States and Canada.
For information on rights, translations, and bulk purchases, contact Matt Pedersen, Director of Sales and Rights, at Syngress Publishing; email matt@syngress.com or fax to 781-681-3585.

Acknowledgments

Syngress would like to acknowledge the following people for their kindness and support in making this book possible.

Syngress books are now distributed in the United States and Canada by O'Reilly Media, Inc. The enthusiasm and work ethic at O'Reilly are incredible, and we would like to thank everyone there for their time and efforts to bring Syngress books to market: Tim O'Reilly, Laura Baldwin, Mark Brokering, Mike Leonard, Donna Selenko, Bonnie Sheehan, Cindy Davis, Grant Kikkert, Opol Matsutaro, Steve Hazelwood, Mark Wilson, Rick Brown, Tim Hinton, Kyle Hart, Sara Winge, Peter Pardo, Leslie Crandell, Regina Aggio Wilkinson, Pascal Honscher, Preston Paull, Susan Thompson, Bruce Stewart, Laura Schmier, Sue Willing, Mark Jacobsen, Betsy Waliszewski, Kathryn Barrett, John Chodacki, Rob Bullington, Kerry Beck, Karen Montgomery, and Patrick Dirden.

The incredibly hardworking team at Elsevier Science, including Jonathan Bunkell, Ian Seager, Duncan Enright, David Burton, Rosanna Ramacciotti, Robert Fairbrother, Miguel Sanchez, Klaus Beran, Emma Wyatt, Krista Leppiko, Marcel Koppes, Judy Chappell, Radek Janousek, Rosie Moss, David Lockley, Nicola Haden, Bill Kennedy, Martina Morris, Kai Wuerfl-Davidek, Christiane Leipersberger, Yvonne Grueneklee, Nadia Balavoine, and Chris Reinders for making certain that our vision remains worldwide in scope.

David Buckland, Marie Chieng, Lucy Chong, Leslie Lim, Audrey Gan, Pang Ai Hua, Joseph Chan, June Lim, and Siti Zuraidah Ahmad of Pansing Distributors for the enthusiasm with which they receive our books.

David Scott, Tricia Wilden, Marilla Burgess, Annette Scott, Andrew Swaffer, Stephen O'Donoghue, Bec Lowe, Mark Langley, and Anyo Geddes of Woodslane for distributing our books throughout Australia, New Zealand, Papua New Guinea, Fiji, Tonga, Solomon Islands, and the Cook Islands.

Lead Author

Jacob Babbin works as a contractor with a government agency filling the role of Intrusion Detection Team Lead. He has worked in both private industry as a security professional and in government space in a variety of IT security roles. He is a speaker at several IT security conferences and is a frequent assistant in SANS Security Essentials Bootcamp, Incident Handling, and Forensics courses. Jake lives in Virginia. Jake is coauthor of *Snort 2.1 Intrusion Detection Second Edition* (Syngress Publishing, ISBN: 1-931836-04-3), *Intrusion Detection and Active Response* (Syngress, ISBN: 1-932266-47-X), and *Snort Cookbook* (O'Reilly, ISBN: 0-596007-91-4).

Technical Editor

Esteban Gutierrez (CISSP) is currently an information security architect at a Fortune 100 company. He works on improving the security architecture of a global computing environment made up of massive amounts of data and tens of thousand of systems. In the past he has worked as a senior network security engineer for a ".mil" network as part of a global network operations and security center, where he focused on daily security operations involving IDS and firewall management, incident response and containment, policy guidance, and network architecture. He has also done security work in e-commerce environments during the "dot-com" boom and bust (Webvan), provided security for Internet service provider networks, and worked as a consultant. Esteban also has experience with Linux, Solaris, BSD, Cisco hardware, routing protocols, DNS, Apache, VPN, and wireless networking. His work, however, has focused primarily on network security architecture in large-scale enterprise networks.

He is most interested in being able to point at packet traces and pick out the "bad" traffic.

Esteban is a graduate of Reed College in Portland, OR. He makes his home in the Pacific Northwest with his wife and daughter.

Contributing Authors

Jeremy Faircloth (Security+, CCNA, MCSE, MCP+I, A+) is an IT Manager for EchoStar Satellite, L.L.C., where he and his team architect and maintain enterprise-wide client/server and Web-based technologies. He also acts as a technical resource for other IT professionals, using his expertise to help others expand their knowledge. As a systems engineer with more than 14 years of real-world IT experience, he has become an expert in many areas, including Web development, database administration, enterprise security, network design, and project management. Jeremy has contributed to several popular Syngress technical books, including *Snort 2.0 Intrusion Detection* (ISBN: 1-931836-74-4), *Security+ Study Guide & DVD Training System* (ISBN: 1-931836-72-8), *Microsoft Log Parser Toolkit* (ISBN: 1-932266-52-6), and *SSCP Study Guide & DVD Training System* (ISBN: 1-931836-80-9).

Dr. Everett F. (Skip) Carter, Jr is President of Taygeta Network Security Services (a division of Taygeta Scientific Inc.). Taygeta Scientific Inc. provides contract and consulting services in the areas of scientific computing, smart instrumentation, and specialized data analysis. Taygeta Network Security Services provides security services for real-time firewall and IDS management and monitoring, passive network traffic analysis audits, external security reviews, forensics, and incident investigation.

Skip holds a Ph.D. and an M.S. in Applied Physics from Harvard University. In addition, he holds two Bachelor of Science degrees

(Physics and Geophysics) from the Massachusetts Institute of Technology. Skip is a member of the American Society for Industrial Security (ASIS). He was contributing author of Syngress Publishing's book, *Hack Proofing XML* (ISBN: 1-931836-50-7). He has authored several articles for *Dr. Dobbs Journal* and *Computer Language,* as well as numerous scientific papers and is a former columnist for *Forth Dimensions* magazine. Skip resides in Monterey, CA, with his wife, Trace, and his son, Rhett.

Dave Kleiman (CAS, CCE, CIFI, CISM, CISSP, ISSAP, ISSMP, MCSE) has worked in the Information Technology Security sector since 1990. Currently, he is the owner of SecurityBreach Response.com, and is the Chief Information Security Officer for Securit-e-Doc, Inc. Before starting this position, he was Vice President of Technical Operations at Intelliswitch, Inc., where he supervised an international telecommunications and Internet service provider network. Dave is a recognized security expert. A former Florida Certified Law Enforcement Officer, he specializes in computer forensic investigations, incident response, intrusion analysis, security audits, and secure network infrastructures. He has written several secure installation and configuration guides about Microsoft technologies that are used by network professionals. He has developed a Windows Operating System lockdown tool, S-Lok (www.s-doc.com/products/slok.asp), which surpasses NSA, NIST, and Microsoft Common Criteria Guidelines. Dave was a contributing author to *Microsoft Log Parser Toolkit* (Syngress Publishing, ISBN: 1-932266-52-6). He is frequently a speaker at many national security conferences and is a regular contributor to many security-related newsletters, Web sites, and Internet forums. Dave is a member of several organizations, including the International Association of Counter Terrorism and Security Professionals (IACSP), International Society of Forensic Computer Examiners® (ISFCE), Information Systems Audit and Control Association® (ISACA), High Technology Crime Investigation Association (HTCIA), Network and Systems Professionals Association (NaSPA), Association of Certified Fraud

Examiners (ACFE), Anti Terrorism Accreditation Board (ATAB), and ASIS International®. He is also a Secure Member and Sector Chief for Information Technology at The FBI's InfraGard® and a Member and Director of Education at the International Information Systems Forensics Association (IISFA).

Additional Contributors

Gabriele Giuseppini is a Software Design Engineer at Microsoft Corporation in the Security Business Unit, where he developed Microsoft Log Parser to analyze log files.

Originally from Rome, Italy, after working for years in the digital signal processing field, he moved to the United States with his family in 1999, and joined Microsoft Corporation as a Software Design Engineer working on Microsoft Internet Information Services.

Mark Burnett is an independent researcher, consultant, and writer specializing in Windows security. Mark is author of *Hacking the Code: ASP.NET Web Application Security* (Syngress Publishing, ISBN: 1-932266-65-8), co-author of *Microsoft Log Parser Toolkit* (Syngress Publishing, ISBN: 1-932266-52-6), co-author of *Maximum Windows 2000 Security*, and co-author of *Stealing The Network: How to Own the Box* (Syngress Publishing, ISBN: 1-931836-87-6). He is a contributor and technical editor for Syngress Publishing's *Special Ops: Host and Network Security for Microsoft, UNIX, and Oracle* (ISBN: 1-931836-69-8). Mark speaks at various security conferences and has published articles in Windows IT Pro Magazine (formerly Windows & .NET Magazine), WindowsSecrets.com newsletter, Redmond Magazine, Security Administrator, SecurityFocus.com, and various other print and online publications. Mark is a Microsoft Windows Server Most Valued Professional (MVP) for Internet Information Services (IIS).

Contents

Foreword

Logs, logs, logs. Ever since I started taking my first steps in the world of security, it has been clear that "the log" plays a crucial—and sometimes under-valued—role in the security management of any IT infrastructure. This fact alone explains the plethora of tools, applications, and solutions whose only purpose is to generate, analyze, and report on logs. Entire software companies were built on nothing but a few valid ideas on how to analyze logs or how to process and aggregate information coming from different logs. I myself spent a great deal of time in this field while developing the Microsoft Log Parser tool to tackle some of these problems.

Despite the proliferation of log-generating, processing, and reporting tools, and partially *because* of it, however, obtaining something useful from "the log" is still a somewhat obscure, complicated, and confusing wizardry, caused by, I believe, the fact that computers are still far from being as smart as we wish they'd be. Wouldn't it be nice if your security sensors told you immediately what's going on as an event was happening, rather than generate a huge log of seemingly worthless data? Wouldn't it be wonderful if you could instruct your Web servers to show you a trend related to a variable over the past 10 weeks rather than have to retrieve, correlate, and aggregate gigabytes and gigabytes of log files?

Unfortunately, that's not the case—yet—with the current state of software engineering. Most of the time, the developer of an IDS can't come up—right-fully so—with a list of all the possible questions you might want to ask the IDS in the future, so the solution is simple: let's log everything, and when users come up with new questions, they can go back to the archive and ask the question directly to "the log." This is especially true in the world of security, where in most cases a single "event" can not be deemed of security importance unless correlated with other "events" occurring at other key places in your network.

In these times of cheap storage and increased processing power and net-work traffic, however, asking a question to "the log" becomes more and more similar to executing a data-mining query. Most of the times "the log" *does* contain the answers you are looking for, but they're buried under countless useless entries, and scattered across innumerable, heterogeneous log files; as Jake Babbin, the lead author of this book, elegantly puts it, the answers you are looking for are *patterns in chaos*. And the news is that someone has to find those patterns. And it might be you.

The purpose of this book is to show you exactly how to do that, at the same time tackling all the various problems pertinent to log generation, storage, processing, and reporting.

Once the right security sensors are in the right places, Jake shows you how to generate reports that both provide management with the data needed to evaluate the ROI of your security infrastructure, while simultaneously feeding vital data to your security staff. The information that needs to be analyzed in these processes comes from different sources (e.g., intrusion detection systems, firewalls, Web servers) and different platforms. As a result, the logs generated by these sources are formatted in different ways and contain different information. Still, Jake manages to provide a unified view of this Babel of logs, showing you how to overcome the inherent "language barriers" with both commercial and low-cost solutions.

In addition, you will find that these solutions are discussed in true Syngress style, with real-world examples and working scripts developed. They're also used in production systems by the author and his staff.

Whether or not you are the one charged with asking questions to "the log," after reading this book, you will agree that finding the *patterns in chaos* is actually not as daunting as you would have believed, and that creative solutions like the ones adopted by Jake will go a long way in making your job, and your quest, easier.

—*Gabriele Giuseppini*
Developer of Microsoft Log Parser
Security Business Unit, Microsoft Corporation

Companion Web Site

Much of the code presented throughout this book is available for download from **www.syngress.com/solutions**. Look for the Syngress icon in the margins indicating which examples are available from the companion Web site.

www.syngress.com

## Chapter 1

Log Analysis:
Overall Issues

Solutions in this chapter:

- **IT Budgets and Results: Leveraging OSS Solutions at Little Cost**

- **Reporting Security Information to Management**

- **Combining Resources for an "Eye-in-the-Sky" View**

- **Blended Threats and Reporting**

- **Code Solutions**

- **Commercial Solutions: ArcSight and Netforensics**

☑ **Summary**

☑ **Solutions Fast Track**

☑ **Frequently Asked Questions**

Introduction

One of the first complaints heard in most security shops is, "there is too much data to look at," and finding out what all the different security "widgets" mean can be very confusing. For example, with reports coming from firewalls, IDS/IPS, AV, policy, and other sources, finding the information pertinent to your network health and wellness is a challenge to say the least. For the technical members of a security staff who live and breathe in the trenches, this is part of your daily battle assessment. As the technical eyes and ears of an organization, you need to be able to communicate useful and meaningful data up the chain to your management and to their management. However, as most management staffs are not network/security engineers/analysts, the technical details of daily operations are beyond the realm of their need to know. The security team provides reliable evidence of threats and attacks to management so they can make educated decisions on network issues. Finally, if security teams can present a balanced and flexible view into network events and changes, they can help save budgets and provide a useful and continuous return on investment (ROI) for the tools and hardware needed to do their jobs.

IT Budgets and Results: Leveraging OSS Solutions at Little Cost

The biggest issues we hear about security groups within organizations include:

- The security budget for tools and hardware is shrinking or nonexistent.

- Upper management is bombarded with vendors trying to sell another security "widget" that can replace everything they currently use.

- All of the good solutions cost money and there are no funds available.

- Open source is not an option because no one in house understands it.

- Most organizations don't have a complete programming/development staff on hand to leverage a custom open source solution.

For example, we were brought in to an organization to set up a security shop. This client had never really had much in the way of a functioning security organization so they were reluctant to create a new budget item for the "security" projects. Therefore, all of the solutions had to be free or low cost, and provide some deliverable(s) that the client hadn't seen before that would give them insightful information about their network(s). The first set of solutions, some of which are still in place today, were all using open source software on machines that were to be inventoried out of commission.

Our first order of business was to set up a working IDS shop to help us provide visibility and understanding about the client network(s). The client already had commercial intrusion detection systems (IDSes) that hadn't been tuned or upgraded for years, and were spewing out garbage. Our solution was to deploy several snort sensors sniffing at key locations around the network(s). Our security engineering (SE) team, consisting of network engineers with backgrounds in security disciplines such as router access control lists (ACLs), firewall rulesets, and secure network design, decided to implement P-SPAN at the key locations. P-SPAN allows a mirrored port on a switch or router to be shared across multiple switch ports. In our case, it allowed our SEs to provide our IDS sensors with the same view of sniffed traffic across eight switch ports. For example, at our inside the firewall span we put a snort sensor, an ISS sensor, a dragon sensor, a Cisco NAM (Network Analysis Module), and four other devices all seeing the same traffic. With this multisensor at each key location setup, we were able to set up new snort sensors that would see the same set of traffic as the commercial IDS.

However, the P-SPAN solution can get very messy in larger organizations. Another solution that can be used on a wider variety of Cisco devices is SPAN, which allows for a one-to-many mirrors setup while taking up less load on the spanning switch/router. SPAN ports are often used for edge or slower links to perform a one-to-one mirror of smaller segments.

Lastly, in larger organizations R-SPAN (Remote Spanning) is the most common choice due to the ease of pushing mirrored data across the organization's network. One of the most common uses of R-SPANing is in organizations that have a "security VLAN" where all security data is centralized from all over the infrastructure. R-SPAN allows a Cisco device to forward mirrored traffic to a switch or VLAN on a different switch than the spanning switch. However, when implementing an R-SPAN solution, you must plan your infrastructure carefully.

Are You 0wned?

Do You Know What Those IDS Alarms Mean?

Imagine our surprise hours after standing up our new sensors when the unconfigured commercial IDS started spewing out "ICMP ECHO" alarms at a rate that most spammers would have been proud of! All of these alarms had packet sizes of 92 bytes and consisted of all "a" in the payload. Not surprising to us, the new security team members, the signature was the characteristic of the then recent Nachi worm. We immediately turned to our new snort sensors that were rapidly identifying the traffic not as low-priority ICMP PING traffic but as hostile high-priority Nachi broadcast traffic. In our first proof of ROI, our sensors were able to provide a graphical view of the attack vector and attack victims. This data was then transformed into an ACL to be placed at all network chock points to contain the worm, while identifying new victims as they attempted to spread.

With these new sensors and the ability to have more than one IDS at each key location at little or no cost to the client, we were able to provide them with a new service. In addition to having enough span points at each location for a multiplatform view into network traffic, our solution allowed enough monitoring taps for network operations to use their own network management tools at those locations.

As this was a new security shop, several other aspects of information assurance came to bear, such as incident response and management. As network events and incidents were investigated, a record of the events and resulting information needed to be kept as well. We were sure that eventually, when funding was available, an official tool would be approved. However, in the meantime, since results had to be shown, we started using an open-source ticketing and reporting tool called elog. This tool comes blank with any example "logbook," which we used to create two basic logbooks—one for IDS events and news, and one for Computer Incident Response Team (CIRT) data from cases. We liked this tool for the multi-user access as well for writing out to time-stamped text files. These files could then be queried by other scripts for, say, the last update to a case or for insertion into an Enterprise Security Manager ticketing system for concise log aggregation.

The last task of the new security shop was to create and help monitor the firewalls and their data streams. Several of our SEs were familiar with iptables and ipchains, so they quickly set up our sensor network on a semi-out-of-band network to protect it from attack and to provide a separation of the sensors and support devices from the rest of network. Then, as the data streams from the firewalls were starting to be fed down to their devices in the security network, our SEs needed a firewall log aggregator and reporting tool. They turned to another open-source tool to provide a queued look at the events per hour in a dynamically updating Web page.

By now, we're sure you are wondering how all of these devices and software were supposed to interact. The better question is, how and what do you provide up the chain to your management from all of these devices and systems?

Reporting Security Information to Management

One of the key problems for most security shops is clearly communicating up the chain of command information that is important to a site's operation. For example, outside a security staff's direct line of management, other managers are not likely to understand threat information or even the differences in products to approve or disprove for use on a network. If a security team cannot come up with simple and easy to understand external reporting methodologies, they will be drowned out by other slicker voices such as the vendor of the day/hour.

As a new security shop being set up, and most of us having come from a large client site where security's input into almost every project and change was required, we had to make sure that the new shop was set up to foster this idea. One of the first examples we found useful was the idea of a short incident report, or white paper. These "white papers" were to be a quick summary of an event after most of the facts had been established, and were used to provide nontechnical management with a quick, repeatable information disclosure of the event, the facts as known, and the teams responding to the event. While it is yet another deliverable to create for every incident, a smart security manager will realize that doing so will take some heat off the security teams to dig into an event without having upper management "hawking" over the security staff. It will also provide upper management with the comfort that your team can handle every event in a thorough, precise manner.

As the white paper idea is great for a quick response during incident reporting, an after-action report is then needed. Reporting is different for each type of company and industry, so details of that report will be unique to your agency or organization.

These reports and others are some of what is needed to help a security team communicate with management.

Example of an Incident Report: IDS Case No. 123, 5 September 2005

```
Background:
At 10:34 AM the event "WEB-CLIENT Microsoft ANI file parsing overflow" entered
the IDS event monitors. Upon searching through the IDS logs no  further
events have identified a successful attack by this site. As well the host-
based Anti-Virus solution seem to have killed 3 hostile files per each
victim. At this time only two client IPs seem to have gone to the hostile
site, exposing them to the hostile code. The attack vector seems to be from
a banner rotation script on "hostilesite.com". The victims seem to have been
browsing another site (unknown at this time) when a banner rotation script
displayed the hostile banner (inst/AD_rotator.php) which had a browser check
script that called (msits.htm) when a vulnerable IE browser was found using
(test.php). This then seems to have called (infect.html) to load a java jar
file (archive.jar) that exploited the .ani file parsing with (infect.anr) most
likely hiding the ani with anr from signature scanners. Lastly upon
successful victimization it broadcasts it with (our.htm) that is killed by
our Host Anti-Virus solution. A last note is source viewing is unable to
happen once the javascript is decoded. This is due to the hostile site using
a session key that is unique per each connection.
```

Also appended to this report is the details of each file found in the investigation, in addition to all other detailed IDS logs related to this case being placed in the case folder.

This vulnerability (MS05-002) is a file type parsing bug in Internet Explorer. More information about this can be found here. http://www.securiteam.com/windowsntfocus/5YP0F0KEKK.html

Timeline:

10:30am - Victim 1 browses the site "classmates.com" when a banner rotation script (inst/AD_rotator.php) from an outside site (xxx.com) performs a browser check. Checking if you are running Internet Explorer using the exploit checking script (msits.htm), if so then it runs (test.php) that determines if the host is vulnerable to the MS04-013 (MS-ITS exploit).

10:31am - Victim 1 has been determined to be vulnerable so it launches (infect.html) that launches 2 seperate attacks at once.
- Runs a hostile java jar file called (archive.jar) that uses IE's implict trust to run java completely on the client machine.
- Runs a renamed ".ani" cursor file called (infect.anr) that attempts to load a hostile executable from another site.
- Lastly upon sucessful takeover it sends a notification to another site using (our.htm) which has a tag for the victim's IP to be recorded.

10:32am - Host-based Anti-Virus reported successful deletion of the web page in temp files, the archive.jar, and the infect.anr file.

12:10pm - Victim 2 browses the same site "classmates.com" and gets the same results as victim 1.

1:00pm - Both events are tied to the same site by CIRT team. After investigation the site owner will be contacted. While the IDS events will be closely monitored for other users browsing to the hostile site and a recommended IP address block will be implemented for all network communications to this netblock.

1:05pm - Closed IDS and CIRT cases.

Personnel involved:

Stan Smith - IDS Analyst

Peter Griffin - CIRT Analyst

File details:

our.htm - it turns out that this file generates a javascript file that mcafee detects as "JS/Exploit-BO.gen" so the risk of spread is mitigated.

infect.anr - is indeed a ani file that tries to call the file "start.exe" from the host "http://www.HOSTILESITE.com/1qswr45/start.exe". The file "start.exe has been submitted for analysis with a virus sandbox test and the results are below.

archive.jar - unknown at this time

infect.html - simply follows the file parsing to load the "cursor" infect.anr...the exploit. "{CURSOR: url("ifect.anr")}"

test.php - simple blank page, used for testing the browser type

msits.htm - checks if you are also vulnerable to the ITS exploit through writing a file "Bao.htm" to your C:\ path.

-----Norman AV sandbox information ------------------------
start.exe : [SANDBOX] contains a security risk - W32/Downloader (Signature: W32/DLoader.DZI)   [General information]
* File might be compressed.
* File length: 1669 bytes.

[Changes to filesystem]
* Deletes file c:\LF00!.exe.
* Creates file C:\LF00!.exe.
* Creates file C:\p!0!.

[Network services]
* Looks for an Internet connection.
* Downloads file from http://www.HOSTILESITE.com/statpath/inr.gif as c:\LF00!.exe.
* Downloads file from http://www.HOSTILESITE2.cc/cnt/erun?{10001} as c:\p!0!.

[Security issues]
* Starting downloaded file - potential security problem.

[Process/window information]
* Creates a mutex arx5.

While the amount of detail in the preceding report seems excessive for just one incident, it will prove invaluable if you have an incident that involves an organization outside your own or even your own law enforcement team. However, if that day ever comes or if an event reaches upper management's level, you will most likely have to provide them with answers quickly. One method is to produce a quick one-page report that covers the high-level overview of the incident in question. This report should be easily distributed and understood among C-level management. It can even be made into a template if you constantly have to explain to management the details of an incident.

Combining Resources for an "Eye-in-the-Sky" View

As your security team begins to build its processes and procedures, upper management might keep popping in to show off their prize security teams. Most upper management is going to expect to see flashy screens with lots of blinking green buttons. Red buttons will attract many questions and even more "attention"… just a word to the wise.

In setting up our new security shop, our first sets of reports were filled with mostly tables and raw text fields, had no graphics, and were based on the need to produce some type of daily and weekly reports. The first problem this solved for us was the ability to create repeatable documentation of network events and security status.

One problem with the reports was that they were all coming from different platforms and technologies. For example, snort events were being created from BASE/ACID graphics by hand, ISS event summaries were copied from Site Protector boxes, and tcpdump data was being generated by tcpdstat and rrdtool, all of which then had to be combined to provide any type of overall security status view.

One goal of our reporting infrastructure was to make it as platform independent as possible, such as a Web-based platform. The idea behind this was twofold: First, security consoles that were dependent on a specific platform in order to view our security data were limited or cut out. One specific example would be the ISS Site Protector console, which requires Windows, a specific version of the Java runtime environment, and several ports open between the consoles and the database backend. This solution may work if your analysts always use the same machines in the same environment consistently. However, if you have ever had to think about a disaster recovery plan or COOP, having a security console that is heavily dependent on certain applications won't fly. For example, to continue using ISS as an example, the new Site Protector has an SSL-enabled Web console that only requires one port for access to the same functionality of the Windows console. This Web client can then be easily used from a disaster recovery/Continuity of Operations/remote site without having to worry about having any extra dependencies other than a working Web browser!

Our second reason for being platform independent was that Web-based platforms could be easily displayed and updated. This can be a simple display of data, but when upper management or other groups come to check out the security shop, they can see the information. As this information is displayed in Web format, almost every application in use can be tuned to output information in a Web format. Some of the examples you will be shown are simply raw text files that are parsed via scripts to create graphics of network data.

By leveraging the platform-independent and browser-based reporting infrastructure you also gain the ability to limit data access and need to know. For example, if you require a username and password to access the security "portal," you can limit what accounts have access to what directories. Moreover, if you are proficient enough, you can create custom "views" at login for each type of user or a user list. In the current environment, a simple "portal" view of events from most of our IDS applications (not all yet) is used by our IDS analysts to give them a global view of events and up-to-date information as can be seen in Figure 1.1.

Figure 1.1 A Light Portal Page

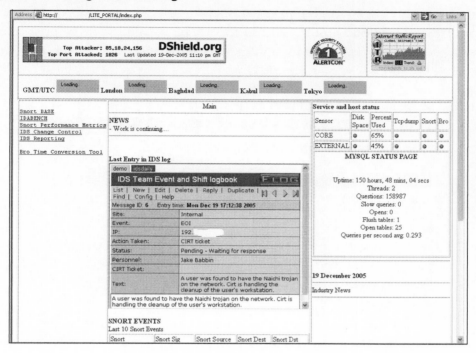

However, for our management reporting we created a "daily report" Web page. This page is where most of the raw IDS data is searched and graphed into meaningful information. This "daily report" can then serve as the main page that management will view for information about security events on their network(s), or provide a "buffet" for information to be combined into other reports. For example, if you needed to create a DNS report, you could copy the graphics and tables out if needed to another report; for example, in a network utilization report from another team. The DNS report could be something as simple as several tables of data, such as the top 10 DNS queries, the breakdown by geo-location, or ".com/.net/.org" domain breakdowns. The idea to keep in mind is that you can change these to be more useful depending on the feedback you get from version .001 of this report. For example, if you are a hosting company, you might be more interested in geo-location and top 10 queries, as these will help in capacity planning. A more globally facing organization would be more interested the geo-location data and the domain breakdowns to help understand where malware and possible attackers are coming from. Another option would be to create a menu of the most commonly accessed graphics and label them as "DNS report," Malware report," "Network load report," and so forth. These could then be preloaded templates that when requested would generate the most up-to-date information graphics and tables (see Figure 1.2).

Figure 1.2 New Preloaded Report Page Menu

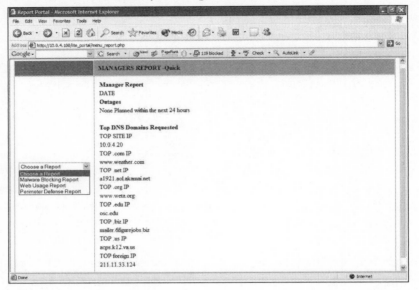

When this information is combined into a "status" page such as Figure 1.2, it can be used as a quick and dirty ESM page. With filtering of events and signatures, an auto-updating view of the highest priority events and event changes can keep up on everything from unused machines to larger "show and tell" displays in the form of a screensaver. Several commercial tools allow you to create a screensaver from a Web page, and there are even some creative JavaScript examples floating around on Google that will create a screensaver in the browser.

Blended Threats and Reporting

Malware has slowly risen to the top of most organizations' concern lists. A recent report by the group mi2g calculates the cost of malware "[sic] at around 600 million Windows-based computers worldwide, which works out to $281 to $340 worth of damage per machine." This works out to several billion dollars in lost revenue for companies worldwide. This type of software can bring in Trojans and viruses, open backdoors, and report your users' browsing preferences to hostile and foreign sites. According to Wikipedia.org, "Malware (a portmanteau of "malicious software") is a software program designed to fulfill any purpose contrary to the interests of the person running it. Examples of malware include viruses and trojan horses. Malware can be classified based on how it is executed, how it spreads, and/or what it does."

Are You 0wned?

How Bad Can Clicking on That One Link Be?

In a recent case, a user triggered a series of alarms in a matter of seconds even across multiple IDS platforms. When we started investigating the events, we quickly realized that the user on our network had been duped into searching on a malicious search page with what could have been disastrous results had the user's machine not been patched. As an exercise in demonstrating the effects of malware, we decided to see how much damage a single click could be…boy, were we in for a surprise! After several hours of sniffing, and following links on pages, we came back with what could have happened if the user wasn't patched. Figure 1.3 outlines the path of destruction that would have been completed in four to five minutes.

    The end score:
    Domains Used: 3
    IPs Used: 7
    Malware file: 13
    Exploits used: 5

Figure 1.3 Malware Path of Destruction

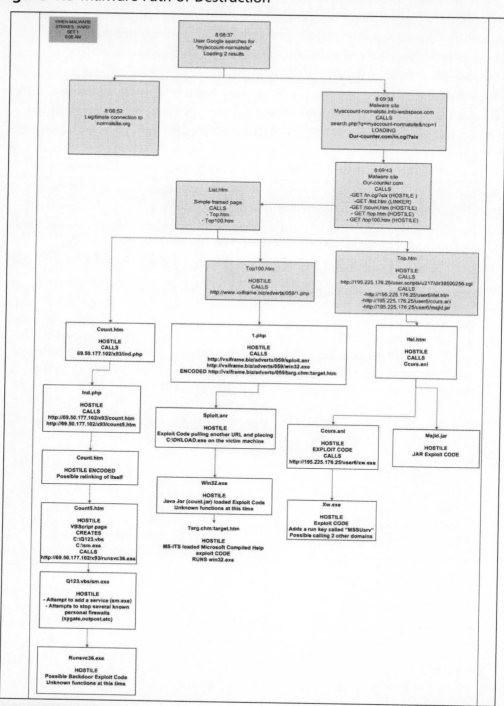

As malware is such a prevalent issue with most organizations, our SEs began to form an idea for how to stop the malware we were aware of and stop traffic to domains we knew were bad. Our solution was to simply "poison" our DNS server with master zones for these hostile domains, and then redirect these now harmless domain requests to a message server that would simply display a "sorry due to policy you have hit a site that is known bad Complaints contact helpdesk" message for every request. These requests and the offenders are logged via IDS logging of DNS sessions and through HTTP requests to the malware server. To display the effectiveness of our malware blocks, we simply comb through the malware logs with Awstats to generate a Web page with loads of charts and graphs to display to management. This page when combined with several charts generated from IDS data can be put into a report for management of the daily effectiveness of the malware blocks. However, we usually simply use the graph in Figure 1.4 to show the number of DNS malware domain requests versus the number of valid DNS requests.

Figure 1.4 Bro Malware

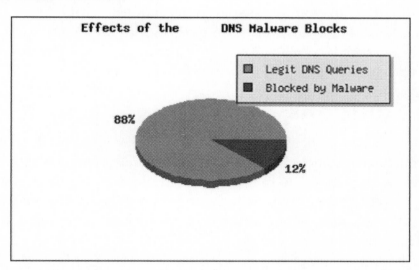

When this data was combined with the CIRT counts of the number of cases over time, we clearly showed a direct correlation between malware and security events. In the specific example after the malware blocks were put in place, the number of CIRT cases being opened dropped steadily. While using the IDS event counts before and after the blocks were put in place, the number of malware and hostile events dropped significantly.

Conclusion

When trying to combine security events from multiple platforms and technologies, the need to create a central repository for these logs becomes apparent. Another requirement is the need to report useful and meaningful data to upper management and other business units. A security organization that fails to report well and often will either go out of business or find budget and political hurdles in place when they need assistance. In addition, if your security organization is trying to figure out what to report on, simply start reporting something such as multiple top 10 lists with a request for feedback. You will find that once your client or organization heads see version .001, they will request one change after the next until you have a format that is meaningful to your organization. Moreover, providing a high-level and technical report of data per incident will help document systematic issues with the network or users. In addition, management will come to expect answers to questions once the situation has been identified, not beforehand...

Finally, if you can provide a platform-independent "view" into security events and cases such as a "status Web page," management will feel that your security organization is performing its duties.

Code Solutions

The examples presented here are drop-in solutions that are dependent on how you implement some of the solutions in subsequent chapters. However, they will work enough so you can see if they would work in your organization. After each example graphic is the code behind it, heavily commented to help give you some ideas of how and where you might want to tweak the code to better suit your organization.

Bird's-Eye View for Management: HTML

As mentioned in the previous section, a high-level view of the information that is clear and concise is needed to enable your management and above to understand the threats facing their network(s). The solution we have been trying with some success is the report-oriented format shown in Figure 1.5.

Figure 1.5 Manager View

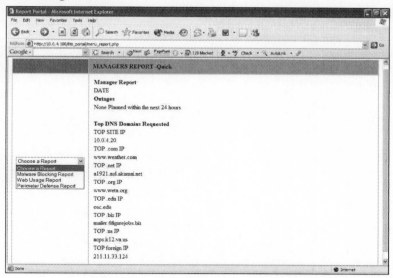

The following is the code needed to create the Managers View in HTML and PHP. However, in this example we have added the table of DNS information manually. In later chapters, we will cover how to "pull" the data dynamically from other files.

```
################ manager_main.php ##################
# This is the file that displays the above example
# Comments are displayed inline to the code
# HTML comments are "<!--Comment -->"
# While the PHP coments are "// "
<HTML>

<HEAD> <TITLE> Report Portal </TITLE>
<SCRIPT TYPE="text/javascript">
<!--This is a javascript function that creates the opening of a new html
window when the user -->
<!--Clicks on the "GO" Button -->
function dropdown(mySel)
{
var myWin, myVal;
myVal = mySel.options[mySel.selectedIndex].value;
```

```
if(myVal)
    {
    if(mySel.form.target)myWin = parent[mySel.form.target];
    else myWin = window;
    if (! myWin) return true;
    myWin.location = myVal;
    }
return false;
}
//-->
</SCRIPT>
</HEAD>
<?php
// This could have been done with just html but…
// This creates an HTML table that has 2 columns with a bluish color
 echo '<table cols="2" border="1" cellpadding="10" cellspacing="0"
align="center" width="100%" ';
 echo '<TR><td width=15% bgcolor="#0099FF" valign="top">';
 echo '</td>' ;
   echo '<td width=65% valign="top" bgcolor="#33CCFF">';
   echo '<B> MANAGERS REPORT -Quick </B></TD></TR>';
echo '<TR><TD>';
// This is using the javascript above in the HTML HEAD space to complete our
forms' actions
?>
<FORM
     ACTION="http://10.0.4.100/lite_portal/litestatus.php"
     METHOD=POST onSubmit="return dropdown(this.gourl)">
<SELECT NAME="gourl">
<OPTION VALUE="">Choose a Report


<OPTION VALUE="http://10.0.4.100/lite_portal/reports/malware.php" >Malware
Blocking Report
<OPTION VALUE="http://10.0.4.100/lite_portal/reports/webusage.php" >Web
Usage Report
<OPTION VALUE="http://10.0.4.100/lite_portal/reports/perimeter.php"
>Perimeter Defense Report
<!--Feel free to add more links to this as you preload more information into
prepared reports -- >
</SELECT>
```

```
<INPUT TYPE=SUBMIT VALUE="Go">
</FORM>

<?php
 echo '</td>';
// This table is filled with static information however with some simple php
scripting you could
// very easily take dynamic data read from a file and put it in an array to
create
// EXAMPLE
// echo '<TR><TD> Top SITE IP </TD></TR>';
// echo '<TR><TD>'; print_r($Top_DNS[2]); </TD></TR>';
// Repeating for each value in the file

echo '<TD>';
echo '<TABLE border=0 width=100% ><TR><TD>  <B> Manager Report
</B></TD></TR>';
echo '<TR><TD> DATE </TD></TR>';
echo '<TR><TD><B> Outages </B> </TD></TR>';
echo '<TR><TD>None Planned within the next 24 hours </TD></TR>';
echo '<TR><TD> <BR> </TD></TR>';
echo '<TR><TD><B> Top DNS Domains Requested </B><BR> </TD></TR>';
echo '<TR><TD>TOP SITE IP  </TD></TR>';
echo '<TR><TD>10.0.4.20</TD></TR>';
echo '<TR><TD>TOP .com IP </TD></TR>';
echo '<TR><TD>www.weather.com </TD></TR>';
echo '<TR><TD>TOP .net IP </TD></TR>';
echo '<TR><TD>a1921.aol.akamai.net</TD></TR>';
echo '<TR><TD>TOP .org IP </TD></TR>';
echo '<TR><TD>www.weta.org</TD></TR>';
echo '<TR><TD>TOP .edu IP </TD></TR>';
echo '<TR><TD>osc.edu</TD></TR>';
echo '<TR><TD>TOP .biz IP </TD></TR>';
echo '<TR><TD>mailer.6figurejobs.biz</TD></TR>';
echo '<TR><TD>TOP .us IP </TD></TR>';
echo '<TR><TD>acps.k12.va.us</TD></TR>';
echo '<TR><TD>TOP foreign IP</TD></TR>';
echo '<TR><TD>211.11.33.124 </TD></TR>';
```

```
echo '</table>';
echo ' </td></TR>';
echo '</table>';

?>

    ################## <Report Name> Report.php ####################
# This basic example can be used to create a preloaded report with your
# data that you want displayed via graphics and tables
# This example uses static ".png" graphics but the graphics are generated
# from dynamic data once a day. See Chapter 2 IDS solutions for the details
# of the dynamic graphic generation
# I keep sticking to using HTML tables because you can nest them to create
# very detailed layout. Also they are easier to template then trying to use
# something fancy to format.
<?php

echo '<CENTER> <B> Malware Blocking Information </B></CENTER>';
echo '<table>';
echo '<TR><TD><img src=dns_malware.png></img></TD>';
echo '<TD><img src=dns_malware_breakdown.png></img></TD></TR>';
echo '</Table>';
?>
```

Birds-Eye View for Security Teams: HTML

For our security teams, we have come up with a "status" page for them to use
as a central point for events, news, and client site information. For our IDS
team, we have to come up with a single Web page that can provide them
with this information. The page in its format today can query events in
MySQL databases, provide status information from the sensors and their processes, provide outside status from USCERT, ISS, and SANS, and query events
from other IDS platforms through searching flat files with word pattern
searches (see Figure 1.6).

Figure 1.6 A Light Status IDS Example

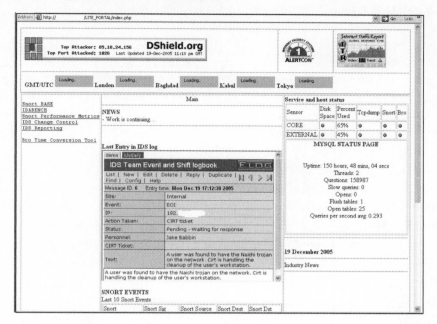

Again, the following is the code needed to create the framework. The difference is that because almost every component of the framework is dynamically loading, we have placed examples of each component in one or more of the included code pages. For example, the tables found on the main page are actually dynamic MySQL queries from the snort BASE setup, while the sensor status is done with a php "exec" function call.

```
############### index.php ############################
# This is the page generated above with most of the database calls
# commented out but still there for notes


    <HTML>


<table cols=3 border=1 cellpadding=10 align=center width=100% >
 <tr><TD>
<?php  include('header.html'); ?>
</TD></tr>
<TR><TD colspan=3>
   <table border=1 width=100% colspan=3>
```

```
    <tr>
      <td width=15% bgcolor="#0099FF" valign="top">
       <?php include('navbar.html'); ?>
      </td>
      <td width=65% valign="top" bgcolor="#33CCFF">
       <?php include ('actualindex.html'); ?>
      </td>
      <td width=20% valign=top>
       <?php include 'feeds.php' ; ?>
      </td>
   </tr>
     </table>
</TD></TR>
<TR><TD colspan=3>
 <?php include ('footer.html'); ?>
</TD></TR>
</TABLE>


</HTML>


##################### Navbar.html #########################
# Again some code either taken out or commented out
<HTML>
<PRE>
<dl>
<dt><A HREF="http://10.0.1.100/base/" target="_blank">Snort BASE</a></dt>
 <dt><A HREF="http://10.0.1.6/idabench/" target="_blank">IDABENCH</A></dt>
<dt><A HREF="http://10.0.1.100/snortperf/" target="_blank">Snort Performance
Metrics</A></dt>
<dt><A HREF="http://10.0.4.100/websvn/" target="_blank">IDS Change
Control</A></dt>
<dt><A HREF="http://10.0.1.100/idsdaily/" target="_blank">IDS
Reporting</A></dt>
<!--- If you have this company's tools enable below
<dt><A HREF="http://10.0.1.10:3994/siteprotector" target="_blank">ISS Web
Frontend</A></dt> -- >
<dt><A HREF="http://10.0.1.100/timeconvert.php" target="_blank">Bro Time
Conversion Tool</A></dt>


</dl>
```

```
</PRE>
</HTML>

###################### Actualindex.html ####################
# This file is where most of the team notifications and hot items
# should be published
# As well where some of the secondary loggging can be reported such
# as the argus data, bro "hot" IP's or keywords, NFR events, etc

<HTML>

<CENTER> Main </CENTER>
<HR></HR>
<B> NEWS </B>
<BR>
- Work is continuing on a full deployment of the change control using
subversion
<BR>
<HR></HR>
<BR>
<BR>
<B> Last Entry in IDS log </B>
<BR>
<!-- <iframe width=100% height=350
src="http://10.0.4.100/idsdaily/0?cmd=Last"></iframe> -->
<BR><BR>
<B> SNORT EVENTS </B>
<BR>
Last 10 Snort Events
<!-- <PRE>
should be a display of the last 10 snort events....No?
</PRE> -->

</HTML>
//<?php

/// Mysql connection This initializes and creates an open Database
/// connection for the page to use
//$link = mysql_connect('10.0.4.100','aciduser','acidweb');
```

```
//if (!$link) {
// die('Could not Connect: '. mysql_error());
// }
//echo 'Connected successfully';


// Mysql Query - This mysql query for our data
//$result = mysql_query('SELECT timestamp, sig_name, ip_src,
ip_dst,layer4_dport FROM acid.acid_event ORDER BY timestamp DESC LIMIT
0,10;');
//if (!$result) {
//die('Invalid query: ($result) ' . mysql_error());
//}
//echo "<HTML><TABLE border=1>";
/// As the results are pulled in a mult-dimensional array we are going to
/// format the way we want the output. Basically for each line of result
/// convert the IP address to dotted notation, and make each line a row
/// in an HTML table
//while ($row = mysql_fetch_assoc($result)) {
// print_r($row); echo "<BR>";
//$sip_address = long2ip($row["ip_src"]);
//$dip_address = long2ip($row["ip_dst"]);

//echo "<TR>";
//echo "<TD>"; echo $row["timestamp"];
//echo "</TD><TD>"; echo $row["sig_name"];
//echo "</TD><TD>"; echo "$sip_address";
//echo "</TD><TD>"; echo "$dip_address";
//echo "</TD><TD>"; echo $row["layer4_dport"];
//echo "</TD>";
// print_r($row); print " \n";
// echo "</TR>";
//}
//echo "</TABLE><BR> Last 10 Unique Events";

// Mysql Query
//$result2 = mysql_query('SELECT
DISTINCT(sig_name),timestamp,ip_src,ip_dst,layer4_dport FROM acid.acid_event
ORDER BY timestamp DESC LIMIT 0,10;
//');
```

```
//if (!$result2) {
//die('Invalid query: ($result2) ' . mysql_error());
//}
//echo "<HTML><TABLE border=1>";
//while ($row = mysql_fetch_assoc($result2)) {
// print_r($row); echo "<BR>";
//$sip_address = long2ip($row["ip_src"]);
//$dip_address = long2ip($row["ip_dst"]);

//echo "<TR>";
//echo "<TD>"; echo $row["timestamp"];
//echo "</TD><TD>"; echo $row["sig_name"];
//echo "</TD><TD>"; echo "$sip_address";
//echo "</TD><TD>"; echo "$dip_address";
//echo "</TD><TD>"; echo $row["layer4_dport"];
//echo "</TD>";
// print_r($row); print " \n";
// echo "</TR>";
//}

//echo "</TABLE></HTML>";

// End connection now that we are all done with the database
// mysql_close($link);

//?>


##################### feeds.php #####################
# This script is basically a sensor check script, and soon
# to be possibly the location for some of the argus events

<?php

?>
<HTML>
<BODY bgcolor="#0099FF">
<B> Service and host status </B>
<BR>
<table border=1 bgcolor=white>
```

```
<TR ><TD>Sensor</TD><TD>Disk Space</TD><td>Percent
Used</TD><TD>Tcpdump</TD><TD>Snort</TD><TD>Bro</TD></TR>
<TR><TD >CORE</TD>
<TD width=5%>
<?php


/// Using the php "exec" function you can perform system commands on the
/// server as un untrusted user. However through the use of the "sudo"
///command the web server can temporarily have access to specific commands

//("sudo -u scripts ssh scripts@10.0.4.18 df -h | head -n 2 | awk '{print
$5}' | sed 's/%//g'", $c_df);
// if ( $c_df[1] > 90 ) {
// print " <img src=off.gif ></img> ";
//} else {
 print " <img src=on.gif></img> <BR>";
//}
?>
</td><td ><?php print_r($c_df[1]); print "%"; ?></td>
<TD width=5%>
<?php
//("sudo -u scripts ssh scripts@10.0.4.18 ps -auxw | grep tcpdump",
$c_tcpdump);
//if ($c_tcpdump[0] == NULL ) {
// print "<img src=off.gif></img>";
//} else {
 print "<img src=on.gif></img> <BR>";
//}
?>
</td>
<TD width=5%>
<?php
//("sudo -u scripts ssh scripts@10.0.4.18 ps -auxw | grep snort", $c_snort);
//if ($c_snort[0] == NULL ) {
// print "<img src=off.gif></img>";
//} else {
 print "<img src=on.gif></img> <BR>";
//}
?>
```

```
</td>
<TD width=5%>
<?php
//("sudo -u scripts ssh scripts@10.0.4.18 ps -auxw | grep bro", $c_bro);
//if ($c_bro[0] == NULL ) {
 //print "<img src=off.gif></img>";
//} else {
 print "<img src=on.gif></img> <BR>";
//}
?>

</td></tr>
<TR><TD >EXTERNAL</TD>
<TD width=5%>
<?php
//("sudo -u scripts ssh scripts@10.0.4.19 df -h | head -n 2 | awk '{print
$5}' | sed 's/%//g'", $e_df);
// if ( $e_df[1] > 90 ) {
// print "<img src=off.gif></img>";
//} else {
 print " <img src=on.gif></img> <BR>";
//}
?>
</td><TD><?php print_r($e_df[1]); print "%"; ?></td>
<TD width=5%>
<?php
//("sudo -u scripts ssh scripts@10.0.4.19 ps -auxw | grep tcpdump",
$e_tcpdump);
//if ($e_tcpdump[0] == NULL ) {
// print "<img src=off.gif></img>";
//} else {
 print "<img src=on.gif></img> <BR>";
//}
?>
</td>
<TD width=5%>
<?php
//("sudo -u scripts ssh scripts@10.0.4.19 ps -auxw | grep snort", $e_snort);
```

```
//if ($e_snort[0] == NULL ) {
// print "<img src=off.gif></img>";
//} else {
 print "<img src=on.gif></img> <BR>";
//}
?>


</td>
<TD width=5%>
<?php
//("sudo -u scripts ssh scripts@10.0.4.19 ps -auxw | grep bro", $e_bro);
//if ($e_bro[0] == NULL ) {
// print "<img src=off.gif></img>";
//} else {
 print "<img src=on.gif></img> <BR>";
//}
?>


</td></tr>

<TR><TD colspan=8 width=100%>
<!--- By using a built-in mysql function called "mysql_stat()" we can get an
idea of the load our MySQL server is under -- >
<?php //include('http://10.0.4.100/mysql_status_lite.php'); ?></TD></TR>

</TABLE>

<HR align=left width=100%></HR><BR>
<!-- <BODY> -->
<B> <?php echo date (" d F Y "); ?> </B>
<br>

<HR algin=left width="100%">Industry News</HR><br>
<!--- When this code is called from java-capable browser such as IE a news
reader will display hyperlinked news articles -- >
<applet CODE="news_java.class" WIDTH=270 HEIGHT=200>
<PARAM NAME="MSGTEXT" VALUE="announce.txt">
<PARAM NAME="BGCOLOR" VALUE="#F4F2F0">
<PARAM NAME="FGCOLOR" VALUE="#000000">
<PARAM NAME="HREFCOLOR" VALUE="#0000FF">
```

```
<PARAM NAME="LINKCOLOR" VALUE="#FF0000">
<PARAM NAME="FONTNAME" VALUE="Dialog">
<PARAM NAME="FONTSIZE" VALUE="10">
<PARAM NAME="SPEED" VALUE="30">
<PARAM NAME="WAITTEXT" VALUE="YES">
<PARAM NAME="PAUSE" VALUE="5500">
</APPLET>


<!-- This is pulling the daily news feeds from the RSS script -->
<!--- Using a small RSS feed client we can get news and updates to
information that could provide us with a clue of what threats are coming
down the pipe. -- >
<!-- <B> CNN Top Stories </B>
<script language=JavaScript
src="http://10.0.4.100/instantfeedreader/instantf
eedreader.php?feed=http://rss.cnn.com/rss/cnn_topstories.rss"></script>
<HR><B> BBC News Top Stories </B></HR>
<script language=javascript
src="http://10.0.4.100/instantfeedreader/instantfeedreader.php?feed=http://n
ewsrss.bbc.co.uk/rss/newsonline_world_edition/front_page/rss.xml"></script>
<HR><B>SecurityFocus Bugtraq</B> </HR>
<script language=JavaScript
src="http://10.0.4.100/instantfeedreader/instantf
eedreader.php?feed=http://www.securityfocus.com/rss/vulnerabilities.xml"></s
cript>
<HR><B> SecurityFocus Incidents </B></HR>
<script language=JavaScript
src="http://10.0.4.100/instantfeedreader/instantf
eedreader.php?feed=http://www.djeaux.com/rss/insecure-
incidents.rss"></script>
<HR><B> Full Disclosure </B></HR>
<script language=JavaScript
src="http://10.0.4.100/instantfeedreader/instantf
eedreader.php?feed=http://www.djeaux.com/rss/insecure-
fulldisclosure.rss"></script>
-->


<hr></hr>
</BODY>
</HTML>
```

Commercial Solutions: ArcSight and Netforensics

For those security teams that have money to spend on a SIM/ESM deployment, there are several available such as Arcsight and Intellitactics, to name a couple.

Tools & Traps...

ESM/SIM Solutions

If your organization is looking to implement an ESM/SIM solution, there are several things to consider:

1. What are you going to push into it? For example, if your organization uses Cisco IDS, then you really should talk to the vendor to make sure that they can get your data and parse your data. If that is your primary IDS solution and the vendor can't read it, you just made a half-a-million-dollar mistake!

2. Capacity planning anyone? One of the easiest traps to get into when deploying an ESM/SIM is that all of the data is going in to the SIM, but how much data can be in there before it starts to affect performance? In one example after the database for the ESM/SIM reached more than 30 million records, search times went from less than 15 seconds to more than 5 minutes!

3. Hardware costs? Once your organization decides to deploy an ESM/SIM and has swallowed the cost for the software don't forget the almost as large cost of hardware, such as a Storage Array or SAN, as well as the support "network" to create this new architecture.

Or, if you are more familiar with Netforensics, you might recognize the example in Figure 1.7.

Figure 1.7 Netforensics Example

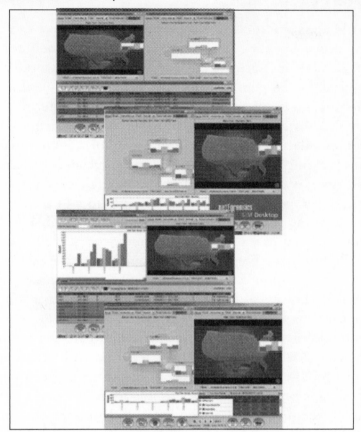

Summary

Hopefully, the ideas and tools that were shown briefly here can help your organization in several ways. The main idea here is that the information coming out of all of the security devices across your network(s) firewalls, IDS/IPS, and ACLs can be much like torrential rain. However, out of that rain, security organizations are supposed to be able to determine attacks and threats, provide clear and concise reporting on the health and wellness of network(s), and provide some meaningful information to upper management. By using some very simple methods outlined in this chapter to manage these flows of data, several clear pictures can be found. For example, the reports an analysis team needs are the easiest to create and should have the highest priority. However, using some simple data manipulation, high-level and general reports can be created to show the effectiveness of a security organization and its policies and processes. For example, a "status page" for each component of your security organization can provide a simple way to show events of higher priority, such as a hot list of IPs to monitor or something as simple as if sensors and applications are running. In addition, preloaded or templates of the most common reports can be easily integrated into a larger reporting structure such as an ESM/SIM platform. Another concern is accessing your applications from a remote or disaster recovery site, so try to keep your security reporting and applications as light as possible to help create a flexible reporting infrastructure. Finally, if you keep all these solutions in mind, your organization should have a flexible, scalable, remotely accessible security reporting infrastructure that can bend to the needs of an organization.

Solutions Fast Track

IT Budgets and Results:
Leveraging OSS Solutions at Little Cost

☑ Cisco P-SPAN allows you to mirror traffic across more than one port on a switch.

☑ P-SPAN and R-SPAN can be used to a security and operations staff advantage to provide a multiplatform view of the network.

☑ By allowing multiplatforms to see the same traffic at each span location, your shop will not be single-solution dependent.

☑ When you can validate the effectiveness of your purchased software with a cheap or free solution, you can assure management that budgets are being spent responsibly.

☑ Having more than one view of a network event or network performance can assist in providing an accurate view. This will help a security team and management from falling into a single vendor mentality.

☑ OSS solutions can help a security organization decide where to spend monies in the right places.

Reporting Security Information to Management

☑ Provide your management with a clear, concise view of network threats and changes.

☑ Provide you security teams with a clear, detailed view of network events and threats.

☑ Make sure your reports are repeatable and automatically followed every time the same way. By doing this, you are assuring that you have a set of procedures and processes to follow.

☑ Try to push your reporting to a platform-independent solution. Doing so will make your solution easy to deploy and manage, and add or remove features from it as well.

Combining Resources for an "Eye-in-the-Sky" View

☑ One goal of our reporting infrastructure was to make it as platform independent as possible, such as a Web-based platform

☑ For our management reporting we created a "daily report" Web page. This page is where most of the raw IDS data is searched and graphed into meaningful information.

☑ With filtering of events and signatures, an auto-updating view of the highest priority events and event changes can keep up on everything from unused machines to larger "show and tell" displays in the form of a screensaver.

Blended Threats and Reporting

☑ Malware has slowly risen to the top of most organizations' concern lists.

☑ As malware is such a prevalent issue with most organizations, our SEs began to form an idea for how to stop the malware we were aware of and stop traffic to domains we knew were bad.

☑ When trying to combine security events from multiple platforms and technologies, the need to create a central repository for these logs becomes apparent. Another requirement is the need to report useful and meaningful data to upper management and other business units.

Code Solutions

☑ A high-level view of the information that is clear and concise is needed to enable your management and above to understand the threats facing their network(s).

☑ For our security teams, we have come up with a "status" page for them to use as a central point for events, news, and client site information.

☑ For our IDS team, we have to come up with a single Web page that can provide them with this information.

Frequently Asked Questions

The following Frequently Asked Questions, answered by the authors of this book, are designed to both measure your understanding of the concepts presented in this chapter and to assist you with real-life implementation of these concepts. To have your questions about this chapter answered by the author, browse to **www.syngress.com/solutions** and click on the **"Ask the Author"** form.

Q: Can we deploy more than one monitoring technology per span location?

A: Yes, using P–SPAN, you can mirror a single port to an entire VLAN, or using R–SPAN, you can mirror a port to an entire VLAN to another VLAN across the enterprise. However, each of these technologies has a different set of pre-requisites depending on the size and scale of your operational network engineering staff.

Q: Do I have to run commercial off-the-shelf (COTS) products in my network?

A: Having an open-source tool to validate the COTS tool can prove invaluable, especially in determining if an attack has occurred; for example, if only one tool is reporting a backdoor alarm in your IDS logs, yet all of the other tools are not. This means that you might want to have an analyst dig into the root cause.

Q: What platforms are these tools able to run on?

A: Almost all of these solutions are running on BSD or Linux using Apache and PHP, and or a MySQL database.

IDS Reporting

Solutions in this chapter:

- Session/Flow Logging with Snort

- Session/Flow Logging with Argus

- Can You Determine When a DDoS/DoS Attack Is Occurring?

- Using Snort for Bandwidth Monitoring

- Using Bro to Log and Capture Application-Level Protocols

- Tracking Users' Web Activities with Bro

- Using Bro to Gather DNS and Web Traffic Data

- Using Bro for Blackholing Traffic to Malware-Infested Domains

- Using Bro to Identify Top E-Mail Senders/Receivers

Introduction

This chapter covers how to get more information out of your passive detection systems. An organization's intrusion detection system (IDS) platform can be used for attack detection and can be leveraged to help in monitoring many different aspects: the health and wellness of a network, policy enforcement, policy effects, utilization of network resources, and providing better visibility of your network(s). All the solutions in this chapter are freeware and should be able to answer at least one of the following questions:

- Do you know if an exploit worked on a victim on your network even if you don't have a signature for the exploit?

- Can a tool like tcpdump be used to create an effective poor man's denial-of-service (DoS) detection tool in your network environment?

- Can you tag and determine how much of your Web traffic is being used by malware and unauthorized software? Can you determine from network monitoring which machines on your network don't have the latest build of your corporate network software (Web clients, SSH clients, telnet/FTP clients, etc)?

- Can you determine your top Web surfer and the site your users are browsing most?

- Can you determine the top .com/.net/.edu/etc. site that your users are requesting? How much of that is malware?   Can you use that information to create a blocklist of bad domains to kill malware before it has a chance to communicate outside your network(s)?

- Can you determine how much mail your SMTP servers are processing? Who are the top sender and top receiver? Are there unusual failed delivery attempts? From where?

We encourage all computer security professionals to use these questions and solutions to better defend and understand their network(s). In addition, these solutions should provide you a point from which to take these apart, improve, and build on them to use in even more imaginative ways. As an example, if you can answer most of these questions, then you are way ahead of the curve in terms of most organizations' security postures.

Session/Flow Logging with Snort

If you follow the defense in depth methodology of network defense, arguably one of the first methods to discover if attacks worked is to use flow or session information about the network traffic. Flow- or session-based logging that can be done even at high speed, such as multigigabit Ethernet, is a type of IDS that can come from different types of tools such as Argus for text-based logging or in graphical format from such companies as Lancope, Arbor Network, Q1 labs, or Mazu Networks. This type of IDS is meant to capture not the packet payload or the single hostile packet but rather record each connection in an "auditable" form. For example, when you use a tool such as Argus or Cisco's Netflow, a logging record is kept for HTTP, FTP, and other connections. However, several key pieces of that connection are recorded when dealing with flow or session logging. This "auditable" portion of the log includes the following pieces:

1. **Duration** How long did this connection last?

2. **Source and destination IPs and ports involved** Who was talking to whom? And over what ports?

3. **Protocol** Was this a TCP? UDP? ICMP? Or other protocol?

4. **Number of packets sent/received** Was this a small connection or a large one?

5. **Amount of packet payload size** How much data was involved in this connection?

6. **TCP flags (optional)** What TCP flags were in use by both client and server in the connection?

This type of information can sometimes be the only indication of a successful attack, especially over uncommon ports. For example, although having a full tcpdump log of all network traffic would be ideal to search through, most organizations can't even begin to store that large size of data for any length of time. In a recent example of using session logging and sizing, a client site was recording full tcpdump logs for a certain heavy load VLAN where per hour the tcpdump logs where between 15 and 20 gigs compressed per hour! This situation was obviously not working, but the company still needed the ability to audit all connections through that VLAN. As a test implementation Argus was placed on the sensor to record all traffic for 24 hours. The session logs for the 24-hour period were about 30MB versus the over 200GB tcpdump logs! With the Argus logger in place the client was able to gain a clearer understanding for the traffic on the VLAN. Although losing the ability to capture full packet payloads, the company made improvements in the host security logging for that VLAN, and the other components in the defense in depth "stack" covered the audit requirements in thatsegment.

The next section of this chapter covers several tools that can be used to create a layered defense-in-depth network defense strategy for your network(s). We recommend that you run at least two of these solutions so that your strategy doesn't have a single point of failure. Another reason is that your network analysts won't then be tied to a single solution or vendor for event data. Running more than one of the network security tools can help the Chicken Little mentality; if one vendor says the network sky is falling, your analysts can use a second tool to verify the first tool's data.

Lastly, when you include session-based logging in your defensive posture, it can serve to benefit your operational teams as well in terms of uptimes, network load, and other measurements that can help them maintain the "5 9's" of acceptable downtime, if they have to adhere to those rules.

Tools & Traps…

Network Downtime in Terms of the "5 9's"

If your operational network support personnel are on certain types of contracts, you are probably familiar with the "5 9's" in terms of network compliance. What this means for network personnel is that the network will be up for 99.999% of a year, or a total downtime of five minutes per year. Although this may seem like a small amount of downtime, you can imagine the loss of revenue for companies such as Yahoo!, CNN, eBay, and others if they were down for longer than that each year.

Did That Exploit Work? Did the Attacker Download Any Data?

One of the least used parts of Snort is to turn on the stream4 preprocessor's statistic logging mechanism. When the Snort engine gets a TCP connection passed through it, the connection needs to be reassembled for the signature engine and other preprocessors to scan it. This function is performed by the stream4 preprocessor, which can also detect TCP scans and TCP abnormalities in the "stream." The preprocessor can log a record of all connections passing through this engine by enabling the *keepstats* directive. These logs are stored in a separate file in the Snort log directory. You can enable or disable several options in the preprocessor, depending on your specific deployment. However, for the course of this discussion, we are concerned with only the variable *keepstats machine*.

Tools & Traps...

stream4 with Barnyard

Barnyard, the popular Snort front end, uses the stream4 keepstats logs to detect anomalies through "unified" logs. These logs are output in snort's "binary" format, which are virtually unreadable to human eyes. However, if you are trying to get a human-readable format in the stream4 logs, then you want to specify the "machine" format. This format will produce space-separated logs that are output on a single line per event. This formatting will enable easy searching from scripts. For more complete information on Barnyard, read the *Snort 2.1* (Syngress Publishing, ISBN:)for almost an entire chapter on Barnyard from its creator.

You might be wondering what information can be stored in these logs that could possibly be useful in the case of an exploit for which you don't have a signature. First, you have to appreciate what information is going to be stored in these files. Table 2.1 shows the format of these log files.

Table 2.1 Format of Log Files

Fields 1–3	Fields 4–8	Fields 9–13	Fields 14–22
Formatting data	Starting and ending time stamp (date and time)	The "server" in the connection information (IP, server port in use, the number of packets received, and the number of bytes of the packets)	The "client" in the connection information (IP, first client port in use, the number of packets sent, and the number of bytes of the packets)

The example log entry can be found from a normal Web (80/TCP) connection.

```
[*] Session => Start: 07/16/05-23:43:18 End Time: 07/16/05-
23:43:19[Server IP: 66.28.250.174  port: 80  pkts: 11  bytes:
11566] [Client IP: 69.243.13.223  port: 49978  pkts: 8  bytes:
1181]
```

Now that you know what the log files store, this data can be pushed into a flat file for later analysis during an investigation. For those who like to be able to query a database with a little coaxing, these logs could also be pushed into a database.

To enable this type of logging, simply edit your snort.conf file and modify the following line in the configuration:

```
######
# Snort.conf enable stream4 statistic logging
example
#
# Default configuration
#preprocessor stream4: disable_evasion_alerts
#
# Loggging enabled change
preprocessor stream4: disable_evasion_alert,
keepstats machine
```

This modified code will then produce a file called session.log in your Snort log directory. With the *machine* keyword set, each log entry will be a single line, which will make scripted searching through these files easier.

A Virus Beta Test

Recently, at a client site we had a user "volunteer" to be a virus beta tester by clicking on an ad on the "work-related" Web site he was browsing. Upon that single click, the IDS sensors fired off about three alarms for the user in a matter of seconds. These events went from bad "IE page spoof" to "code execution" to "MHTML exploit." The alerts then went quiet with no further events from either attacker or victim. We checked the signature alarm systems seeing the same thing, but just to double check, we looked through the snort session logs. These logs showed clearly the connection to the site as can be seen in the next section.

An Example of a Web Connection

The good part of this example is that there is no large upload of data from our victim's machine. However, if there had been, the example would have looked like the following portion of the connection.

An Example of a Web Connection with a Backdoor Snort Session

Another way that is normally faster to check is to look through your application logs with bro, as we will talk about later.

However, these logs are not part of the actively looked through logs, and the information found in these files has sometimes proven to be the only record of a data transfer! If you can afford to keep them, do so, because the first time you don't, will be when you will want or need that data.

Session/Flow Logging with Argus

Argus (www.qosient.com/argus), another session–auditing tool, has two major components: argus and ra*. Argus is the daemon or sniffing component, and several clients can be used for reading and displaying the Argus data. The advantage of using Argus is that it can maintain logs for TCP, UDP, and ICMP IP. Table 2.2 lists Argus clients and their uses.

Table 2.2 Argus Clients and Their Uses

Client Name	Description	Example Use
ra	"Read Argus." This is the base client from which all the others are built.	*ra –r <argus_file> > human_read.txt* Will produce a space formatted text file.
racount	Used to count events from an argus data stream.	*racount –ar <argus_file>* Will produce a summarized -r and protocol sorted -a table.
ragator	Used to combine matching records in an argus flow file.	*ragator –f <argus_file> -w newargus.file* Will produce a smaller aggregate Argus data file.
ramon	The client that is used to create RMON2 reports.	*ramon –r <argus_file> –M TopM or Matrix* Will produce a RMON2 style table.
rasort	Used to produce sorted reports based on criteria fields.	*rasort –r <argus_file> -s srcaddr* Will produce a table of the argus records sorted by source IP.
raxml	The client used to convert argus data records into XML formatted data.	*raxml –r <argus_file> > argus.xml* Will produce an XML output of the argus records. With the -e option, you can specify the data format encoding of either ASCII or Base64.

As mentioned previously, Argus records some interesting information for almost all the common IPs. For example, in the default configuration, each

Argus record has information that would be useful in an investigation, such as connection duration, the number of packets sent and received, and the amount that both sender and receiver got in bytes. Using a configuration file called rarc, you can specify other options such as time formats, data column labeling, display MAC addressing, and the number of seconds you want the ra* client to run. One of the major cases for using Argus is that it provides a poor man's version of flow-based record keeping. This type of data can be invaluable in an investigation because it stores such information as connection start/end/duration times, number of packets and bytes for both sender and receiver, and the flagging of the connection (TCP only). Another thing to keep in mind is that this data doesn't have a large footprint. For example, to keep full packet traces on a sensor even on a 10MB Ethernet link is several GBs of data per hour, while the same information minus the payload content in the form of Argus files is several MBs of data.

On a production sensor, one possible deployment would be to leave an Argus daemon running to, say, /log/argus/argus.raw if on a *nix sensor platform. This file would be the output file for the Argus sniffing daemon monitoring your sniffing interface. Depending on how you are going to use the Argus data, pulling several different feeds off that single data file is possible.

- **Database access** Using the schema presented here and formatting of the ra data file, it is possible to push the data into a MySQL database. This might be smart for those looking to pull the data together from multiple Argus sensors, and for those who have some savvy Web/database developers at their disposal to pull together a Web interface for this data.

- **XML formatted** To pull the ra data into XML formatted files. One possible use would be to talk to your Enterprise Security Manager vendor and see if they could parse this data. However, having heard from a group trying that in production, the XML conversion is painfully slow.

- **Flat text files** This solution would be good for those groups that search through text files with Perl scripts. Using such things as grep pattern files, searching through the text files for a "hot list" of ports and/or IP addresses could be a quick way to determine if a hostile IP was crossing your network or a known backdoor port was in use.

As always, if you have the storage capacity, compress and log the hourly raw Argus files for later searching or to hand over as evidence during an investigation.

Database Setup

Here, we present instructions on how to set up Argus logging to a database and keep hourly compressed raw logs for later evidence using a series of simple scripts and text file manipulations. We encourage people to improve upon and modify them to best serve their deployments.

For those familiar with MySQL, simply create a database called argusdb (at least for this example).

```
Mysql> CREATE DATABASE argusdb;
```

Then, run this code to create the table argus_data in the database.

```
Mysql> DROP table argus_data if exist;
Mysql> CREATE TABLE `argus_data` (
    `starttime` timestamp NOT NULL default CURRENT_TIMESTAMP
on update CURRENT_TIMESTAMP,
    `lasttime` timestamp NOT NULL default '0000-00-00
00:00:00',
    `duration` text NOT NULL,
    `flags` text NOT NULL,
    `type` text NOT NULL,
    `saddr` text NOT NULL,
    `sport` text NOT NULL,
    `direction` text NOT NULL,
    `daddr` text NOT NULL,
    `dport` text NOT NULL,
    `spacket` int(11) NOT NULL default '0',
    `dpacket` int(11) NOT NULL default '0',
    `sbytes` int(11) NOT NULL default '0',
    `dbytes` int(11) NOT NULL default '0',
    `state` text character set latin1 NOT NULL
) ENGINE=MyISAM DEFAULT COMMENT='raw argus data';
```

Next, create a sensor account for each of the sensors you want to have access to the database.

```
Mysql>  GRANT SELECT, INSERT, UPDATE ON argusdb.* TO argus sensor@%
IDENTIFIED BY "password";
```

Finally, refresh the database for your new credentials to work.

```
Mysql> FLUSH PRIVILEGES;
```

Now, to have ra use this client you will have to create a rarc file some-where on your sensor. This file is used by ra* clients to provide formatting and other variables, which override those on the command line. However, to make these variables global to the sensor, an rarc file needs to be created in the /etc directory. The file should look like the following example:

```
# example rarc global file
# Only leave this one enabled if you want to see the
column labels for every hour
RA_PRINT_LABELS=0
RA_FIELD_DELIMITER';'
RA_TIME_FORMAT="%Y%m%d%H%M%S"
```

Once you have enabled this file, your ra files should look like the fol-lowing example with five line examples for each of the three common proto-cols (TCP, UDP, ICMP):

```
StartTime;Flgs;Type;SrcAddr;Sport;Dir;DstAddr;Dport;SrcPkt;DstPk
t;SrcBytes;DstBytes;Status
20050712232320;;tcp;x.x.13.223;2322;-
>;x.x.76.10;110;8;10;481;642;sSEfF
20050712232338;;tcp;x.x.13.223;2325;-
>;x.x.0.17;80;4;3;696;586;sSE
20050712232414;;tcp;x.x.13.223;2326;-
>;x.x.111.225;80;6;5;815;881;sSEfF
20050712232415;;tcp;x.x.13.223;2327;-
>;x.x.240.42;80;11;16;1314;16201;sSEfF
20050712232536;s;tcp;x.x.108.150;1650;<-
>;x.x.13.223;3527;3;0;186;0;s

20050712232046;;udp;x.x.160.1;67;->;x.x.255.255;68;1;0;346;0;INT
20050712232052;;udp;x.x.160.1;67;->;x.x.255.255;68;1;0;346;0;INT
20050712232100;;udp;x.x.160.1;67;->;x.x.255.255;68;1;0;389;0;INT
20050712232112;;udp;x.x.13.223;57628;->;x.x.0.4;53;1;0;93;0;INT
```

```
20050712232114;;udp;x.x.13.223;57628;-
>;x.x.27.33;53;1;0;93;0;INT

20050712233301;;icmp;x.x.13.223;;->;x.x.202.148;;1;0;90;0;URH
20050712234614;;icmp;x.x.168.90;;->;x.x.13.223;;3;0;210;0;URP
20050713001752;;icmp;x.x.168.90;;->;x.x.13.223;;3;0;210;0;URP
20050713011111;;icmp;x.x.38.152;;<->;x.x.13.223;;1;1;106;106;ECO
20050713022353;;icmp;x.x.21.166;;->;x.x.13.223;;2;0;140;0;URH
```

These files are now ready to go into the database. Simply place this modified argusarchive file in the default path of "/usr/local/bin" on the sensor. Argusarchive is distributed as part of the stock build, and is a simplified version that outputs several formats of data per run. The following file can perform several data outputs such as :

- Sorted ASCII plain text, useful for searching with Perl and other scripting tools
- Database insertion into mysql using mysqlimport, does timed bulk insertions into the database to enable long-term storage and searching.
- Copies of each hour's raw Argus file compressed and with a time stamp on the filename, this is helpful if evidence is needed or if data needs to be run through again for errors.

```
# Jake Modified argusarchive
#!/bin/sh
#
#  Copyright (c) 2000-2004 QoSient, LLC
#  All rights reserved.
#
#  This program is free software; you can redistribute it and/or
modify
#  it under the terms of the GNU General Public License as
published by
#  the Free Software Foundation; either version 2, or (at your
option)
#  any later version.
```

```
#
#   This program is distributed in the hope that it will be
useful,
#   but WITHOUT ANY WARRANTY; without even the implied warranty
of
#   MERCHANTABILITY or FITNESS FOR A PARTICULAR PURPOSE.  See the
#   GNU General Public License for more details.
#
#   You should have received a copy of the GNU General Public
License
#   along with this program; if not, write to the Free Software
#   Foundation, Inc., 675 Mass Ave, Cambridge, MA 02139, USA.  */
#
#

PATH=/bin:/usr/bin

#
# Try to use $ARGUSDATA and $ARGUSARCHIVE where possible.
# If these are available, the only thing that we need to
# know is what is the name of the argus output file.
#
# If ARGUSDATA set then don't need to define below.  For
# cron scripts however, $ARGUSDATA may not be defined, so
# lets do that here.

ARGUSBIN=/usr/local/bin
ARGUSDATA=/log/argus
ARGUSARCHIVE=/log/argus/GZIP
ARGUSSORTARCHIVE=/log/argus/SORT
ARGUSDBARCHIVE=/log/argus/DB

RAGATOR=$ARGUSBIN/ragator
RASORT=$ARGUSBIN/rasort
RA=$ARGUSBIN/ra

COMPRESSOR=gzip
```

```
COMPRESSFILEEXT=gz

#COMPRESSOR=bzip2
#COMPRESSFILEEXT=bz2

#COMPRESSOR=compress
#COMPRESSFILEEXT=Z

DATAFILE=argus.raw

ARCHIVE=argus.`date '+%Y%m%d%H'`
ARCHIVE_DB=argus.db.`date '+%Y%m%d%H'`
#ARCHIVE_SORT=argus.sort.`date '+%Y%m%d%H'`
ARCHIVEZIP=$ARCHIVE.$COMPRESSFILEEXT

if [ -d $ARGUSDATA ] ; then
   cd $ARGUSDATA
else
   echo "argus data directory $ARGUSDATA not found"
   exit
fi

if [ -f $DATAFILE ] ; then
   mv $DATAFILE $ARCHIVE.tmp >> /log/argus/archive.log 2>>
/log/argus/archive.log
else
   echo "argus data file $ARGUSDATA/$DATAFILE not found"
   exit
fi

if [ -f $ARCHIVE.tmp ]; then
#  $RAGATOR -VRr $ARCHIVE.tmp -w - | $RASORT -w $ARCHIVE
#   $RASORT -r $ARCHIVE.tmp > $ARGUSSORTARCHIVE/$ARCHIVE_SORT
   $RA -nn -z -Z b -s +1lasttime -s +2dur -r $ARCHIVE.tmp >
$ARGUSDBARCHIVE/$ARCHIVE_DB
# hackjob for mysql support
 cp $ARGUSDBARCHIVE/$ARCHIVE_DB /tmp/argus_data
```

```
 cd /tmp/
 /usr/local/bin/mysqlimport --local --fields-terminated-by=";" -u
argus_sensor -ppassword -h localhost argusdb argus_data
argus_data >> /log/argus/archive.log 2>> /log/argus/archive.log
# rm -f /tmp/argus_data
 cd $ARGUSDATA

else
   echo " All of the sort and DB scripts failed to run"
   exit
fi
mv $ARCHIVE.tmp $ARCHIVE >> /log/argus/archive.log 2>>
/log/argus/archive.log

if [ -e $ARGUSDATA/$ARCHIVE ]; then
#    rm -f $ARCHIVE.tmp
   $COMPRESSOR $ARCHIVE
   mv $ARCHIVEZIP $ARGUSARCHIVE
else
   echo "argus data file not moved."
   exit
fi
```

Argus allows its output file to be "taken" from it and will simply create a new named file to write more data to. This will allow us to capture data on an hourly queue without having to constantly stop and restart the sniffing process.

```
    # example crontab entry
         # This entry runs every hour on the hour
    0 * * * * /bin/sh /script/location/jargusarchive >>
/log/argus/archive.log
```

With Argus now running and its output being inserted into a database and being stored on a sensor, the next logical thing would be to offload the zipped raw log files to a central backup server. Doing so will protect the data from hitting possible disk storage limits on your sensor, or if a sensor is compromised. However, for those feeling creative, a proper Web interface to search and display this information is not available at this time. The simple solution currently would be to create a Web interface that would display several pieces of information useful to an organization, including:

- Total bandwidth—can be in the form of a daily total count in MBs and GBs

- Top 10 source IPs of traffic

- Top 10 destination IPs of traffic (second column with DNS name for each)

- Top 10 host-pairs of communication

- Top 10 TCP destination ports

- Top 10 UDP destination ports

- Hits on IPs in a "hotlist"—can be simply a pull of the dshield Top 10 IP page or from a list unique to your organization

The page might look something like Figure 2.1 if you include a limited search capability.

Figure 2.1 Argus Web (Prototype Example)

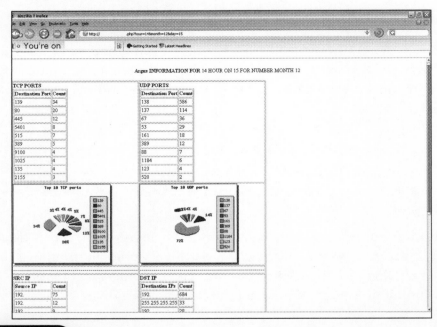

Can You Determine
When a DDoS/DoS Attack Is Occurring?

Another part to your defense-in-depth strategy is to use all your layered defensive tools to your greatest advantage. One of the ways you can do that is to use your tcpdump logs—if they are available—to augment the session-based logging and application logging. One of the ways you can leverage the tcpdump logging is to use it to help detect bandwidth problems such as a DoS or to help detect large network utilization from other means such as a backup to a hot-site or a download of several CDs' worth of an operating system. When first deploying your tcpdump logging application, you should find out what other information you could get out of that data. One solution was to use a tool called tcpdstat (http://staff.washington.edu/dittrich/talks/core02/tools/tools.html) written by Dave Dittrich of the University of Washington. This tool produces a text output from reading and parsing a tcpdump file such as the one shown here:

```
Id: 200406010000
StartTime: Tue Jun  1 00:00:00 2004
EndTime:   Tue Jun  1 01:00:00 2004
TotalTime: 3599.73 seconds
TotalCapSize: 102.27MB  CapLen: 1514 bytes
# of packets: 632499 (102.27MB)
AvgRate: 238.22Kbps  stddev:499.02K   PeakRate: 12.52Mbps
```

Several more lines in the output can be culled later for other reports, but for the DoS detection, the value you need to be concerned with is PeakRate. This value is the highest throughput during that hour; when compared with the rest of the day, or even the previous hour, you can come up with a rough idea if you are under attack. For example, you can have a simple script called via cron to check the hour-to-hour max rate with something such as:

```
#!/bin/sh
# Simple Script to check on the max bandwidth hour-to-hour
#
#
 filedate=`date '+%Y%m%d%H'`
prevhour=`cat /tmp/lasthour`
curhour=`cat /tmp/curhour`
```

```
echo " "


if   [ $prevhour -gt $curhour ]
then
echo "All Clear"
else
echo "Possible Attack"
echo "1" > /log/Dos.txt
fi

  # using tcpdstat to generate the curhour file
  /path/to/tcpdstat -r
/path/to/hourjustcompressed_tcpdump.file > /log/tcpdstat.$filedate
   cat /log/tcpdstat.$filedate >> /log/daily_proto.txt
  mv /tmp/curhour /tmp/lasthour
  tmpcurhour=`grep "PeakRate" /log/tcpdstat.$filedate | awk
'{ print $6 }' | sed -e 's/Mbps//g' > /tmp/curhour `


# all ready for the next hour
```

The Dos.txt file could then be checked by a status page/script to alert
you to possible attacks. Using this script called every hour, your team would
then know to take a closer look at the amount and type of traffic that
occurred during the last hour.

To provide some statistics on the traffic over each day as a whole, you
simply write out each 24-hour period to /log/daily_proto.txt. This file could
then be parsed with a simple shell script to return 24 entries for PeakRate,
one per hour, such as:

```
HOUR   PEAKRATE
00     9.3
01     8.2
02     3.7
03     3.4
04     2.1
05     16.7
```

Then, if you wanted to graphically display this information, a PHP script that could take the values and plot them on a bar graph could query this data. If you have deployed BASE for displaying your Snort alerts, you can simply use the graphing library of JpGraph to run your code as can be seen in the following example:

```php
<?php

// INCLUDES FOR GRAPH
include ( "/var/www/html/SUPPORT/jpgraph/src/jpgraph.php");
include ( "/var/www/html/SUPPORT/jpgraph/src/jpgraph_bar.php");

// DATA
// read from file

// Create blank arrays for place holders
$hour = array();
$Mbps = array();

$f = fopen("/log/daily_proto.txt", "r");
while ($array= fgetcsv($f, 24," ")) {
// Print out each variable
// print "HOUR: $array[0] Mbps: $array[1] <br>";

// create/add to two arrays
//$hour = array();
//$Mbps = array();
array_push($hour, $array[0]);
array_push($Mbps, $array[1]);

// print "$hour[0] <br>";
// print "$Mbps[0] <br>";

}
fclose($f);
```

```
$data = $Mbps;

//// CREATE GRAPH SIZING AND FEATURES
$graph = new Graph (400,250,"auto");
$graph->SetScale("textlin");

// Add drop shadow
$graph->SetShadow();

// Create bar plot
$bplot = new BarPlot($data);
$graph->Add($bplot);

// Titles and x/y axis labels
$graph->title->Set("Daily Hourly Bandwidth (SENSOR)");
$graph->xaxis->title->Set("Hour 24-hour clock");
$graph->yaxis->title->Set("Amount of Usage (Mbps)");

// Fonts
$graph->title->SetFont(FF_FONT1,FS_BOLD);
$graph->yaxis->title->SetFont(FF_FONT1,FS_BOLD);
$graph->xaxis->title->SetFont(FF_FONT1,FS_BOLD);

// Display the graph
$graph->Stroke();

?>
```

This code will generate a bar graph of the data as in Figure 2.2, which can be used for such things as bandwidth monitoring over time or graphically showing bandwidth spikes such as those in a DoS attack.

Figure 2.2 Bandwidth Monitoring and DoS Detection

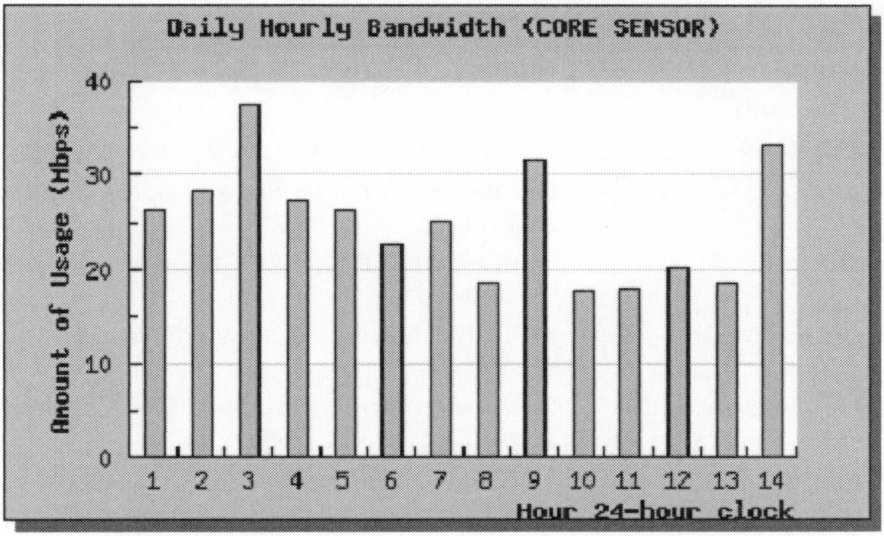

Finally, if you can archive the data over a period of a week or possibly longer if you push it into a database, you can show bandwidth trending. Using this data, you can determine such things as peak usage, unusual levels of traffic at odd times, or even for planning based on the lowest usage time frames.

Using Snort for Bandwidth Monitoring

Can you determine when your network segments are experiencing drops in connectivity? Can you determine trends in traffic utilization? Using the Perfmonitor preprocessor on your Snort sensors, you can determine this as well as an entire laundry list of information about your sensors as seen in Table 2.3.

Table 2.3 Output to the Snort File

Field Name	Description
Unixtime	Used for duration and runtime calculations
%pkts dropped	Percentage of packets the snort process has dropped

Continued

Table 2.3 continued Output to the Snort File

Field Name	Description
Alerts/second	Number of IDS events per second
K-packets/second	
Avg-bytes/packet	Average amount of data in each packet
Syns/second	Number of TCP SYN flagged packets per second
Synacks/second	Number of TCP SYN/ACK flagged packets per second
New-sessions/second	STREAM4 number of new TCP sessions per second
Deleted-sessions/second	STREAM4 number of closed TCP sessions per second
Total-sessions	STREAM4 total number of TCP sessions opened
Max-sessions	STREAM4 the highest number of total TCP sessions
Streamflushes/second	STREAM4 the number of connections passed through the preprocessor per second
Streamfaults/second	STREAM4 the number of failed TCP sessions per second
Fragcompletes/second	FRAG2 number of fragmented packets that were reassembled per second
Fraginserts/second	FRAG2 number of fragmented packets that were inserted into partial packets per second
Fragdeletes/second	FRAG2 number of fragmented packets that were deleted from the packet assembler of FRAG2 per second
Fragflushes/second	FRAG2 number of fragmented "sessions" that were dropped out per second
Fragcreates/second	FRAG2 number of fragmented "sessions" that were created per second
Fragtimeouts	FRAG2 the number of fragmented "sessions" that timed out before they could be assembled
Fragfaults	FRAG2 the number of failed fragmented "sessions"
Number of cpus	Number of CPU's on the sensor

Continued

Table 2.3 continued Output to the Snort File

Field Name	Description
%user-cpu usage	Percentage of the cpu being used for userlevel applications
%sys-cpu usage	Percentage of the cpu being used for system and kernel activity
%idle-cpu usage	Percentage of the cpu that is idle
Mbits/sec (wire)	Number of Megabits per second on the wire
Mbits/sec (ip fragmented)	Number of megabits per second that are fragmented
Mbits/sec (app layer)	Number of megabits per second that are application level such as HTTP/FTP/SMTP
Kpackets/sec (ip fragmented)	

Using this information, you can determine the load a Snort sensor is under, which can be very useful in gauging what type and size of machine to deploy at that location. Another use of this data is to show dropped packets, which could be caused by network outages planned or unplanned, as well as giving a detailed view of network usage. This data is generated in two forms: a "real-time" format that outputs a table of data to standard output every five minutes, and a csv (comma-separated version). The "real-time" formatting can be used for tuning and testing if you grab the Snort output as in the following example:

```
Sensor# echo $SHELL
/bin/bash
Sensor#snort -c snort.conf -l /log/snort -i eth0 2>1
snort_output.log
```

Using this example, all of the output from Snort will be written to the file snort_output.log. In the Snort configuration file the following line was added to output log information every five minutes (time 300) or 100 packets (pktcnt 100) based on the amount of traffic passing the sensor (flow) to the screen (console):

```
# Sample Snort.conf file perfmonitor
preprocessor perfmonitor: time 300 flow console pktcnt 100
```

Once you enable this output and run Snort with the output log file enabled for several minutes, you should get a wealth of information from startup output and errors to preprocessor and postprocessor output information. Another part of this output will look like the following example; this is a formatted view of the same data that is generated in csv format for later analysis.

```
Snort Realtime Performance  : Thu
--------------------------
Pkts Recv:   397
Pkts Drop:   0
% Dropped:   0.00%

Mbits/Sec:   0.00 (wire)
Mbits/Sec:   0.00 (ip fragmented)
Mbits/Sec:   0.00 (ip reassembled)
Mbits/Sec:   0.00 (tcp rebuilt)
Mbits/Sec:   0.00 (app layer)

Bytes/Pkt:   122 (wire)
Bytes/Pkt:   0 (ip fragmented)
Bytes/Pkt:   0 (ip reassembled)
Bytes/Pkt:   0 (tcp rebuilt)
Bytes/Pkt:   122 (app layer)

KPkts/Sec:   0.00 (wire)
KPkts/Sec:   0.00 (ip fragmented)
KPkts/Sec:   0.00 (ip reassembled)
KPkts/Sec:   0.00 (tcp rebuilt)
KPkts/Sec:   0.00 (app layer)

PatMatch:    34.53%

CPU Usage:   0.01% (user)  0.02% (sys)  99.97% (idle)

Alerts/Sec              :  0.0
Syns/Sec                :  0.0
Syn-Acks/Sec            :  0.0
```

```
New Cached Sessions/Sec:    0.0
Cached Sessions Del/Sec:    0.0
Current Cached Sessions:    1
Max Cached Sessions    :    3
Stream Flushes/Sec     :    0.0
Stream Cache Faults/Sec:    0
Stream Cache Timeouts  :    7
Frag Creates()s/Sec    :    0.0
Frag Completes()s/Sec  :    0.0
Frag Inserts()s/Sec    :    0.0
Frag Deletes/Sec       :    0.0
Frag AutoFrees/Sec     :    0.0
Frag Flushes/Sec       :    0.0
Current Cached Frags   :    0
Max Cached Frags       :    0
Frag Timeouts          :    0
Frag Faults            :    0


Protocol Byte Flows - %Total Flow
-----------------------------------
TCP:    46.12%
UDP:    22.61%
ICMP:   0.00%
OTHER:  31.27%


PacketLen - %TotalPackets
-------------------------
Bytes[60]  73.74%

TCP Port Flows
--------------
Port[80] 62.04% of Total, Src:  75.18% Dst:  24.82%
Port[139] 3.38% of Total, Src:  41.37% Dst:  58.63%
Port[445] 2.59% of Total, Src:  44.64% Dst:  55.36%
```

```
Port[721] 0.56% of Total, Src: 100.00% Dst:    0.00%
Ports[High<->High]: 31.43%


UDP Port Flows
--------------
Port[53] 3.58% of Total, Src:  76.52% Dst:   23.48%
Port[67] 3.24% of Total, Src: 100.00% Dst:    0.00%
Port[68] 9.68% of Total, Src: 100.00% Dst:    0.00%
Port[137] 8.79% of Total, Src: 100.00% Dst:    0.00%
Port[138] 73.59% of Total, Src: 100.00% Dst:    0.00%
Port[161] 1.12% of Total, Src:   0.00% Dst: 100.00%


ICMP Type Flows
---------------

    <real-time output>
```

The problems with this data are that it is not easy to record for later use, and is not easy to script for, say, trending of the information. However, the other format "csv" allows for easier scripting and for trending. When used with the perfmon-graph tool called, this data can be used to generate a Web page for each sensor. This page graphs information such as dropped packets, detailed bandwidth, size of packets, and other information as in Figure 2.3.

Figure 2.3 Perfmon Graph Example

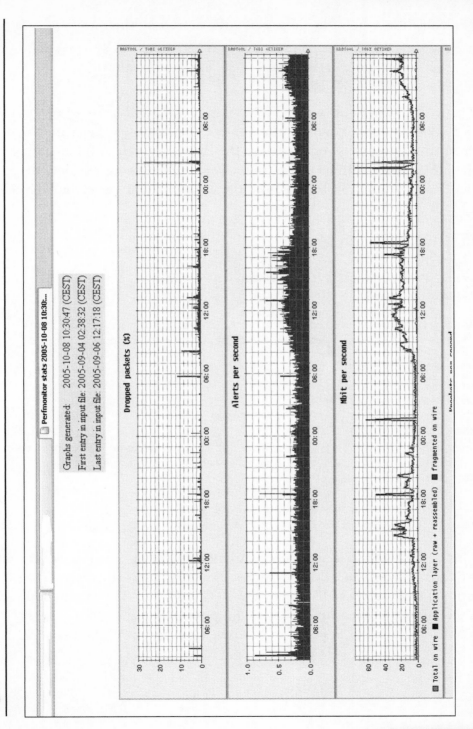

To enable this type of logging, edit your snort.conf file:

```
# snort.conf file change for perfmonitor preprocessor
preprocessor perfmonitor: flow time 300 snortfile
snort_stat_flow pktcnt 1000
```

This will enable Snort to log the csv format of data (snortfile) every five minutes (300 seconds), counting the number of packets (packets) and creating the "real-time" output (console). Once the data is written to the file, it can be graphed using the perfmon-graph tool. Using the following example script, the performance data can be displayed on an hourly basis; as an added bonus, the old file is archived to a dated file.

```
#!/bin/sh

# Jake Babbin
# Basic script to pull then graph the snort
# perfomance data to the web interface
#
# Insert into Root's crontab the following to call each hour
# 0 * * * * /bin/sh /path/to/this/script < /dev/null
#

# date variable
mydate=`date +"%m%d%Y%H"`

# Snort Sensor Name
scp user@sensorIP:/log/snort/snortstat_flow sensor_name_flow_perf;
perl perfmon-graph.pl /var/www/html/snortperf/sensor_name
sensor_name_flow_perf

# Move old file to archive that is dated
mv sensor_name_flow.file /log/archive/sensor_name_flow.file.$mydate
```

This type of information can be extremely useful in showing weekly and daily trends and outages. It creates a checks-and-balances situation for the operational tools such as HP Openview or CiscoWorks. The graphs and data from the Snort preprocessor show match up with the active data from the operational tools; if not, it's time to examine both tools and the network.

Using Bro to Log and Capture Application-Level Protocols

Using an open-source tool called Bro (www.bro-ids.org), the logging and capture of application-level protocols is now possible. For example, when using the Bro HTTP module and its submodule for "http-header," you can capture several useful pieces of Web traffic for every connection. Such information as the server name, user-agent, HTTP commands issued, and other information is captured for each connection, as shown in the following example:

```
1126121446.333380 %1580 start x.x.x.22 > x.x.x.104
1126121446.333380 %1580 > ACCEPT:  */*
1126121446.333380 %1580 > REFERER:  www.google.com/ig
1126121446.333380 %1580 > ACCEPT-LANGUAGE:  en-us
1126121446.333380 %1580 > ACCEPT-ENCODING:  gzip, deflate
1126121446.333380 %1580 > IF-MODIFIED-SINCE:  Tue, 06 Sep 2005
06:37:45 GMT; length=10704
1126121446.333380 %1580 > USER-AGENT:  Mozilla/4.0 (compatible;
MSIE 6.0; Windows NT 5.0; .NET CLR 1.0.3705)
1126121446.333380 %1580 > HOST:  www.google.com
1126121446.333380 %1580 > CONNECTION:  Keep-Alive
1126121446.333380 %1580 > COOKIE:  IGPC=ET=hjlqEWZI3AM;
IGAT=PI=0;
IGTP=H4sIAAAAAAAAG2PQQ6DIBBFr2JYNwqiCydN1z1AF12QNBOg1UQBAWO8fdH
WuumCZH4y782HA82q9Bo4MyjrjAPbcg2EARO0oiUI0sbooCjmec7HyUaMnTXB4Uv
n0g6FwojFaKPKfQiCkMvXViVbudvMNDzQx072OsDq5cIELVfTFqkwO9gkju9cbyX
-lgS5onPLaZ1vd0EOZqu-Qux_ddVtp9AvuddP7bWRn_Kz9co-
Y6sVLikcn3gDNp28shoBAAA;
PREF=ID=2911b04d733ad670:TB=2:TM=1109377476:LM=1112645061:S=t0bv
d40u7M-OORUS; testcookie=; IGDND=1
1126121446.351660 %1580 < CONTENT-TYPE:  text/javascript
1126121446.351660 %1580 < LAST-MODIFIED:  Tue, 06 Sep 2005
06:43:46 GMT
```

The rest is kept out for brevity.

Now you're probably wondering how to enable this tool and what other information you can obtain by using it. As mentioned before BRO is an application-level IDS that at its lowest levels is a series of protocol decoders. These decoders then have a policy built around them; for example, in the case of SMTP, the decoder knows the order and SMTP commands to expect in a typical mail session. If the connection uses different commands such as use of authentication between active directory windows mail servers, then BRO will still record the connection but having fired off several "alarms" for unknown SMTP commands. Although in the case of its DNS decoder, which seems to be one of the few applications that has one, it can determine when a DNS Pointer (PTR) scan is being performed against your DNS server(s). All this information is about the policy files for each "protocol," though there are some application policies as well for such things as gnutella peer-to-peer or blaster worm traffc. If you want to enable several policies and supporting decoders automatically, you would edit a file called "mt.bro" in the policy subdirectory of the bro distribution. To enable HTTP logging like the previous example, you would create an mt.bro file like the following example:

```
# Example BRO mt.bro file
@load http
@load http-request
@load http-reply
@load http-header
```

This would then tell the bro daemon to load:

Generic HTTP decoding policy (http),
```
   1126121446.333380 %1580 start x.x.x.22 > x.x.x.104
```
Client or browser request,
```
1126121446.333380 %1580 GET /index.html (200 "OK" [8183])
```
Server response,
```
   1126121446.333380 %1580 > ACCEPT:  */*
   1126121446.333380 %1580 > HOST:  www.google.com
```
HTTP Header information, the real value add,
```
   1126121446.333380 %1580 > REFERER:  http://www.google.com/ig
   1126121446.333380 %1580 > ACCEPT-LANGUAGE:  en-us
   1126121446.333380 %1580 > ACCEPT-ENCODING:  gzip, deflate
   1126121446.333380 %1580 > IF-MODIFIED-SINCE:  Tue, 06 Sep
2005 06:37:45 GMT;
   length=10704
   1126121446.333380 %1580 > USER-AGENT:  Mozilla/4.0
(compatible; MSIE 6.0; Windows
```

```
    NT 5.0; .NET CLR 1.0.3705)
    1126121446.333380 %1580 > HOST:  www.google.com
    1126121446.333380 %1580 > CONNECTION:  Keep-Alive
    1126121446.333380 %1580 > COOKIE:  IGPC=ET=hjlqEWZI3AM;
IGAT=PI=0;
     Y6sVLikcn3gDNp28shoBAAA; testcookie=; IGDND=1
    1126121446.351660 %1580 < CONTENT-TYPE:  text/javascript
```

With all of these enabled you can search for and find Browsers that are not approved "USER-AGENT" or track spyware such gator or claria based on their unique user-agent string. You can use the "HOST" field to track domains or top servers to either block or to add to your network webcaching server. Another use of these logs is to help debug web-based applications if they talk unencrypted. The full potential of these logs and the BRO application logs is limited only by policy of your organization and the readers' imagination.

Tracking Malware and Authorized Software in Web Traffic

If your organization is trying to fight malware or enforce policy by using only approved software, this data can be useful in determining and detecting hosts that are in violation. The user-agent field is according to the w3c.org site:

"Any software that retrieves and renders Web content for users. This may include Web browsers, media players, plug-ins, and other programs—including assistive technologies—that help in retrieving and rendering Web content."

What this means is that we now have a method to track what type of clients are using the Web through your network. For example, all Internet Explorer browsers have the user-agent string "MSIE," while the Firefox/Netscape/Opera browsers have the string "Mozilla." However, if we eliminate these common strings, forgetting for a moment the Browser Helper Object malware, we quickly find a way to detect such problem applications as gator, streaming media applications such as Real Player, and others. This information can then be searched and displayed as a count of how many times each user-agent was seen (see Figure 2.4).

Figure 2.4 BRO Counts of Unique User-Agents Seen on a Network

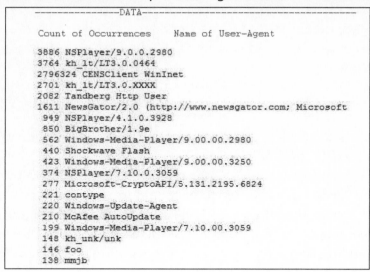

Another way this information can be useful is showing over time a drop or rise in unapproved software. For example, if your organization is actively trying to get rid of the malware running over its network, a simple pie chart like the one shown in Figure 2.5 should show the effects of the removal.

Figure 2.5 Bro Malware Effects

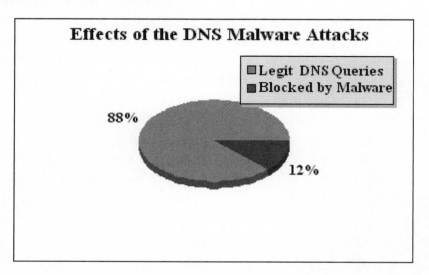

Here is an example of the code related to the pie chart in Figure 2.5.

```php
// INCLUDES FOR GRAPH
include ( "/path/to/base/jpgraph/src/jpgraph.php");
include ( "/path/to/base/jpgraph/src/jpgraph_pie.php");
include ( "/path/to/base/jpgraph/src/jpgraph_pie3d.php");

// DATA
// read from file
$d1=`grep "UNIQUE" dailymalware.txt | awk '{ print $9}'`;
$d2=`grep "Security" dailymalware.txt | awk '{ print $13 }'`;

$data = array("$d1", "$d2");
$leg = array("Legit DNS Queries", "Blocked by Malware");

//// CREATE GRAPH SIZEING AND FEATURES
$graph = new PieGraph (400,250,"auto");
//$graph->SetShadow();
$graph->title->Set(" Effects of <YOUR ORGANIZATIONS> DNS Malware
Blocks");
$graph->title->SetFont(FF_FONT1,FS_BOLD);


$p1 = new PiePlot3D($data);
$p1->SetSize(.3);

// LEGENDS
$p1->SetLegends($leg);

$p1->value->SetFont(FF_FONT1,FS_BOLD);
$p1->value->SetColor("blue");
$p1->SetLabelType(PIE_VALUE_PER);
$p1->SetSliceColors(array('green','red'));

$graph->Add($p1);
$graph->Stroke();

?>
```

However, if your organization has been trying to get rid of malware and is trying to show the effects over time, the graph in Figure 2.6 and the related code might be more helpful.

Figure 2.6 Bro Malware Effects by Day of Week

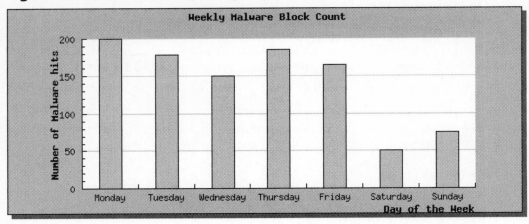

Here is an example of the code related to Figure 2.6.

```php
<?php

// INCLUDES FOR GRAPH
include ( "/path/to/base/jpgraph/src/jpgraph.php");
include ( "/path/to/base/jpgraph/src/jpgraph_bar.php");

// DATA
// read from file

// Assumes that each day's "dailymalware.txt" file was added to
// a new file with only the values for the UNIQUE DNS queries
value
// and the MALWARE values
//

// Create blank arrays for place holders
$uniquedns = array();
$malwaredns = array();

$f = fopen("/tmp/weekly_malware.txt", "r");
while ($array= fgetcsv($f, 7," ")) {

array_push($uniquedns, $array[0]);
array_push($malwaredns, $array[1]);
```

```
// print "$uniquedns[0] <br>";
// print "$malwaredns[0] <br>";


}
fclose($f);


$data = $malwaredns;

//// CREATE GRAPH SIZING AND FEATURES
$graph = new Graph (400,250,"auto");
$graph->SetScale("textlin");

// Add drop shadow
$graph->SetShadow();

// Create bar plot
$bplot = new BarPlot($data);
$graph->Add($bplot);

// Titles and x/y axis labels
$graph->title->Set("Weekly Malware Block Count");
$graph->xaxis->title->Set("Number of Malware DNS requests");
$graph->yaxis->title->Set("Number of Unique DNS requests");

// Fonts
$graph->title->SetFont(FF_FONT1,FS_BOLD);
$graph->yaxis->title->SetFont(FF_FONT1,FS_BOLD);
$graph->xaxis->title->SetFont(FF_FONT1,FS_BOLD);

// Display the graph
$graph->Stroke();

?>
```

Determining Which Machines Use a Provided/Supported Browser

Using this same logging, you can also determine which machines on your network are not using the provided/supported browser. This information is useful on a network where there is no easy way to get to remote machines to clean them. Using this information, a security team can have the needed arguments for implementing Web content filtering such as with Websense, or a squid proxy to limit the amount of malware data leaving their networks. For example, if you are looking to see how much of your Web traffic is being done with your approved Web browser, you might have a chart like the one shown in Figure 2.7 and the related code.

Figure 2.7 Amount of Web Traffic with Approved vs Unapproved Applications

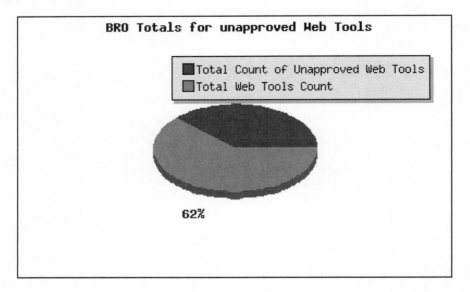

Here is an example of the code related to the chart in Figure 2.7:

```php
<?php
```

```php
// INCLUDES FOR GRAPH
include (
"/usr/local/apache2/htdocs/SUPPORT/jpgraph/src/jpgraph.php");
include (
"/usr/local/apache2/htdocs/SUPPORT/jpgraph/src/jpgraph_pie.php")
;
include (
"/usr/local/apache2/htdocs/SUPPORT/jpgraph/src/jpgraph_pie3d.php
");


// DATA
```

```
// read from file
$d1=`grep "UNAPPROVED" dailysnort.txt | awk '{ print $2}'`;
$d2=`grep "TOTAL" dailysnort.txt | awk '{ print $2 }'`;


$data = array("$d1", "$d2");
$leg = array("Total Count of Unapproved Web Tools", "Total Web
Tools Count");


//// CREATE GRAPH SIZING AND FEATURES
$graph = new PieGraph (400,250,"auto");
//$graph->SetShadow();
$graph->title->Set(" BRO Totals for unapproved Web Tools");
$graph->title->SetFont(FF_FONT1,FS_BOLD);



$p1 = new PiePlot3D($data);
$p1->SetSize(.3);
//$p1->SetCenter(0.45);
//$p1->SetStartAngle(20);
//$p1->SetAngle(45);


// LEGENDS
$p1->SetLegends($leg);


$p1->value->SetFont(FF_FONT1,FS_BOLD);
$p1->value->SetColor("blue");
$p1->SetLabelType(PIE_VALUE_PER);
$p1->SetSliceColors(array('red','green'));


$graph->Add($p1);
$graph->Stroke();



?>
```

Tracking Users' Web Activities with Bro

We have already shown you how you can use the Bro IDS tool to enforce policy, but how about helping to track things like the top sites your users visit, or which user is your top Web surfer? When you run Bro with the HTTP module enabled, tracking each connection is quite easy—the connection details are harder.

To track the top site using this module, you need to search in the first line in the next example:

```
1126121446.333380 %1580 start 10.0.4.100 > 64.233.161.104
... (cut for brevity)
1126121446.333380 %1580 > USER-AGENT:  Mozilla/4.0 (compatible;
MSIE 6.0; Windows NT 5.0; .NET CLR 1.0.3705)
1126121446.333380 %1580 > HOST:   www.google.com
1126121446.333380 %1580 > CONNECTION:  Keep-Alive
1126121446.351828 %1580 GET /ig/f/1Pb00AJmja0/ig.js (200 "OK"
[3732])
... (cut for brevity)
```

Tools & Traps...

BRO Leaks....Memory

Several versions of BRO have a limitation: if you let BRO run for long periods of time (more than three hours) without a restart, several of the policies will start to leak larger and larger sections of memory. Another hangup of BRO is when you restart it, it will delete and recreate the empty files for logging! To correct both of these problems a simple script is needed when to schedule BRO restarts and log moves. In all of my examples, BRO is restarted every 10 minutes. While this may seem excessively short to some, this actually will help make data searches easier and faster. For example at a recent client site with only a T3 connection the daily HTTP logs were around 15 to 20 GB per day!

The following script is called from cron every 10 minutes on each sensor that is running BRO to rotate the log files.

```sh
#!/bin/sh


####################################
# Jake Babbin
####################################


#######################################################
# This script is a meant to be used at a template for starting
and stopping
# the bro processes that are running on the system. This script
# also does some of the maintainence of the logs and rotates the
old files
# with datestamps then places a blank one in it's place.
#
# Example cron job run every 10 minutes on the 10s
# 0,10,20,30,40,50 * * * * /bin/sh /this_script.sh
#
# The date and other system variables are ment for BSD platforms
# You will have to tweak for Linux platforms
#######################################################

mydate=`date +%H%M%m%d%G`

#echo "This should be my date in its proper format here $mydate
"


# First this is going to kill the running bro process
# Ugly but it works as until bro is put into a daemon process no
pid is recorded

#find the pid for the bro process
pidofbro=`ps -ax | grep bro | grep -v "grep" |head -n 1 | awk
'{print $1}'`
rpidofbro=$pidofbro
```

```
echo "This should be the bro pid number $rpidofbro "

# now we kill it
killbro=`kill -9 $rpidofbro`

# Move the current files to their archive places
mv /path/to/bro/dns.log /path/to/bro/dns/dns.log.$mydate
mv /path/to/bro/http.log /path/to/bro/http/http.log.$mydate
mv /path/to/bro/smtp.log /path/to/bro/smtp/smtp.log.$mydate

# create the blank ones for the new process to use
touch /path/to/bro/dns.log
touch /path/to/bro/http.log
touch /path/to/bro/smtp.log

# now restart bro
export BROPATH=/path/to/bro/distribution/policy
/path/to/bro/distribution/bro -i <SNIFFING_INTERFACE>
/path/to/bro/distribution/policy/mt.bro >
/path/to/bro/BRO_RUN.err &

# Make a note for myself when it was last run
date > /path/to/bro/LASTRUN

# All done
```

If you are storing the Web traffic by hour, http.<dateHour>", searching for the top site can be done in two ways.

The first way is to count the total destinations or the sixth field in the line starting with the word *start*, and then count the total number of lines called "total web" as in the following example:

```
1126121446.333380 %1580 start 10.0.4.100 > 64.233.161.104
... (cut for brevity)
1126121446.333380 %1580 > USER-AGENT:  Mozilla/4.0 (compatible;
MSIE 6.0; Windows NT 5.0; .NET CLR 1.0.3705)
1126121446.333380 %1580 > HOST:  www.google.com
1126121446.333380 %1580 > CONNECTION:  Keep-Alive
```

```
1126121446.351828 %1580 GET /ig/f/lPb00AJmja0/ig.js (200 "OK"
[3732])
```
… (cut for brevity)

Then, count the top 10 sites using simple parsing of the data as in:

```
# Count the total number of lines in http logs
cat http.<date> | grep "start" | cat -n | tail -n 1  >
totalwebIP.txt
# Count the top 10 destinations
cat http.<date> | grep "start" | awk '{ print $4 }' | sort
| uniq -c | sort -nr | head -n 10  > top10_Ips.txt
```

The second way to count the total destinations is the search the HTTP log files for the line "HOST:". This is the name of the Web server being connected to as it is "told" to each Web browser. The advantage of this data is that the DNS name of the Web server being connected to is already filled in without having to perform a second step. This can be useful when trying to show misuse of network resources, such as your top hostname is images.monster.com or update1.gator.com.

```
1126121446.333380 %1580 start 10.0.4.100 > 64.233.161.104
```
… (cut for brevity)
```
1126121446.333380 %1580 > USER-AGENT:  Mozilla/4.0 (compatible;
MSIE 6.0; Windows NT 5.0; .NET CLR 1.0.3705)
```
1126121446.333380 %1580 > HOST: www.google.com
```
1126121446.333380 %1580 > CONNECTION:  Keep-Alive
1126121446.351828 %1580 GET /ig/f/lPb00AJmja0/ig.js (200 "OK"
[3732])
```
… (cut for brevity)

The problem with this type of logging is that not every host, especially those used by malware hosts, returns a "HOST" field, possibly to make them harder to block for content or URL filtering. However, if you are going to use this type of searching, is should be counted much like the destination IP using a script like the following to determine the top 10 hosts:

```
# Count the total number of connections with a "HOST" line
cat http.<date> | grep "HOST: " | cat -n | tail -n 1
# Count the top 10 destinations
cat http.<date> | grep "HOST: " | awk '{ print $5 }' |
sort | uniq -c | sort -nr | head -n 10 > top10_HOSTS.txt
```

Finally, if your organization is trying to provide this type of information to management to show, for example, how much of your Web traffic is being used by malware, this is easy to do. Taking the data from the previous examples, assume that your top host is gator7.gatornet.com. The simple answer is to take the count for the gator host and divide it by the total number of Web requests. However, to graph this data for a daily report, for example, we can use the JpGraph library that is already installed on our Web server for BASE/ACID using the code in the following examples (see Figures 2.8 and 2.9):

Figure 2.8 A Pull-in Real-Time Picture Is Generated for Every Refresh

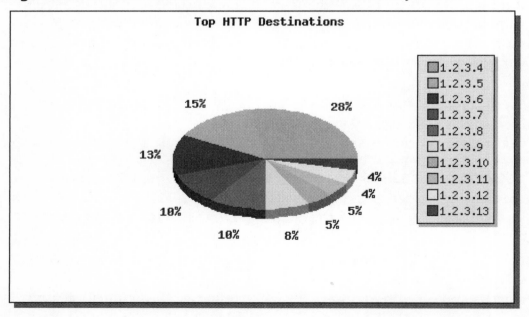

Figure 2.9 A Daily Picture Link to a Picture File Is Easier to Script for a Daily Report

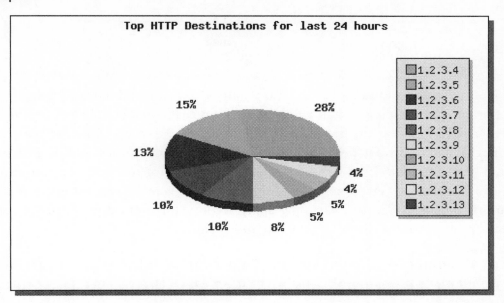

Using Bro to Gather DNS and Web Traffic Data

Can you determine the top .com/.net/.edu/etc. site that your users are requesting? How much of that is malware?   Can you use that information to create a blocklist of bad domains to kill malware before it has a chance to communicate outside your network(s)?

Since your organization is using Bro, what other "cool" information can we gather with this tool? Since Bro is logging all this information about a DNS and Web traffic, can we generate statistics about this data? How about showing how many sites are being accessed by domain (.com/.net/.xxx)? The short answer to these questions is a definitive "yes." Again, using the DNS requests or "A record" queries, we can determine and count the breakdown of DNS domains through scripts. In the following example, we are simply gathering a total number of DNS queries per 24-hour period:

```
#!/bin/bash
total_dns=`grep "?A " /path/to/bro/dns/dns.log.*<date> |
cat -n | tail -n 1 | awk '{ print $1 }' `
```

This count alone can be used as leverage in swaying an organization into using their own caching servers, as a caching DNS server can cut down on the amount of bandwidth being used by an organization's Internet pipe. Another reason to use a caching DNS server is that it is easier to poison the server with bad domains for known malware hosts or policy violating hosts (discriminating, sexual, political(?) sites). Another report that could be generated from the DNS Bro data is a breakdown by site for hits against a known list of malware servers. Take a list of known domains from, say, castlecops.com, and then using a Perl script, simply apply a count for every domain in the list from highest to lowest hit, such as the following:

PERL SCRIPT TO TAKE A LIST OF DOMAINS AND ADD A COUNT TO EACH DOMAIN AFTER SEARCHING THROUGH BRO WEB LOGS.

```
For each line
Search column 1 value in 'daily domain file'
If found then return line from 'daily domain file' to
'malware temp list file'
Repeat until end of file
Run sort +1 -nr on 'malware temp list file' output to
'malware list file'
```

Another report that could come out of this data is a breakdown of DNS domains being accessed from your organization. While the value of this report is going to differ for each organization, it can be another piece of information in your reporting infrastructure. Examples are shown in Figures 2.10 and 2.11; the first is an unsorted list of the domains being accessed, and the second is the same list sorted for unique domains. The reason for the second domain is that the first graph doesn't take into account all of the same calls to the same site, such as when your users have www.google.com set to their home-page every time they open a new browser.

Figure 2.10 Unsorted DNS Domain Breakdown

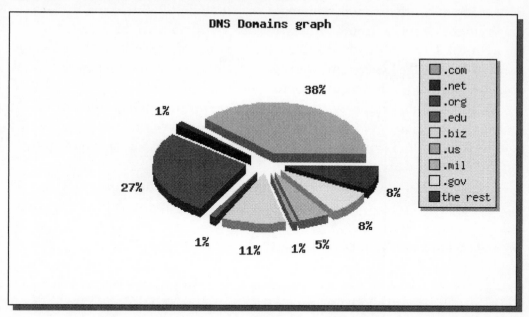

Figure 2.11 Sorted List of DNS Domains

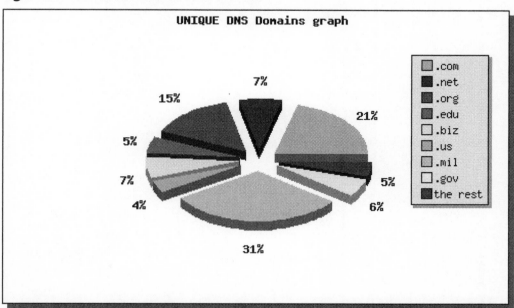

The usefulness of these graphs can be vary, depending on the organiza-tion. If yours has the default homepage set on all the workstations, the second graph might be more useful. Otherwise, the first graph would show an inac-curate breakdown of the domains, having counted all 90 million hits to your assigned homepage every time your users opened a new browser in the domain counts.

To generate this graph, we are again relying on the JpGraph library to render the data. However, this data first comes from Bro on the sensor by counting each DNS domain total and placing it in a file for later pickup by the Web server's daily scripts.

```
#!/bin/sh

###############################
#
# This is a script that calculates for jpgraph presentation the DNS
# domains being accessed such as ".com",".net",etc
#
# As well a then sorting through to knock out all of the repeats and
# finding out how much is then being accessed.
#
#    Jake Babbin
#    06/02/2004
#
###############################
        # Variables (BSD DATES)
yesdate=`date -v -1d +"%m%d%Y"`
yeslongdate=`date -v -1d +"%c"`
        # Remove the old report
rm /logs/DAILY_DNS_DOMAINS.txt
rm /logs/DAILY_UNIQUE_DNS_DOMAINS.txt
rm /tmp/domains_daily.txt
rm /tmp/unique_domains.txt
```

```
# Sort through the dns bro logs and find the amounts then insert
into # a file (GRAPH 1 UNSORTED DATA)
grep "?A " /log/bro/dns/dns.log.*$yesdate  | awk '{ print $4 }'
| grep "[.]" | grep -c "[.]com$" >> /tmp/domains_daily.txt


grep "?A " /log/bro/dns/dns.log.*$yesdate | awk '{ print $4 }' |
      grep "[.]" | grep -c "[.]net$" >> /tmp/domains_daily.txt


grep "?A " /log/bro/dns/dns.log.*$yesdate | awk '{ print $4 }' |
      grep "[.]" | grep -c "[.]org$" >> /tmp/domains_daily.txt


grep "?A " /log/bro/dns/dns.log.*$yesdate | awk '{ print $4 }' |
grep "[.]" | grep -c "[.]edu$" >> /tmp/domains_daily.txt


grep "?A " /log/bro/dns/dns.log.*$yesdate | awk '{ print $4 }' |
      grep "[.]" | grep -c "[.]biz$" >> /tmp/domains_daily.txt


grep "?A " /log/bro/dns/dns.log.*$yesdate | awk '{ print $4 }' |
           grep "[.]" | grep -c "[.]us$" >>
/tmp/domains_daily.txt


grep "?A " /log/bro/dns/dns.log.*$yesdate | awk '{ print $4 }' |
      grep "[.]" |grep -c "[.]mil$" >> /tmp/domains_daily.txt


grep "?A " /log/bro/dns/dns.log.*$yesdate | awk '{ print $4 }' |
      grep "[.]" |grep -c "[.]gov$" >> /tmp/domains_daily.txt


grep "?A " /log/bro/dns/dns.log.*$yesdate | awk '{ print $4 }' |
      grep "[.]" |grep -v -e "[.]com$" -e "[.]net$" -e "[.]org$"
-e "[.]edu$" -e "[.]biz$" -e "[.]us$" -e "[.]mil$" -e "[.]gov$"
| grep -c "[.]" >> /tmp/domains_daily.txt
# Copy for distribution
cp /tmp/domains_daily.txt /logs/DAILY_DNS_DOMAINS.txt
# Now we take that and we knock out all of the repeats.
# GRAPH 2 DATA
grep "?A " /log/bro/dns/dns.log.*$yesdate | awk '{ print $4 }' |
      grep "[.]" | sort | uniq |grep -c "[.]com$" >>
/tmp/unique_domains.txt
```

```
grep "?A " /log/bro/dns/dns.log.*$yesdate | awk '{ print $4 }' |
     grep "[.]" | sort | uniq | grep -c "[.]net$" >>
/tmp/unique_domains.txt

grep "?A " /log/bro/dns/dns.log.*$yesdate | awk '{ print $4 }' |
     grep "[.]" |sort | uniq| grep -c "[.]org$" >>
/tmp/unique_domains.txt

grep "?A " /log/bro/dns/dns.log.*$yesdate | awk '{ print $4 }' |
      grep "[.]" | sort | uniq |grep -c "[.]edu$" >>
/tmp/unique_domains.txt

grep "?A " /log/bro/dns/dns.log.*$yesdate | awk '{ print $4 }' |
     grep "[.]" | sort | uniq | grep -c "[.]biz$" >>
/tmp/unique_domains.txt

grep "?A " /log/bro/dns/dns.log.*$yesdate | awk '{ print $4 }' |
     grep "[.]" | sort | uniq |grep -c "[.]us$" >>
/tmp/unique_domains.txt

grep "?A " /log/bro/dns/dns.log.*$yesdate | awk '{print $4 }' |
grep "[.]" | sort | uniq |grep -c "[.]mil$" >>
/tmp/unique_domains.txt

grep "?A " /log/bro/dns/dns.log.*$yesdate | awk '{ print $4 }' |
     grep "[.]" | sort | uniq|  grep -c "[.]gov$" >>
/tmp/unique_domains.txt

grep "?A " /log/bro/dns/dns.log.*$yesdate | awk '{ print $4 }' |
grep "[.]" | grep -v "[.]com$" | grep -v "[.]net$" | grep -v
"[.]org$" | grep -v "[.]edu$" | grep -v "[.]biz$" | grep -v
"[.]us$" | grep -v "[.]mil$" | grep -v "[.]gov$" | grep -v
"[.]arpa$" | sort | uniq | grep -c "[.]" >>
/tmp/unique_domains.txt

# Copy for distribution
cp /tmp/unique_domains.txt /logs/DAILY_UNIQUE_DNS_DOMAINS.txt
# All done
```

After creating these two scripts, we can have a cron script that grabs these files every day before the start of work. Then, having the files on the Web server, they are prepared for graphs using the following scripts in PHP.

Example of code for the daily DNS domains:

```php
<?php
// INCLUDES FOR GRAPH
include ( "/path/to/BASE/jpgraph/src/jpgraph.php");
include ( "/path/to/BASE/jpgraph/src/jpgraph_pie.php");
include ( "/path/to/BASE/jpgraph/src/jpgraph_pie3d.php");
// DATA
// read from file (/tmp/domains_dns.txt)
// blank array (needed for placeholding )
$rawdata = array();
$data2 = array();
$rawfile = file("/tmp/domains_dns.txt","r");
foreach ($rawfile as $row) {
array_push($data2, $row);
}
// Static (the "Legend" for each entry in the array above)
$leg2 =
array(".com",".net",".org",".edu",".biz",".us",".mil",".gov","th
e rest");
// CREATE GRAPH SIZEING AND FEATURES
$graph = new PieGraph (500,300,"auto");
$graph->SetShadow();
$graph->title->Set(" <ORGANIZATION NAME> DNS Domains graph");
$graph->title->SetFont(FF_FONT1,FS_BOLD);
$p2 = new PiePlot3D($data2);
// adjust color theme can be: earth,pastel,sand or water
$p2->SetTheme('sand');
$p2->SetSize(.3);
$p2->value->Show();
$p2->value->SetFont(FF_FONT1,FS_BOLD);
$p2->value->SetColor("blue");
$p2->SetLabelType(PIE_VALUE_PER);
```

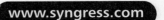
www.syngress.com

```php
//$p2->SetLabelType(PIE_LABEL_ABS);
// LEGENDS
$p2->SetLegends($leg2);
// Find and highlight large use
// $a = array_search(max($data2), $data2);
// Find and highlight smallest slice
//$a = array_search(min($data2), $data2);
// $p2->ExplodeSlice($a);
$graph->Add($p2);
$graph->Stroke();
?>
```

Here is an example of the code for the sorted DNS domain break-downs:

```php
<?php
// INCLUDES FOR GRAPH
include ( "/path/to/BASE/jpgraph/src/jpgraph.php");
include ( "/path/to/BASE/jpgraph/src/jpgraph_pie.php");
include ( "/path/to/BASE/jpgraph/src/jpgraph_pie3d.php");
      // DATA
// read from file (/tmp/domains_unique.txt)
// blank array
$rawdata = array();
$data2 = array();
$rawfile = file("/tmp/domains_unique.txt","r");
foreach ($rawfile as $row) {
array_push($data2, $row);
}
// Static
$leg2 =
array(".com",".net",".org",".edu",".biz",".us",".mil",".gov","th
e rest");
// CREATE GRAPH SIZEING AND FEATURES
$graph = new PieGraph (500,300,"auto");
$graph->SetShadow();
$graph->title->Set("<ORGANIZATION NAME> UNIQUE DNS Domains ");
```

```
$graph->title->SetFont(FF_FONT1,FS_BOLD);
$p2 = new PiePlot3D($data2);
// adjust color theme can be: earth,pastel,sand or water
$p2->SetTheme('sand');
$p2->SetSize(.3);
$p2->value->Show();
$p2->value->SetFont(FF_FONT1,FS_BOLD);
$p2->value->SetColor("blue");
$p2->SetLabelType(PIE_VALUE_PER);
// LEGENDS
$p2->SetLegends($leg2);
// Find and highlight large use
// $a = array_search(max($data2), $data2);
// Find and highlight smallest slice
//$a = array_search(min($data2), $data2);
// $p2->ExplodeSlice($a);
$graph->Add($p2);
$graph->Stroke();
?>
```

A spin-off of this script could be a total DNS traffic versus counts of the top 10 "please I need more work to do" sites, such as games.yahoo.com, popcap-games.com, or others more specific to your organization such as washingtonpost.com. This data would be grabbed with the following script for later generation via the same type of script as those used for the DNS domain listings.

The top 10 useless site script:

```
#!/bin/bash
# Simple example script for generating a hit list for
useless sites
#
# Variables
total_dns=`grep "?A " /path/to/bro/dns/dns.log.*<date> |
cat -n  | tail -n 1 | awk '{ print $1 }' `
```

```
       <site1>=`grep "?A " /path/to/bro/dns/dns.log.*<date> |
grep "<site1>"     | cat -n | tail -n 1 | awk '{ print $1 }'
       <site2>=`grep "?A " /path/to/bro/dns/dns.log.*<date> |
grep "<site1>"     | cat -n | tail -n 1 | awk '{ print $1 }'
       <site3>=`grep "?A " /path/to/bro/dns/dns.log.*<date> |
grep "<site1>"     | cat -n | tail -n 1 | awk '{ print $1 }'
       <site4>=`grep "?A " /path/to/bro/dns/dns.log.*<date> |
grep "<site1>"     | cat -n | tail -n 1 | awk '{ print $1 }'
       <site5>=`grep "?A " /path/to/bro/dns/dns.log.*<date> |
grep "<site1>"     | cat -n | tail -n 1 | awk '{ print $1 }'
       <site6>=`grep "?A " /path/to/bro/dns/dns.log.*<date> |
grep "<site1>"     | cat -n | tail -n 1 | awk '{ print $1 }'
       <site7>=`grep "?A " /path/to/bro/dns/dns.log.*<date> |
grep "<site1>"     | cat -n | tail -n 1 | awk '{ print $1 }'
       <site8>=`grep "?A " /path/to/bro/dns/dns.log.*<date> |
grep "<site1>"     | cat -n | tail -n 1 | awk '{ print $1 }'
       <site9>=`grep "?A " /path/to/bro/dns/dns.log.*<date> |
grep "<site1>"     | cat -n | tail -n 1 | awk '{ print $1 }'
       <site10>=`grep "?A " /path/to/bro/dns/dns.log.*<date> |
       grep "<site1>" | cat -n | tail -n 1 | awk '{ print $1 }'

       # Delete the old file and create a placeholder file
       rm /log/useless_site.txt
       touch /log/useless_site.txt
       # OUTPUT TO File the totals
       site1_total=$total_dns-$site1
       echo "$site1_total <site1_name>" > /log/useless_site.txt

       site2_total=$total_dns-$site2
       echo "$site2_total <site2_name>" >> /log/useless_site.txt

       site3_total=$total_dns-$site3
       echo "$site3_total <site3_name>"  >> /log/useless_site.txt

       site4_total=$total_dns-$site4
       echo "$site4_total <site4_name>"  >> /log/useless_site.txt

       site5_total=$total_dns-$site5
```

```
    echo "$site5_total <site5_name>"  >> /log/useless_site.txt

    site6_total=$total_dns-$site6
    echo "$site6_total <site6_name>"  >> /log/useless_site.txt

    site7_total=$total_dns-$site7
    echo "$site7_total <site7_name>"  >> /log/useless_site.txt

    site8_total=$total_dns-$site8
    echo "$site8_total <site8_name>"  >> /log/useless_site.txt

    site9_total=$total_dns-$site9
    echo "$site9_total <site9_name>"  >> /log/useless_site.txt

    site10_total0=$total_dns-$site10
    echo "$site10_total <site10_name>"  >>
/log/useless_site.txt
```

Then, you could simply add this file to the list that your daily cron job pulls from the sensor(s) the create a graph of this amount of traffic each site takes on your network such as the following example:

```
<?php
// INCLUDES FOR GRAPH
include ( "/path/to/BASE/jpgraph/src/jpgraph.php");
include ( "/path/to/BASE/jpgraph/src/jpgraph_pie.php");
include ( "/path/to/BASE/jpgraph/src/jpgraph_pie3d.php");
    // DATA
// read from file (/tmp/useless_site.txt)
// blank array
$rawdata = array();
$data2 = array();
$rawfile = file("/tmp/useless_site.txt","r");
foreach ($rawfile as $row) {
array_push($data2, $row[0]);
```

```
array_push($leg2, $row[1]);
}
// CREATE GRAPH SIZEING AND FEATURES
$graph = new PieGraph (500,300,"auto");
$graph->SetShadow();
$graph->title->Set("<ORGANIZATION NAME> top 10 useless site
access ); $graph->title->SetFont(FF_FONT1,FS_BOLD);
$p2 = new PiePlot3D($data2);
// adjust color theme can be: earth,pastel,sand or water
$p2->SetTheme('sand');
$p2->SetSize(.3);
$p2->value->Show();
$p2->value->SetFont(FF_FONT1,FS_BOLD);
$p2->value->SetColor("blue");
$p2->SetLabelType(PIE_VALUE_PER);
// LEGENDS
$p2->SetLegends($leg2);
// Find and highlight large use
// $a = array_search(max($data2), $data2);
// Find and highlight smallest slice
//$a = array_search(min($data2), $data2);
// $p2->ExplodeSlice($a);
$graph->Add($p2);
$graph->Stroke();
?>
```

Using Bro for Blackholing Traffic to Malware-Infested Domains

Finally, if your organization is trying to combat malware traversing across its network and has implemented a blacklist of DNS domains for known mal-ware sites, you can determine the effectiveness of the blacklist simply by looking through the DNS requests, "A records" again, for all those that return for your blackhole host.

Tools & Traps…

DNS Block Lists

There are several options if you want to use DNS domain blacklists to stop malware. The first would be to create your own list based off of your organizations "intelligence". This list can be based off of something as simple at the list of the top software removal request that come into the helpdesk or from other resources. Another option would be to get one from a site or organization that already has done that process and is updating their list often such as the Spyware listening post from Bleedingsnort.org (http://www.bleedingsnort.com/staticpages/index.php?page=listeningpost).

To figure out what to do with your blacklist and how to configure your DNS server there are several guides at the Bleedingsnort Black Hole DNS projects' page (http://www.bleedingsnort.com/blackhole-dns/).

If you chose to set up the "malware host" to blackhole traffic to all known malware domains, a search through the Bro DNS or even HTTP logs will show how many hosts have malware loaded on them. If your security team is trying to demonstrate the effectiveness of the blackholing, a search through the logs for the "malware host" such as the following script can be used:

```
      #!/bin/sh

###################
#
# Jake Babbin
# 07 July 2004
# This calculates the total numbers for the malware dns
# requests being stopped
#
###################
```

```
# Variables (BSD date)
yesdate=`date -v -1d +"%m%d%Y"`
yeslongdate=`date -v -1d +"%c"`
# TEMP
mydate=`date +"%m%d%Y"`
longdate=`date +"%c"`


# Gather the previous day's total DNS record
yesDNSTOTAL=`grep "?A " /log/bro/dns/dns.log.*$yesdate | grep -v
"Xnam" | awk '{ print $6 }' | grep "[.]"  | cat -n | tail -n 1 |
awk '{ print $1 }' `
# Gather the previous day's total UNIQUE DNS records
yesDNSUNIQUE=`grep "?A " /log/bro/dns/dns.log.*$yesdate | grep -
v "Xnam" | awk '{ print $6 }' | grep "[.]"  | sort | uniq -c |
sort -nr | cat -n | tail -n 1 | awk '{ print $1 }' `
# Gather the previous day's count for the total UNIQUE that
resolved to
# The malware host
yesDNSSEC=`grep "?A " /log/bro/dns/dns.log.*$yesdate | grep -v
"Xnam" | awk '{ print $6 }' | grep "[.]"  | sort | uniq -c |
sort -nr | grep "<IP of the malware host>" | awk '{ print $1 }'
`


# MAIN
     echo "Generating data for $yeslongdate on DNS queries" >
/logs/DAILY_MALWARE.txt
echo "" >> /logs/DAILY_MALWARE.txt
echo "This is the total DNS queries made yesterday: $yesDNSTOTAL
" >> /logs/DAILY_MALWARE.txt
echo "" >> /logs/DAILY_MALWARE.txt
echo "This is the UNIQUE DNS queries made yesterday:
$yesDNSUNIQUE " >> /logs/DAILY_MALWARE.txt
echo ""  >> /logs/DAILY_MALWARE.txt
echo "This is the Total DNS queries that resolved to the Malware
HOST box: $yesDNSSEC " >> /logs/DAILY_MALWARE.txt
echo "" >> /logs/DAILY_MALWARE.txt
echo "----------------------ALL DONE!" >>
/log/DAILY_MALWARE.txt
```

```
# SIMPLER FORMAT - just 3 values easier to parse for the
graphing php # script
        # FORMAT OF THE FILE IS
# VALUE1= TOTAL DNS QUERIES YESTERDAY
# VALUE2=TOTALE UNIQUE DNS QUERIES YESTERDAY
#VALUE3=TOTAL QUERIES THAT RESOLVED TO THE MALWARE HOST
echo "$yesDNSTOTAL $yesDNSUNIQUE $yesDNSSEC" >
/logs/DAILY_MALWARE_SIMPLE.txt
```

Tools & Traps…

It's Better to Have an Actual Blackhole Host than Not

In the world of Microsoft-centric networks, if you choose to implement a DNS blackholing of malware domains, you have two choices.

First, if you choose to set the blackhole host to loopback 127.0.0.1, you will get almost no indication if a host on your network has malware and will simply create traffic to your DNS server.

Second, you can implement a "malware host" to redirect and log the traffic. This box will be a *nix machine with no services running other than Apache. Apache has to be configured to answer every request with the same response, such as "Sorry known malware site. Complaints contact helpdesk" in a simple HTML document.

The second solution will limit the amount of traffic generated by malware agents on your network for a few reasons:

- When Internet Explorer tries to access a domain such as *www.cnn.com*, if it can't get an HTTP reply such as in the case of solution number 1, it tries several more iterations of the domain, such as *www.cnn.com.com*, *www.cnn.com.net*, *www.cnn.com.us*, and *www.cnn.com.biz*. When this happens, you have simply created five or more times the amount of traffic on your network.

- If you have a "malware host," you can grab statistics off it using a tool such as AWSTATS to parse the Web logs. Using this tool, you can generate a detailed set of information such

Continued

as amount of traffic per client, top client, user-agents, and others all in ready-made graphs and nicely formatted tables.

■ If users continue to try to load and run malware, the site can be tweaked to redirect them to an update server for "auto-patching" (although this solution is seen more on university networks having to do with IP assignment).

Whichever method you chose, each organization should be able to find the setup most useful to its operations and requirements.

Then, using the data from either file (simple for this example), we can create a graphic that is easy to understand—green is good, red is bad. Green will be the total DNS queries made the previous day, and red will be the total DNS queries for the malware host (see Figure 2.12).

Figure 2.12 Malware Traffic Graph

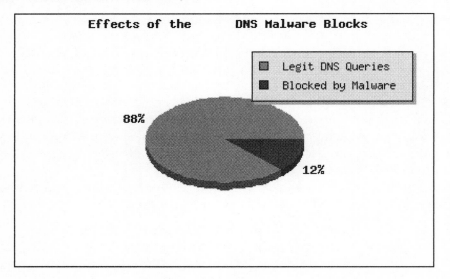

Again, the data from the previous script is added to our daily cron job to pull from the sensors. Then, we are going to create the graphic from the following script:

```php
    <?php
// INCLUDES FOR GRAPH
include ( "/path/to/BASE/jpgraph/src/jpgraph.php");
include ( "/path/to/BASE/jpgraph/src/jpgraph_pie.php");
include ( "/path/to/BASE/jpgraph/src/jpgraph_pie3d.php");

// DATA
// read from file using the format with wording
$d1=`grep "UNIQUE" dailymalware.txt | awk '{ print $9}'`;
$d2=`grep "Security" dailymalware.txt | awk '{ print $13 }'`;

    // DATA
    // read from file using the simple format
// blank array
//$data2 = array();
//$rawfile = file("/tmp/dailymalwaresimple.txt","r");
//foreach ($rawfile as $row) {
//array_push($data2, $row);
//}

    // MYSQL INSERTION
$link = mysql_connect('host','DB_username','password');
if (!$link) {
 die('Could not Connect: '. mysql_error());
 }
//echo 'Connected successfully';
web_date = date ("dmY");
$result = mysql_insert("INSERT
"$webdate","$data2[0]","$data[1]","$data[3]" INTO
<database>.<table>;");
```

```
// Method 1
$data = array("$d1", "$d2");
// Method 2
//$data = array($data2[1],$data2[3]);
$leg = array("Legit DNS Queries", "Blocked by Malware");

//// CREATE GRAPH SIZEING AND FEATURES
$graph = new PieGraph (400,250,"auto");
//$graph->SetShadow();
$graph->title->Set(" Effects of the <Organization Name> DNS
Malware Blocks");
$graph->title->SetFont(FF_FONT1,FS_BOLD);
$p1 = new PiePlot3D($data);
$p1->SetSize(.3);
//$p1->SetCenter(0.45);
//$p1->SetStartAngle(20);
//$p1->SetAngle(45);

// LEGENDS
$p1->SetLegends($leg);
$p1->value->SetFont(FF_FONT1,FS_BOLD);
$p1->value->SetColor("blue");
$p1->SetLabelType(PIE_VALUE_PER);
$p1->SetSliceColors(array('green','red'));
$graph->Add($p1);
$graph->Stroke();
?>
```

One last suggestion to make this more useful to an organization is going
to be to create a trending report on this data. For example, showing a weekly
total of malware in a line chart format or a monthly format. To accomplish
this goal we can use the "simple format" of the data and insert it into a
database (mysql) using the following script, which is a modification to the
previous graph report.

However, the script modification in the previous example inserts the data only into the database that was created with the following schema:

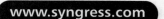

```
# Trending Mysql database trending.mssql
CREATE DATABASE trending;
# Now we create our single table for the data
# First field is the date
# Second field is the DNS total count
# Third field is the DNS unique total count
# Forth field is the Malware host total count
CREATE TABLE `trend` (
`trdate` text NOT NULL,
`dns_total` text NOT NULL,
`uniq_dns_total` text NOT NULL,
`malware_dns_total` text NOT NULL,
) TYPE=MyISAM COMMENT='daily data for DNS Malware';
# Done
```

```
<?php
// INCLUDES FOR GRAPH
include ( "/path/to/BASE/jpgraph/src/jpgraph.php");
include ( "/path/to/BASE/jpgraph/src/jpgraph_pie.php");
include ( "/path/to/BASE/jpgraph/src/jpgraph_pie3d.php");

// DATA
// read from file using the format with wording
$d1=`grep "UNIQUE" dailymalware.txt | awk '{ print $9}'`;
$d2=`grep "Security" dailymalware.txt | awk '{ print $13 }'`;

    // DATA
    // read from file using the simple format
// blank array
//$data2 = array();
//$rawfile = file("/tmp/dailymalwaresimple.txt","r");
//foreach ($rawfile as $row) {
//array_push($data2, $row);
```

```
//}

        // MYSQL INSERTION
$link = mysql_connect('host','DB_username','password');
if (!$link) {
 die('Could not Connect: '. mysql_error());
 }
//echo 'Connected successfully';
$web_date = date ("dmY");
$result = mysql_insert("INSERT
"$webdate","$data2[0]","$data[1]","$data[3]" INTO
<database>.<table>;");

// Method 1
$data = array("$d1", "$d2");
// Method 2
//$data = array($data2[1],$data2[3]);
$leg = array("Legit DNS Queries", "Blocked by Malware");

//// CREATE GRAPH SIZEING AND FEATURES
$graph = new PieGraph (400,250,"auto");
//$graph->SetShadow();
$graph->title->Set(" Effects of the <Organization Name> DNS
Malware Blocks");
$graph->title->SetFont(FF_FONT1,FS_BOLD);
$p1 = new PiePlot3D($data);
$p1->SetSize(.3);
//$p1->SetCenter(0.45);
//$p1->SetStartAngle(20);
//$p1->SetAngle(45);

// LEGENDS
$p1->SetLegends($leg);
$p1->value->SetFont(FF_FONT1,FS_BOLD);
$p1->value->SetColor("blue");
$p1->SetLabelType(PIE_VALUE_PER);
$p1->SetSliceColors(array('green','red'));
```

```
$graph->Add($p1);
$graph->Stroke();
?>
```

One possible method that we could use to show this data over time would be a weekly report (seven-day report) in the form of a bar chart (see Figure 2.13). If your malware blocking is effective, over the period of the week the total malware should go down.

Figure 2.13 Trending of Malware Data

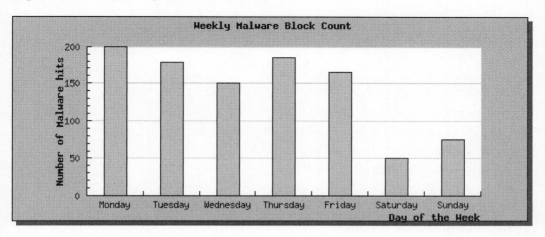

The script would look something like the following example:

```php
<?php

// INCLUDES FOR GRAPH
include ( "/path/to/BASE/jpgraph/src/jpgraph.php");
include ( "/path/to/BASE/jpgraph/src/jpgraph_bar.php");

// DATA

// Create blank arrays for place holders
$day = array();
```

```php
$dnstotal = array();
$malwaretotal = array();

// Database query
//$result = mysql_query("SELECT * FROM trending.trend LIMIT 7");
//mysql_fetch_array("$result");
// $dnstotal = $fetch_result[2];
// $malwaretotal = $fetch_result[4];

//STATIC TESTING
$day =
array("Monday","Tuesday","Wednesday","Thursday","Friday","Saturd
ay","Sunday");
//$dnstotal =
array("1000","1234","1456","1998","1345","556","334");
$malwaretotal = array("200","178","150","185","165","50","75");
        //// CREATE GRAPH SIZEING AND FEATURES
$graph = new Graph (600,250,"auto");
$graph->SetScale("textlin");

// Add drop shadow
$graph->SetShadow();
        // Create bar plot
$bplot = new BarPlot($malwaretotal);
$graph->Add($bplot);
        // Titles and x/y axis labels
$graph->title->Set("Weekly Malware Block Count");
$graph->xaxis->title->Set("Day of the Week");
$graph->yaxis->title->Set("Number of Malware hits");
$graph->xaxis->SetTickLabels($day);
        // Fonts
$graph->title->SetFont(FF_FONT1,FS_BOLD);
$graph->yaxis->title->SetFont(FF_FONT1,FS_BOLD);
$graph->xaxis->title->SetFont(FF_FONT1,FS_BOLD);
        // Display the graph
$graph->Stroke();
        ?>
```

With some experimentation, several other reports can be generated off this data; for example, a monthly metric report, or a peak malware use hours report.

Using Bro to Identify Top E-Mail Senders/Receivers

As Bro is capturing and logging several application protocols, one that has mixed results is the SMTP module. When combined with the MIME module, the SMTP module can be very powerful in helping to identify several of the "Marcus Ranum" top mail-related statistics (Chapter 1). These are useful statistics such as top mail sender, top mail receiver, top mail server sender, and top mail server receiver. These types of data can be helpful and beneficial to both the security teams as well as to the operational side of the house. For example, if you were to show the mail administrators those top statistics they could more than likely discover a spam host and issue a block for that domain or IP space. Although showing who the top mail sender is could be useful in discovering the user who is sending out the most e-mails, this could be dug into deeper to find out what they are sending out. As for the top mail receiver this could be useful in determining targeted or compromised e-mail accounts. As you can see these are only some examples of what type of information you can get out of BRO smtp logs.

Some of the information that can be gathered from Bro for e-mail includes:

- Top mail server—inbound and outbound
- Top e-mail address—inbound (sometimes not as useful as you might think) and outbound (who sends the most e-mails in the organization)
- Track e-mail virus attachment du jour—look for specific e-mail attachments with MIME logs

Top Mail Server

When using Bro SMTP logs, a quick and easy method to track the top mail servers can be to simply apply the same set of code for an HTTP session. The following is an example log from a normal Comcast e-mail user to a corporate network.

```
1135011969.179949 #1 192.168.x.x/57776 > 192.x.x.x/smtp +1: [end
entity]
1135011969.179949 #1 192.168.x.x/57776 > 192.x.x.x/smtp +0:
[finish]
1135011969.179949 #2 192.168.x.x/57776 > 192.x.x.x /smtp +0:
[start]
1135012008.142149 #2 192.168.x.x/57776 > 192.x.x.x/smtp +0:
[state remove]
```

The easiest method to track the top e-mail servers inbound would be to use a script such as:

```
        #!/bin/sh
Inbound_email=`cat /path/to/bro/smtp/smtp.log.<date> | grep
"start"  | awk '{ print $4 }' | sort | uniq -c | sort -nr | head
-n 1`
Outbound_email=`cat /path/to/bro/smtp/smtp.log.<date> | grep
"start"  | awk '{ print $6 }' | sort | uniq -c | sort -nr | head
-n 1`
#
# DNS resolution
Inbound_DNS=`grep "$Inbound_email"
/path/to/bro/dns/dns.log.<date> | grep "?A "  | awk '{ print $4
}' |  head -n 1
```

```
# DNS resolution
Outbound_DNS=`grep "$Outbound_email"
/path/to/bro/dns/dns.log.<date> | grep "?A "   | awk '{ print $4
}' |  head -n 1


     #
     # Print out the results to a file
     echo " Top Inbound server is: $Inbound_email IP and this
DNS name $Inbound_DNS" > /logs/email_report.txt
     echo " " >> /logs/email_report.txt
     echo "Top Outbound server is: $Outbound_email IP and this
DNS name $Outbound_DNS" >> /logs/email_report.txt


1127648312.713213 #1369 137.161.251.34/8828 > 64.18.4.10/smtp
start internal
1127648314.169163 #1370 137.161.251.34/8835 >
216.235.250.57/smtp start internal
1127648314.600289 #1371 137.161.251.34/8836 > 211.43.197.46/smtp
start internal
```

Which makes the output of awk {print $4) be ">" .

This table could then be fed into a report Web site or another combined report to be used for a more comprehensive status of the network resources.

Top E-Mail Address

Another notable off Marcus' list is the top e-mail address sending and receiving in your organization, and the most e-mail outside your organization. When enabled, the MIME logs are quite detailed in what they record per e-mail session as can be seen here:

```
1135012325.724943 #1 192.168.x.x/62842 > 192.x.x.x/smtp start
external
1135012355.081285 #1 error: '<" not found in argument to RCPT:
TO:address@gmail.com
1135012429.988783 #1 192.168.x.x/62842 < 192.x.x.x/smtp: unusual
command/reply: HELP() --> 214(2.3.0 Availab
le commands:^M^J2.3.0 ^M^J2.3.0 DATA, EHLO, EXPN, HELO, HELP,
MAIL FROM^M^J2.3.0 NOOP, QUIT, RCPT TO, RSET, SAML
FROM^M^J2.3.0 SEND FROM, SOML FROM, TICK, TURN^M^J2.3.0 VERB,
```

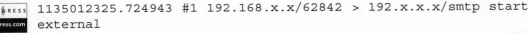

```
VRFY, XADR, XSTA, XCIR, ETRN^M^J2.3.0 XGEN, LHLO, A
UTH^M^J2.3.0)
1135012444.819962 #1 192.168.x.x/62842 > 192.x.x.x/smtp: unusual
command: VRFY(name@mycompany.com)
1135012444.821862 #1 192.168.x.x/62842 < 192.x.x.x/smtp: unusual
command/reply: VRFY( name@mycompany.com)
--> 550(5.1.1 String does not match anything.)
1135012452.238063 #1 finish
```

One method to track the top e-mail address is to search looking for and counting the "TO:" field, eliminating those records that don't have your organization's DNS name. This will return the top receiving e-mail for your domain, while searching through the same logs for the "FROM:" field and knocking out any records not from your DNS domain will return the user sending the most e-mail.

```
#!/bin/sh
#
# Variables
Top_company_sender=`grep "FROM: "
/path/to/bro/mime/mime.log.<date> | awk '{ print $4 }' | grep
"CompanyDNSname" | sort | uniq -c | sort -nr | head -n 1 `
    Top_company_receiver=`grep "TO: "
/path/to/bro/mime/mime.log.<date> | awk '{ print $4 }' | grep
"CompanyDNSname" | sort | uniq -c | sort -nr | head -n 1 `
    # More than likely this is your top spam relayer through
your network
    Top_outside_sender=`grep "FROM: "
/path/to/bro/mime/mime.log.<date> | awk '{ print $4 }' | grep -v
"CompanyDNSname" | sort | uniq -c | sort -nr | head -n 1`
    Top_Spam_address=`grep "TO: "
/path/to/bro/mime/mime.log.<date> | awk '{ print $4 }' | grep -v
"CompanyDNSname" | sort | uniq -c | sort -nr | head -n 1 `


    # Place into a simple report
    echo "The top email user in the organization (Sender) is:
$Top_company_sender" > /logs/email_report.txt
    echo "" >> /logs/email_report.txt
    echo "The Top email user in the organization (Receiver)
is: $Top_company_receiver" >> /logs/email_report.txt
    echo ""
```

```
     echo "The Top email address not from your organization is:
$Top_outside_sender " >> /logs/email_report.txt

     echo ""

     echo "The Top address coming through your mail server
(relay) not to someone in your organization is:
$Top_Spam_address" >> /logs/email_report.txt
```

Virus Attachment Du Jour

When enabled, the MIME logs will allow tracking of several aspects of an e-mail message throughout your networks. This type of logging enables an entire other bit of information gathering such as top sender and receiver, top mail server, etc. This can also help us track emails that could have sensitive attachments or virus attachments. With the ability to record the subject and the attachment name this goes along way in tracking and remediation of virus infections throughout your network(s). Though one question that comes up in some organizations is, are we seeing X virus on our network?

Are You Owned?

E-Mail Virus Detection

In a recent example, a new variant of the Beagle e-mail virus was being distributed. After a quick look through our antivirus vendor's updates, we realized we could detect it. Being a curious security shop, we wanted to see if any of our users were affected by the virus. In the initial virus outbreak, it always used the same filename new_price.zip. A search through the Bro MIME logs for "ATTACHMENT:" and then filtering for "new_price" revealed several users getting the virus from external (spam) sources. To make sure the antivirus was picking these up, we checked with our mail server admins to make sure they had blocked or quarantined all of the messages in question. The result was that they had picked them all up easily and none of our users had been infected with the virus.

One method of trying to find these viruses in a very reactionary method would be to use the BRO MIME logs to search through. These logs store some useful parts of every mail connection that can be used in a search for viruses and Trojans. As most shops have predominately windows workstations and users will traditionally click on anything in their inboxes monitoring mail connections would serve as the best way to detect and audit virus threats. As a recent example of a virus du jour, once a user had clicked on a malicious mail message a silent "ping" email was sent out to a specific email address for record keeping of victims. With BRO MIME logs a simple search through the daily logs can be used to determine when the first email was sent as well as to whom else. This data can then be handed over to your CIRT team and they have an immediate list of users and machines to go clean for remediation.

Damage & Defense…

Be Careful What Your Security Team Is Monitoring

As with most IDS work, monitoring network resources is a privileged task. However, as hopefully has been seen with the Bro data, this is considered privacy data at some organizations. At least one site has told its security team to disable all applications that could log e-mail traffic. The reason for this was that the content of the e-mail traffic was confidential and the assumption of privacy by the user community was more than upper management was willing to fight! For some reason, most organizations are very sensitive when it comes to monitoring e-mail but are not concerned with other protocols…go figure.

In another example if you are trying to determine if anyone in your organization has gotten a hostile mail message attachment then a search through the BRO MIME logs will help determine if any users were affected. In another example if the name of the attachment were to change while leaving the attachment size the same the attachment size could then be searched to find infection email addresses.

Lastly, if you can't use any of the email based methods to track a virus or Trojan, most phone home now over the web. This means that you can look for a specific URL string such as "…&port=356&name=victim1" from a compromised machine with a new backdoor running, or look for something as begin as "/5.php" from a listing of IP's such as with the beagle worms. There are multiple ways in which this BRO data can be leveraged to detect and prepare remediation to the virus or Trojan of the day.

Summary

Hopefully, in this chapter there have been some takeaways that you can use or implement in your organization to improve the level of informed security measures are in place. Another key point in this chapter was to illustrate the effectiveness of a true defense in depth IDS architecture while at the same time having a checks-and-balances system of validation of data through use of multiple tools. One good example is the use of session logging from Argus and Lancope to validate that they both see the same thing on the same span port. Another important takeaway is to report in useful and distributable information from your security devices. One example that is used over and over is to translate the "technical" information into an understandable format such as graphs and charts. If the data is presented in that format, it is easily distributed to other interested parties, and then, hopefully, upper management and/or the client will have a better understanding about threats to the networks. This type of understanding can lead to management knowing the return on investments (ROI) that they have made to the security teams in such forms as firewalls, IDS, router and ACLs, just to name a few line items.

Solutions Fast Track

Session/Flow Logging with Snort

- ☑ Using snort session logging, you can determine if a connection occurred and how much data was sent by the client and server in the connection.

- ☑ One of the least used parts of Snort is to turn on the stream4 preprocessor's statistic logging mechanism. When the Snort engine gets a TCP connection passed through it, the connection needs to be reassembled for the signature engine and other preprocessors to scan it.

☑ Snort's stream4 preprocessor can log a record of all connections passing through this engine by enabling the keepstats directive. These logs are stored in a separate file in the Snort log directory. You can enable or disable several options in the preprocessor, depending on your specific deployment.

Session/Flow Logging with Argus

☑ Using Argus a very detailed flow log is created for each connection such as source and destination packets and bytes and other information.

☑ Snort and Argus data can be used to identify anomalous data traffic by looking at variations in packet counts and data amounts transferred.

☑ The advantage of using Argus is that it can maintain logs for TCP, UDP, and ICMP IP.

Can You Determine When a DDoS/DoS Attack Is Occurring?

☑ If capturing tcpdump logs, you can use the tcpdstat tool to create hourly statistics such as "PeakRate." When using an open-source graphing library called JpGraph, we can create a 24-hour view of network peak rates. This information is used to show possible spikes in traffic normally associated with DoS attacks.

☑ If you have deployed BASE for displaying your Snort alerts, you can simply use the graphing library of JpGraph to run your code

☑ When first deploying your tcpdump logging application, you should find out what other information you could get out of that data.

Using Snort for Bandwidth Monitoring

☑ Can you determine when your network segments are experiencing drops in connectivity? Can you determine trends in traffic utilization? Using the Perfmonitor preprocessor on your Snort sensors, you can determine this as well as an entire laundry list of information about your sensors

☑ This data is generated in two forms: a "real-time" format that outputs a table of data to standard output every five minutes, and a csv (comma-separated version).

☑ The "real-time" formatting can be used for tuning and testing if you grab the Snort output

Using Bro to Log and Capture Application-Level Protocols

☑ Using an open-source tool called Bro (www.bro-ids.org), the logging and capture of application-level protocols is now possible.

☑ When using the Bro HTTP module and its submodule for "http-header," you can capture several useful pieces of Web traffic for every connection.

☑ BRO is an application-level IDS that at its lowest levels is a series of protocol decoders. These decoders then have a policy built around them; for example, in the case of SMTP, the decoder knows the order and SMTP commands to expect in a typical mail session.

Tracking Users' Web Activities with Bro

☑ When you run Bro with the HTTP module enabled, tracking each connection is quite easy.

☑ Using Bro HTTP logging, you can track the "user-agents" on your network. If you are looking for a specific build (i.e., your company build), search for all Web traffic that is not using that build.

☑ Several versions of BRO have a limitation: if you let BRO run for long periods of time (more than three hours) without a restart, several of the policies will start to leak larger and larger sections of memory.

Using Bro to Gather DNS and Web Traffic Data

☑ Using Bro HTTP logging, we can track the "USER-AGENT" field for software compliance, while looking through SMTP, FTP, and even the SSH logs can help searching for known banners of information to determine software compliance.

☑ Using Bro and JpGraph, you can create an easily understandable format to show the top "surfer" and Web site—information that your management will surely be interested in seeing.

☑ When combined with a policy of blocking or disallowing use of certain sites, the BRO Web logs can provide a security team the information needed to find the users.

Using Bro for Blackholing Traffic to Malware-Infested Domains

☑ Using Bro software and DNS poisoning, it's very easy to track clients on your network that have been affected with malware.

☑ Using the Bro DNS policy, we can easily break down and count DNS domains, top sites being requested, and other information.

☑ When this information is used when combined with DNS blackholing for known malware sites, you now have an immediate method of combating malware.

☑ Another use of this data is to find and clean malware off your user community's machines.

Using Bro to Identify Top E-Mail Senders/Receivers

☑ Using the Bro SMTP and MIME policies, much information is available, from statistics on the top e-mail address, the top spammer, to several other "top" lists that different organizations will find useful.

☑ Another use of these logs can be to track through the MIME logs the virus/Trojan e-mail attachment of the day. Such information can be passed throughout other security teams for coordination with anti-virus deletes and captures of the virus/Trojan.

☑ As with most IDS work, monitoring network resources is a privileged task. However, as hopefully has been seen with the Bro data, this is considered privacy data at some organizations.

Frequently Asked Questions

The following Frequently Asked Questions, answered by the authors of this book, are designed to both measure your understanding of the concepts presented in this chapter and to assist you with real-life implementation of these concepts. To have your questions about this chapter answered by the author, browse to **www.syngress.com/solutions** and click on the **"Ask the Author"** form.

Q: What are some other tools in the open source community similar to Argus and Snort's Keepstats directive:

A: SANCP (Security Analyst Network Connection Profiler) is a tool in development that looks promising: http://www.metre.net/sancp.html. Netstate is another tools that is being developed at Sandia National Labs: http://net-state.ca.sandia.gov/. A very complex tool that does a lot of the statistical analysis needed for worm detection is ourmon: http://ourmon.cat.pdx.edu/ourmon/

Q: Are there any commercial tools that capture flow-based traffic?

A: Yes, they are the products in the "behavioral IDS" market, such as Lancope Stealthwatch, Arbor Networks Peakflow X, Mazu Profiler, or Q1 Labs Qvision products. These all perform at the lowest level, very similar to how Argus performs; however, they have engines that sit on top of that data that do a variety of other tasks as well, such as detecting port scans, monitoring the ebb and flow of a network, and generating network visualizations of that data.

Q: Where is a good resource to get malware-related signatures and IP listings?

A: The bleedingsnort.org site remains an extremely good resource for malware-related snort stuff. This site maintains the most actively updated sets of malware signatures and configurations. It is also home to the DNS blackhole and spyware listening post projects that are both entirely driven to detecting and stopping malware.

Q: Where can I find out more information about generating some graphs for IDS data like the ones in the chapter?

A: Almost all graphs and charts in the chapter were generated from jpgraph (jpgraph.sourceforge.net). If you simply download the distribution to a directory on a Web server, a subdirectory is the complete function list in Web format. This directory has every function with examples, as well as some examples of common graphs. The jpgraph Web site has a huge FAQ section with most of the common questions here as well as a forum where you can post questions.

Q: I'm a little confused about Bro and its policy files. Where can I get more information about Bro?

A: Answers for most of the smaller setup questions are on the FAQ page of the main Bro Web site, **www.bro-ids.org**. The newer versions of Bro attempt to automatically themselves up at installation (make install time). When they are doing that, they simply load all your needed customizations into a "site.bro" file. The installation scripts will walk you through configuration during setup.

Firewall Reporting

Solutions in this chapter:

- **Firewall Reporting: A Reflection of the Effectiveness of Security Policies**

- **The Supporting Infrastructure for Firewall Log Management**

- **Parsing the Data**

- **Tools for an Overview of Activity**

- **Reporting Statistics**

☑ Summary

☑ Solutions Fast Track

☑ Frequently Asked Questions

Firewall Reporting: A Reflection of the Effectiveness of Security Policies

Your firewall is configured to protect your network and seems to be running properly, but how is it behaving and what threats is it facing? Is your firewall adequate to handle the load, or is it being overwhelmed? Is your network being specifically targeted, or are you just seeing "normal" scanning activity?

To answer these questions, the firewall's logs must be monitored and analyzed in a timely manner. Your firewall should be configured to log anytime it blocks or rejects a connection,—for both inbound and outbound network traffic. Three or four years ago, a typical firewall was configured to deny by default inbound traffic and allow by default outbound. Now, however, we have to cope with virus-worm hybrids, malicious e-mail, and malicious Web pages, all of which can cause dangerous outbound traffic. Consequently, a firewall should also deny by default outbound as well. Any firewall policy violation should be logged so it can be analyzed for the threat it might represent. The only exception to the "log-it-all" rule is benign (attempted) outbound things like broadcasts for NetBIOS connections to the firewall itself (NetBIOS attempts to computers outside your network *should* be logged, since they indicate a possible misconfiguration or potential compromise of an internal system).

Are You 0wned?

Watching What You Send

By implementing a deny-by-default policy in *both directions* on the firewall, you go a long way in helping detect whether there are compromises on your LAN. Any unauthorized service that begins to run on your LAN will not be allowed and will be logged. The catch is that if you are infected with a worm or have a backdoor compromise that happens to use a normal network port for its actions (say, port 80), most firewalls will not detect it. Some firewalls have a "deep inspection" feature, which looks at those port 80 connections and verifies that actual HTTP protocols are

Continued

being used as expected. Other firewalls can be coupled with an intrusion detection system (IDS) that does the inspection for the firewall.

While this seems like a good idea, it is problematic because many applications run private protocols on port 80 because it is expected that most LAN firewalls will allow outbound Web traffic. These applications can be vital to your organization; they include virus update programs, and application or operating system patch systems. The response to this situation is typically to configure the network so that normal Web traffic goes through a proxy server on the LAN (which verifies that the traffic is actually HTTP), and some server is designated at the official patch/update manager. Only the patch manager and the proxy server are allowed to go outbound on port 80.

That will work okay, until someone develops a worm that communicates over SOAP (Simple Object Access Protocol) messages (which appear as HTTP communications)—it's kind of like an episode of Spy-vs.-Spy.

Reporting firewall activity serves several purposes. First, it gives security administrators an overview of what is currently happening on all the networks and firewalls for which they are responsible. Which firewall needs attention first? Is anything unusual happening on a firewall?

The second purpose is to understand what kinds of activity are typical for a given firewall and how that activity changes over time. Armed with the knowledge of what is typical, the security administrator can quickly spot something new happening (such as a new worm) and can quickly react to adjust the firewalls if necessary.

To handle the reporting requirements, the firewall logs must be automatically digested and summarized on a regular basis. By *regular*, we mean that real-time or near real-time summary status information on a given firewall should be available at least hourly. The analysis needs to be automatic because raw firewall logs are tedious to wade through. Consider the task of manually looking through a megabyte of logs that look like the following *single* NetScreen firewall log entry.

```
Oct 25 08:37:38 10.0.0.1 ns25: NetScreen device_id=ns25
[Firewall1]system-    notification-00257(traffic):
start_time="2005-10-25 08:38:09" duration=0 policy_id=29
service=tcp/port:445 proto=6 src zone=Untrust dst zone=Trust
action=Deny sent=0 rcvd=0 src:10.42.180.17 dst:192.168.32.86
src_port=1672 dst_port=445 session_id=0
```

All alone, it's easy to understand that this log event represents a port 445 probe from the Internet along with where it tried to go and then to access its threat as an individual event. However, in the real world, this log event will be buried along with thousands of other entries in the log file, so it could easily be missed. Further, we need to look at many such entries to determine if the destination server is being targeted, if there is a port scan going on or widespread port 445 activity, or if it is just an isolated event.

In addition, the most important information needs to be archived so it is available for a deeper analysis when necessary.

The Supporting Infrastructure for Firewall Log Management

To make sense of the security status of your network, you need to set up some supporting infrastructure beyond the firewall itself. First, you need a log server for the firewall; this is usually a syslog server, but occasionally some other logging system is used (probably the most common alternative is the use of SNMP traps). If your firewall is built on a regular operating system such as Solaris or Linux, it is reasonable to syslog to the firewall itself. If your firewall is an appliance, such as a Cisco PIX, you should syslog to some syslog server on your internal network. The syslog protocol is not secure (and neither is SNMP; in fact, in security circles SNMP is described to mean "Security is Not My Problem"!), so the connection between your firewall and the syslog server should be a trusted one. There are security enhanced syslog systems, but these will probably not be available if you are using a firewall appliance.

What constitutes a trusted network connection depends on your circumstances (and perhaps corporate policy or regulatory requirements). We want to achieve three security goals when creating a trusted network. The first is *confidentiality*; we do not want the log information to be read by unauthorized users. The second is data *integrity*, assuring that the log data is not modified. The third goal is *nonrepudiation*, assuring that the syslog server is actually receiving the data from where it thinks it is coming from. Implementing a trusted network could be based on something as simple as a special VLAN on your network that is dedicated to carrying just security management traffic. A stronger approach would be to have a dedicated network interface on the firewall and syslog server connected on an isolated network, again dedicated to carrying only security traffic. Yet another approach is to set up an IPsec VPN tunnel between the firewall and syslog server; if you manage remote firewalls with a local syslog server, this is the only approach.

The log files should be rotated daily, and kept online for at least two weeks.

TIP

Incident management will be simpler if the firewall logs are rotated at midnight local time or midnight GMT. Your firewall system clock should match whatever time zone you use.

Second, you need a system to analyze the logs themselves. This is most naturally done on the syslog server. If the syslog server is the firewall itself, you should be careful about doing the analysis locally since the priority is for the firewall to protect the network behind it. Depending on the types of queries and reports you will be creating and the size of the logs you are analyzing, performing the analysis could take a lot of processing time. If the burden of the analysis starts to overload the firewall, the analysis should be moved to another system. A tool such as rsync over ssh or scp can be used to copy the logs from the syslog server to the log analysis system if you use a distributed approach.

The third component of the system is a console to display the status reports. The most natural place to implement the console is on the internal (LAN) Web server. Do *not* put this on the firewall, as it adds another service that needs to be properly administered and secured—the firewall is the last place you want to have a large collection of services each with separate security issues. In addition, resist the temptation to place this in a password protected area of your public Web server. A misconfiguration error or poor implementation of the password mechanism could expose your firewall summaries to the outside world. Again, securely implemented rsync or scp can be used to make sure the Web server has the most recent copy of the analysis results.

The final component is a database server for storing the firewall event data for deeper analysis or historical archiving. This should never be placed on the firewall itself, because of the complications in keeping it secure (just like the Web server), and most importantly because the database server will be working very hard. If you have the CPU cycles to spare, you could place this on the internal Web server, but you should consider setting up a dedicated (internal) security database server for this role. Any SQL database server package (such as PostgreSQL or MySQL) will work.

TIP

If you are new at using SQL databases, you might want to consider using PostgreSQL since it has native data types for IP addresses, MAC addresses, netmasks, and so forth.

Parsing the Data

A good open source tool for parsing and summarizing the firewall logs is fwlogwatch. This C program can read the firewall logs from several firewalls (ipchains, iptables, ipfw, ipfilter, PIX, NetScreen, Windows XP); if you know how to work with the lexical analyzer generator, Lex, it is easy to add others. The program generates a table (or an HTML file) output that summarizes the events as seen in the log file. Fwlogwatch should run on the firewall log server. It is lightweight enough to easily run on the firewall itself without overloading it.

If you run fwlogwatch hourly with a command such as

```
/usr/local/sbin/fwlogwatch -s -d -t -z -y -p -w >
/var/security/firewall1.html
```

you will get a cumulative hourly report on the overall status of what events are happening on your firewall.

Table 3.1 is a small sample of such a report from a NetScreen firewall.

Table 3.1 A Log Watch Summary from a NetScreen Firewall

fwlogwatch summary

Generated Thu Oct 27 12:01:09 PDT 2005 by root of eltanin.
2167 (and 130 malformed) of 2297 entries in the file "/var/log/firewall1.log" are packet logs, 1634 have unique characteristics.
First packet log entry: Oct 27 00:04:03, last: Oct 27 12:00:18.
All entries were logged by the same host: "ns25".
All entries are from the same chain: "-".
All entries are from the same interface: "-".

#	start	end	interval	target	proto	source	port	destination	port	opts
5	Oct 27 06:07:22	Oct 27 06:08:07	00:00:00:45	Deny	tcp	10.164.74.210	43549	192.168.32.85	25	-
5	Oct 27 06:08:22	Oct 27 06:09:07	00:00:00:45	Deny	tcp	10.164.74.210	43585	192.168.32.85	25	-
4	Oct 27 10:54:09	Oct 27 10:54:39	00:00:00:30	Deny	tcp	10.75.2.34	2448	192.168.32.84	12345	-
4	Oct 27 10:54:10	Oct 27 10:54:40	00:00:00:30	Deny	tcp	10.75.2.34	2451	192.168.32.85	12345	-
4	Oct 27 10:54:11	Oct 27 10:54:41	00:00:00:30	Deny	tcp	10.75.2.34	2455	192.168.32.86	12345	-
3	Oct 27 00:40:39	Oct 27 00:40:48	00:00:00:09	Deny	tcp	10.54.16.6	4637	192.168.32.86	111	-
3	Oct 27 00:40:39	Oct 27 00:40:48	00:00:00:09	Deny	tcp	10.54.16.6	4636	192.168.32.85	111	-
3	Oct 27 09:37:32	Oct 27 09:37:37	00:00:00:05	Deny	tcp	10.114.125.36	51683	192.168.32.85	113	-
3	Oct 27 11:01:19	Oct 27 11:01:28	00:00:00:09	Deny	tcp	10.10.188.152	3131	192.168.32.84	4899	-
3	Oct 27 11:01:20	Oct 27 11:01:28	00:00:00:08	Deny	tcp	10.10.188.152	3133	192.168.32.86	4899	-
3	Oct 27 11:01:20	Oct 27 11:01:28	00:00:00:08	Deny	tcp	10.10.188.152	3132	192.168.32.85	4899	-
2	Oct 27 00:05:25	Oct 27 00:05:28	00:00:00:03	Deny	tcp	10.168.37.202	3069	192.168.32.85	135	-
2	Oct 27 00:13:08	Oct 27 00:13:11	00:00:00:03	Deny	tcp	10.168.37.202	4755	192.168.32.86	135	-
2	Oct 27 00:13:48	Oct 27 00:13:52	00:00:00:04	Deny	tcp	10.248.186.48	3140	192.168.32.84	1433	-
2	Oct 27 00:16:53	Oct 27 00:16:56	00:00:00:03	Deny	tcp	10.168.38.227	2233	192.168.32.84	445	-
2	Oct 27 00:19:52	Oct 27 00:19:55	00:00:00:03	Deny	tcp	10.168.37.207	3066	192.168.32.85	135	-
2	Oct 27 00:20:48	Oct 27 00:20:51	00:00:00:03	Deny	tcp	10.168.37.207	3327	192.168.32.86	445	-
2	Oct 27 00:21:20	Oct 27 00:21:23	00:00:00:03	Deny	tcp	10.168.37.202	2688	192.168.32.86	135	-

fwlogwatch 0.9.3 2003/06/23 © Boris Wesslowski, RUS-CERT

The columns in the preceding table show the number of events, their start and end times, and the average time interval between them. These are particularly useful entries to watch for automated scans of your network. The "target" column is actually the type of firewall rule that triggered the log entry. For the NetScreen, you can only have the basic deny, reject, or accept rule. Other firewalls, such as the Linux Iptables, can have much more information, such as a "MAC address violation" statement in this column. In our example, the protocol column just shows TCP events, but other protocols such as UDP and IPsec can show up here. The "source" column shows the IP address of the origin of the security event. For an outbound policy violation, this address will be from a system on you LAN; for an inbound policy violation, it will be a system somewhere on the Internet. Remember, for protocols such as UDP and ICMP it is trivial to spoof the origin IP address. For other protocols such as TCP, the attacker may be using a proxy to hide his true location. In any case, one should use judgment when using the source IP address information when conducting a security incident follow-up. The "port" column after the "source" column is the source port number of the network connection. This is supposed to be a randomly chosen value, so at first glance, it seems like it would not be that useful. However, many scanning and exploit tools do not randomize the source port number. Instead, they use a fixed value, or just simply increment the value by one with each connection. Therefore, if you see a simple pattern with the source port number, you can usually do a little Internet research at various security sites and determine if you are being probed by a specific tool. The "destination" is the IP address that is being targeted by the policy violation. If it is an outbound violation, an external address is the target. If it is an inbound violation, this column will show the public address of the destination system. The "port" column following the "destination" column is the port number the service was probed for. Finally, the "opts" column shows the packet flags that were set if the firewall is capable of logging that information. This information is useful for detecting attacks from tools that manipulate the packet flags (e.g., using illegal or nonsensical combinations) in an attempt to bypass or crash a firewall.

As useful as fwlogwatch is, it is not enough by itself; we still need a way to store each of the firewall events in a way that is convenient for further analysis. This is best done using an SQL database, which means we need to parse the log files and turn them into a series of SQL INSERT statements. For example, we need to convert the NetScreen syslog entry given earlier into:

```
insert into firewall1 values ( '8:38:09', '2005-10-25',
'10.42.180.17', '192.168.32.86','tcp', 445, 1672 );
```

This parsing can be done in a variety of ways; for example, a Perl or AWK script could be written to do so. For performance reasons, however, we want to use a compiled C program using lex/flex to do the parsing if the logs are very large. The parser can also be run once per hour and insert the newest data into the database (we will show a script for doing this later in this chapter).

As an example of a lex parser, consider the following, which will parse the logs from an OpenBSD firewall.

```
/* Parser for OpenBSD PF firewall output from,
        tcpdump -neq -ttt -r /var/log/pflog


        Skip Carter */

%option prefix="pf"
%option outfile="pf.c"
%option noyywrap

%{
#define YY_NO_UNPUT

#include <unistd.h>
#include <string.h>
#include <ctype.h>

#include "pf_utils.h"

extern int verbose;
extern struct conn_info info;

static int state;


void pf_parse_start(char *input);
void pf_parse_proto(char *input);
void pf_parse_ips(char *input, unsigned int mode);
void pf_parse_interface(char* input);

%}
```

```
MONTH
"Jan"|"Feb"|"Mar"|"Apr"|"May"|"Jun"|"Jul"|"Aug"|"Sep"|"Oct"|"Nov
"|"Dec"
STRING[a-zA-Z][a-zA-Z0-9.-]*
DIGIT [0-9]
NUMBER{DIGIT}+
OCTET {DIGIT}{1,3}
PORT  {DIGIT}{1,5}
PROTO "tcp"|"udp"|"icmp"
IPADDRESS          {OCTET}.{OCTET}.{OCTET}.{OCTET}
IP        {IPADDRESS}.{PORT}


%%


{MONTH}[ ]{1,2}{DIGIT}{1,2}[
]{DIGIT}{2}:{DIGIT}{2}:{DIGIT}{2}\.{NUMBER}
pf_parse_start(pftext);
{PROTO}                        pf_parse_proto(pftext);
"on "{STRING}":"
pf_parse_interface(pftext+3);
{IP}[ ]                        pf_parse_ips(pftext,
PF_OPT_SRC);
{IP}":"[ ]            pf_parse_ips(pftext, PF_OPT_DST);
[ ]                    /* ignore whitespace */
[\n]                   info.active = (state ==
(PF_DATE|PF_PROTO|PF_IF|PF_SRC_IP|PF_SRC_PORT|PF_DST_IP|PF_DST_P
ORT) ) ? -1 : 0; print_info();
{STRING}               if(verbose) fprintf(stderr,
"Unrecognized token: %s\n", pftext);
.                      if(verbose) fprintf(stderr,
"Unrecognized character: %s\n", pftext);


%%


void pf_parse_start(char *input)
{
   int retval, day, hour, minute, second;
   char smonth[4];
```

```
    retval = sscanf(input,
                "%3s %2d %2d:%2d:%2d",
                smonth, &day, &hour, &minute, &second);

    if (retval != 5)
        return;

    build_time(smonth, day, hour, minute, second);

    state = PF_DATE;
}

void pf_parse_proto(char *input)
{

    strncpy(info.protocol,input,4);

    state |= PF_PROTO;
}

void pf_parse_interface(char* input)
{
    char *pnt;

    if ( (pnt = rindex( input,':')) == NULL ) return;
    *pnt = '\0';

    strncpy(info.interface, input, SHOSTLEN);

    state |= PF_IF;

}

void pf_parse_ips(char *input, unsigned int mode)
{
```

```
   char *ptr;
   int n = strlen(input) - 1;

   fprintf(stderr,"pf_parse_ips(<%s>, %d)\n", input, mode);

   n = n > 15 ? 15 : n;

   if (mode == PF_OPT_SRC)
   {
        strncpy(info.src_ip,input,n);
        fprintf(stderr,"\tcopied src ip to <%s>\n",
info.src_ip);
        state |= PF_SRC_IP|PF_SRC_PORT;


   }
   else if (mode == PF_OPT_DST)
   {
        strncpy(info.dst_ip,input,n);
        if ( (ptr = rindex(info.dst_ip,':') ) )
                   *ptr = '\0';

        fprintf(stderr,"\tcopied dst ip to <%s>\n",
info.dst_ip);
        state |= PF_DST_IP|PF_DST_PORT;
   }


}
```

This file is separated into sections by %%. The section before the first %% is the declarations section, which contains global definitions and declarations. Most of this section looks like normal C code except the last part (between the %} and the dividing %%). This part of the file is a list of token definitions (for example, we are defining an OCTET to be 1 to 3 DIGITs) that can be used symbolically later in the file. The second section of the file (between the two %% markers) is the rules section, where we list a set of rules on how to parse a line of text from the log file. Any text that matches a rule on the left side is passed to the C code on the right side as a string called "pftext." The final section of the file is the programs section, which is where supporting C code (typically functions called in the rules section) is defined. Once you get used to it, it's really quite simple and easy to work with. With a little experience, you can write a new parser from scratch in about 20 minutes.

When the file is passed to the lex analyzer, the output is a C program that implements the parser. The rules section is converted into a large C switch statement. When invoked, the program is given a line of input text, which is passed through the rules repeatedly. Each pass through a rule consumes the parsed text from the line, and each subsequent pass gets whatever is left. In its simplest form, the main C program just invokes the parser by calling `pflex()`, which reads the log file from standard input (stdin).

A vitally important aspect of moving the data into a database is that once it is there, everything we subsequently do to analyze our firewall activity is neutral to the kind of firewalls with which we are dealing. As the security administrator, you will find life less complicated if your security architecture is designed to support multiple firewall types. For example, you might be working for an organization that has a mandate to use more than one firewall type to enhance security. Or, you may have a mixture of networks of different ages and so were built with different firewalls. If you are security consultant or contractor, multiple firewall products are a fact of life.

We need to decide on a database table schema for storing the firewall information. At the minimum, this should include the time and date of the event, the source and destination IP addresses, the source and destination port numbers, and the protocol being used. Other information that could be useful to capture includes the protocol flag settings and the packet size. We will create a different table for each firewall, and for firewalls with multiple network interfaces there will be one for each interface as well. The table name will reflect the firewall/interface with which we are working.

A minimal table definition (for PostgreSQL) would look like the following basic table template:

```
CREATE TABLE firewalls (
      time time,
      date date,
```

```
        source inet,
        destination inet,
        protocol varchar(7),
        dport int4,           -- used for 'type' for ICMP protocol
        sport int4            -- used for 'code' for ICMP protocol
        action char;          -- 'd' drop, 'r' reject, 'a' accept
);

-- create the working instances (3 here) from the basic
template
CREATE TABLE firewall1 () INHERITS (firewalls);
CREATE TABLE firewall2 () INHERITS (firewalls);
CREATE TABLE firewall3 () INHERITS (firewalls);
```

The action entry in the table in the previous section allows us to record what action the firewall took when the event occurred. Generally, this is just what kind of blocking action the firewall took, drop the packet as if it never arrived, or reject the packet by sending a TCP reset packet back to the source (for TCP protocol packets). Distinguishing and recording the two types of block actions can be useful for some kinds of analysis. Usually, there is not much interest in logging the accepted packets; however, there are exceptions, so having an entry to record what packets are acceptable gives us flexibility for analyzing the unusual cases.

For database performance reasons, it is useful to rotate these tables annually, or depending on the amount of data you have, more frequently—say, quarterly. These tables would be active for the current year and then moved to long-term archives at the end of each year. Then, a new set of fresh tables are generated for the new year.

Tools for an Overview of Activity

Now we can get an overview of what is happening on the firewall as it happens, and a way to save the important firewall event information in a database. The question then is, what can we do with the data? Pretty much anything. We can look for patterns in the activity, see where the connections are coming from, determine if we are being specifically targeted, look for slow scans, or see what networks are particularly active in creating security events. We will look at some of these ways to analyze the information we have.

Time History Graphics

Having a time history of the events on the firewall is a very revealing way to analyze the data. It will show how active your firewalls are, and makes it visually easy to see trends and bursts of activity. In addition, time history graphs are very easy for nontechnical managers to understand. One can see the consequence of a new worm, such as the one shown in Figure 3.1, which shows the impact of the Zobot worm on a firewall at the end of week 32.

Figure 3.1 A Firewall Responds to the Zobot Worm in Late Summer 2005*

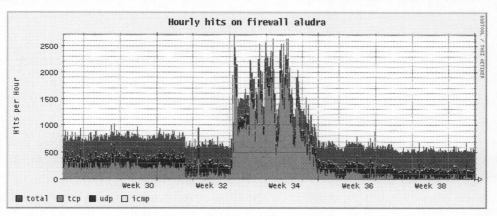

* The impact from the Zobot worm lasted about two weeks.

One can even see historical events on firewalls, such as how the Internet changed in 2001 (see Figure 3.2).

Figure 3.2 The Year 2001 as Seen from a Single Firewall (Only the TCP Events Are Shown for Clarity)

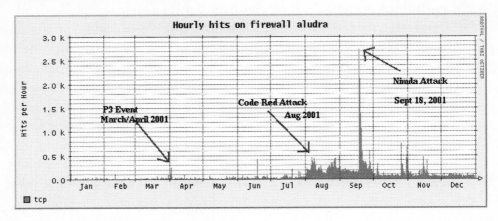

In Figure 3.2 we see the U.S.-China cyberwar that was a consequence of the collision of a U.S. Navy plane and a Chinese Air Force fighter, the attempted Code Red attack against the White House, and the Nimda Worm attack.

Figures 3.1 and 3.2 were created with the RRD (Round Robin Database) tool suite, which is a general-purpose tool for storing and graphing time series data. It has many similarities to the program MRTG (Multi Router Traffic Grapher), which is most often used for graphing time histories of bandwidth utilization. RRD is much easier to use when trying to handle a custom set of data, such as our history of firewall activity. With RRD, you use the rrdtool program to create and initialize a binary file with a given number of data slots in it (say, 8784 slots) to hold hourly TCP, UDP, ICMP, and total activity data for one year. We then start filling the file with our data as we do the hourly analysis of the firewall logs. Once all the slots are full, the tool starts reusing the slots by treating them as a circular buffer and overwriting the oldest data. Our hourly analysis script will place data in both the SQL database and in the RRD database.

```
#!/bin/sh
# summarize_deny    Creates a list of packet DENY and REDIRECT
messages
```

```
#                        parses them and places them into an RRD
and SQL database
#
#   usage: summarize_deny
#
DBCMD='/usr/bin/psql -q'
firewall="firewall1"


pid=$$
lockfile=/var/run/summarize_deny.pid
if [ -f $lockfile ]; then
    exit 0
fi

echo $pid > $lockfile

from=`date +%b\ %e\ %H:%M:%S --date='1 hour ago'`
stime=`date +%Y-%m-%d\ %H:%M:%S --date='1 hour ago'`
param=`date +%e\ %H: --date='1 hour ago'`
then=`echo $from | cut -f 2 -d ' '`
when=`date +%d`

if [ $when -eq $then ]; then
# same date
  logfile=/var/log/messages
else
#   yesterday
#   if the logfiles are rotated BEFORE this is run
#     logfile=/var/log/messages.1
# if the logfiles are rotated AFTER this is run
    logfile=/var/log/messages
fi

tmpfile=/var/tmp/$$
```

```
# filter for only the last hour
grep "$param" $logfile | grep " Netscreen " > $tmpfile

size=`wc -l $tmpfile | awk '{ print $1 }'`
if [ $size = 0 ]; then
     rm -f $lockfile
     exit 0
fi

tcp=`grep "service=tcp" $tmpfile | wc -l | awk '{ print $1 }'`
udp=`grep "service=udp" $tmpfile | wc -l | awk '{ print $1 }'`
icmp=`grep "service=icmp" $tmpfile | wc -l | awk '{ print $1
}'`

# uncomment this to get hourly email reports
#{
#    date
#    echo "there were $size DENY/REDIRECT messages at the
$firewall firewall in the hour since $from"
#    echo $tcp TCP hits, $udp UDP hits, $icmp ICMP hits
#} | mail -s"firewall summary -- $firewall" fwadmin@example.com


# move to the directory that contains all the data and graphs
# this is to be rsync'd with the security display console
cd /var/adm

epoch=`/usr/local/bin/epoch_time $stime`

echo "update " $firewall\_hits.rrd "   "
$epoch":"$size":"$tcp":"$udp":"$icmp   | /usr/local/bin/rrdtool
- > /dev/null

now=`date +%Y-%m-%d\ %H:%M:%S --date='1 hour ago'`
stop_epoch=`/usr/local/bin/epoch_time $now`
```

```
onow=`date +%Y-%m-%d\ %H:%M:%S --date='30 hours ago'`
start_epoch=`/usr/local/bin/epoch_time $onow`


now=`date +%Y-%m-%d\ %H:%M:%S`
title="Hourly hits on firewall $firewall -- last day"


gfile=totalDay\_$firewall.gif


/usr/local/bin/rrdtool graph $gfile --title="$title" -w 550 -h
200 --start $start_epoch --end $stop_epoch \
                    --vertical-label="Hits per Hour" \
                    DEF:total=$firewall\_hits.rrd:total:AVERAGE
\
                    DEF:tcp=$firewall\_hits.rrd:tcp:AVERAGE
\
                    DEF:udp=$firewall\_hits.rrd:udp:AVERAGE    \
                    DEF:icmp=$firewall\_hits.rrd:icmp:AVERAGE
\
            AREA:total#FF0000:"other" AREA:tcp#00FF00:"tcp"
STACK:udp#0000FF:"udp" \
            STACK:icmp#FFFF66:"icmp" COMMENT:"last update
$now" \
                    COMMENT:"current total: $size  tcp: $tcp
udp: $udp  icmp:  $icmp" > /dev/null


rm -f $lockfile


psqllock=/var/run/summarize_deny.psql
if [ ! -f $psqllock ]; then
   echo $pid > $psqllock
   /usr/local/bin/netscreen_ingest < $tmpfile | $DBCMD
   rm -f $psqllock
fi


rm -f $tmpfile


exit 0
```

The preceding script is called once per hour to extract the hourly firewall data and place it in both the SQL database and the RRD database. It generates the graph of the activity of the last 30 hours as well, and is easy to extend this to add other time intervals. You could also enhance this script so if a threshold of the number of events is exceeded, or some other undesired event happens, it will send an e-mail or a page alert that the firewall and the network that it protects needs special attention.

Reporting Statistics

With the history of firewall events residing in a database, it is easy to do a deeper analysis of these events. For the most part, this type of analysis is used for monthly, quarterly, or annual reports, long-term planning, or for historical analysis, and not so much for the real-time or near real-time reports we have described so far.

Statistics by Country

It is often useful to understand where various firewall events originated. For some organizations, it is of vital importance to know if they are being scanned or probed from other countries. A useful tool for determining the country of origin is the GeoIP library and database. GeoIP consists of a binary database of the country to which all the network address blocks are assigned, plus a set of APIs (application programming interfaces) in several languages for accessing the database. The API and basic database are available for free. For a nominal subscription fee, you can get automatic database updates. Also by subscription, you can get a more detailed database that gives locations down to the city.

A simple program to read IP addresses from standard input and indicate the country is just a few lines of code:

```
/* geoip.c
        Return the country code and name for a given network
address

    to compile:   gcc -Wall -O2 -o geoip geoip.c -
L/usr/local/lib -lGeoIP
```

```
     to run give a newline delimited list of addresses from
stdin
 */

#include <stdio.h>
#include <stdlib.h>

#include <GeoIP.h>


int main(int argc, char** argv)
{
    GeoIP * gi;
    const char * returnedCountry;
    char hostip[256];
    char *p;

    gi = GeoIP_open("/usr/local/share/GeoIP/GeoIP.dat",
GEOIP_STANDARD);


    while ( fgets(hostip,255,stdin) )
    {
      if ( (p = rindex(hostip,'\n') ) ) *p = '\0';

      if ( (returnedCountry =
GeoIP_country_name_by_addr(gi,hostip)) == (char *)NULL )
          returnedCountry ="(unknown)";

      printf("%s    %s\n", hostip, returnedCountry);

    }

     GeoIP_delete(gi);

      return 0;
```

```
}
```

To get our list of countries, we can use a short script such as:

```
#!/bin/sh
# country_audit
#
# Note: customize the following as is appropriate for your
setup
# The table containing the firewall of interest
FIREWALL="firewall1"
# The command to start the database client, connected to the
proper database
# and to produce an unadorned output
DBCMD="psql firewalls -At -F ' '"

#
# you can pass the desired analysis date as an argument to
this script,
# otherwise the current date is used

if [ "$#" -lt 1 ]; then
    date="CURRENT_DATE"
else
    date=$1
fi


echo "select distinct(source) from $FIREWALL where
date='$date'" | $DBCMD \    | geoip

exit 0
```

This will generate the list of IP addresses and countries. It is a simple matter to take the first element of the list and get the count as well.

Statistics by Business Partner

Most organizations have special relationships with other businesses—vendors, clients, or partners of some sort. Typically, such partners have dedicated VPN connections or special access rules on the firewall that will allow them to connect to your LAN, whereas the general Internet population is not allowed. What are the activity patterns of these special connections and how much traffic is moving through them? While this type of network auditing is most naturally done on an IDS, we can use the firewall to watch and measure some of this activity. This is an example where you may find it helpful to log *allowed* connections instead of just the denied connections, giving you the ability to perform some measure of an audit trail on when these partners have connected and what they did. If you are using an hourly analysis script like the one described previously, you will have the information you need almost available to you automatically. The script will require modification so it distinguishes logged allows from denies at the point where the **grep** filters are being applied. The logged allow data is then saved separately for counting the number of connections, the remote end of the connection, and the protocol being used.

Tools & Traps…

Review Your Special Access Rules

If your network has special rules for partners, etc., make sure these rules are carefully periodically reviewed, preferably by an independent third-party security auditor. We once audited the firewalls of an organization that had nothing to do with retail sales, and discovered that it had very liberal access rules for Victoria's Secret. Some investigation revealed that the IP address once belonged to a genuine business partner who gave up the IP address, which was subsequently given to Victoria's Secret.

What Is "Normal" and What Is Threatening

With information about each firewall event in a database, we can do more sophisticated analyses on the security status of our network. Consider the case of the port 445 events. We can determine if the activity on our firewall is typical of the Internet as a whole, or is out of profile. To do this, we calculate a "threat index" that compares the total number of events and sources from our firewall with data published at SANS. There are two threat index values: one for destination port numbers, and one for source IP addresses.

For the port threat index, we calculate the ratio of the number of firewall hits on port 445 to the total number of firewall hits.

Now we go to the SANS Port Report page (http://isc.sans.org/port_report.php) and sum up the "Reports" column. The SANS page by default only shows the first 20 reports. This should be sufficient unless the port number you are interested in is not in the first 20, in which case you will need to include more data from their Report page.

Next, we take our ratio and divide it by the SANS ratio to arrive at our Port Threat Index (PTI). For example, on 26 October 2005, the SANS Port report had a total of 12,112,956 reports and 4,422,422 port 445 reports.

SANS Port Index = 4422422 / 12112956 = 0.365

Now, let's suppose on the same date we had a total of 7950 firewall events, of which 2000 were port 445 hits.

Our Port Index = 2000 / 7950 = 0.251

Therefore, our threat index is:

PTI = 0.251 / 0.365 = 0.68

Therefore, we are getting about 70 percent of what is typical on the Internet with port 445 probes. This is not especially worrisome, but if our number was significantly larger than 1.0, for some reason we are being targeted for port 445 probes.

The Source IP address Threat Index (SITI) works in a similar way, except that we count the number of distinct IP addresses hitting us and compare it to the number of sources that SANS is reporting (the "Source" column in their table). Therefore, for our port 445 analysis, SANS reported a total of 930,325 sources of firewall events and a total of 97,194 sources for port 445.

SANS Source Index = 97194 / 930325 = 0.104

Now suppose that our firewall saw 250 different IP addresses logged in one day, and 8 of them were probing on port 445. That would make our Source Index = 8 / 250 = 0.032.

So, our source threat index is:

SITI = 0.032 / 0.104 = 0.31

The interesting thing about the Source IP Threat index is that both very large and very small values are threat indicators. A large value means that many more Internet sites than usual have decided that your network is interesting to probe on port 445. This could be the result of some new worm that happens to start out scanning your network block, and so you are seeing the activity before the rest of the Internet . Conversely, it could mean that your network has some kind of port 445 vulnerability and it has been discovered. A small value of the SITI means that somebody in particular is interested in your network on that port. If the SITI is much smaller than one and the PTI is smaller than one, you just haven't seen many port 445 scans and only a few sources were responsible. On the other hand, if the SITI is very small and the PTI is *larger* than one, you are looking at a threat because you are getting a more than your share of probes and they are only coming from a few sources. In other words, you are being targeted.

Therefore, in our example, a SITI value of 0.31 is a little lower than expected. However, our PTI was also low. Therefore, we conclude that we just had a relatively quiet day, at least in terms of the *ratio* of port 445 hits to others. Clearly, there is something wrong if your normal number of logged events is 800 and now you are seeing 7950—do not let a little mathematical analysis be a substitute for common sense.

If you write a script to automatically query and parse the SANS port report page once a day, you can automatically generate RRD graphs of your threat indices and put them on your security console Web pages. Then, you can watch for changes and easily recognize when you are experiencing a situation that calls for specific attention.

Tools and URLs

Here is a list of security log management tools and URLs:

- **MRTG** The Multi Router Traffic Grapher: http://people.ee.ethz.ch/~oetiker/webtools/mrtg/
- **RRD Tool** Round Robin Database tool: http://people.ee.ethz.ch/~oetiker/webtools/rrdtool/
- **fwlogwatch** http://fwlogwatch.inside-security.de/
- **GeoIP** www.maxmind.com/app/country
- **PostgreSQL** www.postgresql.org/
- **MySQL** www.mysql.com/
- **Rsync** http://rsync.samba.org/
- **Ssh (scp)** www.openssh.org/

Summary

Firewall logs provide valuable information about potential violations of your security policies. To be effective, these logs need to be reviewed frequently and regularly. Manually reviewing firewall logs is tedious and prone to missing patterns. Consequently, an automated approach to parsing and analyzing the logs must be used.

The logs are analyzed for two purposes. The first is to generate quick reports about what is currently happening on the firewall. This can be reported as summary tables of the events that are happening, graphs showing the time history, or if something particularly unusual happens, an e-mail or page can be sent. The second purpose of the firewall log analysis is for long-term storage in a database. This information can be used to provide the backup evidence to detect trends and patterns or special events on the firewall.

With the log data stored in a database, it is easy to retrieve the event information to do a deeper analysis of the firewalls beyond the events that are currently occurring. Examples of this include determining the countries of origin of the security events and establishing whether the observed events are typical of the Internet these days or are targeted probes of your network.

Solutions Fast Track

Firewall Reporting: A Reflection of the Effectiveness of Security Policies

☑ A firewall should report both inbound and outbound policy violations to its logs.

☑ To be effective and practical, firewall logs must be automatically parsed and analyzed.

☑ Firewall status summaries should be available on at least hourly intervals.

The Supporting Infrastructure of Firewall Log Management

- ☑ The supporting services for firewall log management require a syslog server, a database server, and a Web server.

- ☑ The syslog server parses the logs for analysis and storage in the database. It can reside on the firewall if desired.

- ☑ The database server should not be on the firewall; it can be on the security Web server if desired. The security Web server should not be on the firewall and should be internal as opposed to a password-protected section of a public Web server.

Parsing the Data

- ☑ Firewall log parsing can be achieved with scripting languages such as AWK or Perl, but a parser based on lex (which generates a C program that can be compiled) will have much higher performance.

- ☑ The tool fwlogwatch contains parsers for several firewall types and can be extended for other firewalls by writing a lex parser for the new firewall.

Tools for an Overview of Activity

- ☑ fwlogwatch is useful for generating a tabular (text or HTML) summary of firewall log events.

- ☑ The rrdtool utilities can be combined with a stand-alone parser to generate easy-to-understand time history graphs of firewall activity.

Reporting Statistics

- ☑ Statistics by country of origin for log events can be determined by extracting the source IP addresses from the database and using the GeoIP library to resolve the country.

☑ If the firewall logs allowed activity with business partners, the firewall can be used to supplement an IDS in determining the patterns of activity with those partners.

☑ You can determine if you are being targeted on a TCP port by comparing the ratio of hits on that port to the total number of firewall hits and then relating that ratio with the same calculated from data at SANS.

Frequently Asked Questions

The following Frequently Asked Questions, answered by the authors of this book, are designed to both measure your understanding of the concepts presented in this chapter and to assist you with real-life implementation of these concepts. To have your questions about this chapter answered by the author, browse to **www.syngress.com/solutions** and click on the **"Ask the Author"** form.

Q: What information does a typical firewall log contain?

A: Different types of firewalls log different pieces of information about the events they see. At a minimum, they will record a timestamp of when the event happened, source and destination IP addresses, the network protocol (for example, TCP, UDP, ICMP), and the source and destination port numbers (or the equivalent). The log entry will typically give some firewall identification indication so one can distinguish between multiple firewalls all being logged to the same location. Some firewalls also log information about the packet involved, such as the header flags, the packet state, and packet size.

Q: How long should firewall logs be retained?

A: Your organization may have regulatory requirements that dictate how long logs need to be retained. If not, the daily raw logs should be kept online for at least 14 days and then either rotated to offline storage or deleted. The database tables should be rotated anually, keeping the current year and last year online. Older database tables can either be rotated to deep storage or deleted as is appropriate for your organization.

Q: What infrastructure is required to support long-term firewall log management?

A: You need a *syslog server* to gather and parse the logs; this can be the firewall itself if you can install software or scripts on it. You need a *database server* to handle long-term data records. You also need a *Web server* for displaying the firewall status and information derived from the database. Depending on your setup, the Web server and database servers could be implemented on the same machine, but these two services should *not* be installed on the firewall.

Q: Can firewall logging be done on Windows systems as opposed to various forms of the Unix operating system?

A: Yes with some effort. Since most firewall logs use the syslog service, you need to run a syslog server on the Windows machine. One such server is available from Kiwi Enterprises (www.kiwisyslog.com). The log summary tool, fwlog-watch, can compile on Windows if the cygwin environment is used. Cygwin (www.cygwin.com) provides a Unix-like environment within Windows. The rrdtools have been ported to both Cygwin and native Windows environments.

Systems and Network Device Reporting

Solutions in this chapter:

- Web Server Logs
- Recon and Attack Information
- Correlating Data with the Host System

☑ Summary

☑ Solutions Fast Track

☑ Frequently Asked Questions

Introduction

Systems and network device reporting is important to the overall health and security of our systems. In this chapter, we explore finding key events in the log files of our Web servers and their host systems, and correlating that data to give us useful reports. Further, we discuss different methods of report outputs that will be meaningful to senior management.

Modern software applications and Web servers have, at least, basic logging features. It is in the best interest of organizations to have policies in place that effectively and efficiently manage these logs and collect them appropriately. It would also be wasteful not to capitalize on these logging capabilities. The policies adopted need to provide for the proper storage and management of the log data collected. A lapse in this area might result in compromise and render any type of "post-mortem" forensic analysis useless, and hinder legal prosecution. Optimally, all log collection and consolidation efforts should be performed on an independent and dedicated log server. Additionally, any network connection information and the actual contents of the log data should be properly encrypted for protection and digitally signed to ensure integrity.

When it comes to log files, it is considered best practices to set log files to be "append only" to avoid deletions, purges, and overwrites. A good suggestion would be to have the logs written to a WORM (Write Once Read Many) device, such as a CD; this way, accidental deletions are prevented via physical means. Regular backups of all log files should be conducted at scheduled intervals (daily, weekly, monthly, and so forth) and follow a naming convention conveying information about the date, type, server, and anything else that may be relevant. Integrating the log backup with the overall corporate backup strategy would be beneficial, as there would not be a requirement to "reinvent the wheel." Additionally, the organization's secure disposal policies should be used when wiping and shredding log data and media. Finally, regular management reports should be generated to properly track backup and disposal events and detect any anomalies that might arise. This organization of data will allow an investigator to track intrusions and discover when incidents first appeared.

NOTE

Some Unix file systems also include the capability to modify file attributes to be append only (this is supported in modern versions of Solaris and Linux through the use of Extended File Attributes).

After the initial setup and configuration of the logging system(s), verifying that logging is still active needs to be on an administrator's agenda. A simple scheduled task can perform this through the Task Scheduler on MS-Windows or cron on Unix systems. It is very important, though, that all systems and logs have synchronized clocks; otherwise, the timestamps will be meaningless. This can be achieved by having a hardened timeserver on the network with which all servers synchronize their internal clocks.

Detailed transaction and access logs are important for, among other things, user accountability by tracking a user's actions across servers (Web applications, database access, file access, and so forth). They can be used to reconstruct the sequence of events that preceded a problem and everything that occurred after it. This reconstruction can assist security administrators to assess the full extent of an intrusion. They may be required to be brought forward in any legal action undertaken against someone. In this event, the way the log data is handled may make or break the case.

What Should the Logs Log? Everything?

Log files can easily become tremendous in size if set to monitor every detail. Sometimes, this is considered a burden; however, with storage capacity costs decreasing at an incredible rate, and compliance issues requiring immense audit trails, it might be easier to log all events, and have tools available to filter out and bring key events to our attention.

The 5 Ws (Who, What, When, Where, and Why)

Including the most information in your log files is essential. When determining the actions of reading, writing, deleting, and modification of data, we need to be able to determine the process, who owns it, when it was initiated, where the action occurred, and why the process ran. Additionally, we should be monitoring all administrative, authentication, authorization, and communication events.

It is vital that you set your Web servers and their host systems to keep proper logging. If using Apache, you should set the log settings to NCSA Combined format; if using Internet Information Server (IIS), you should set the log settings to W3C Extended format. This will ensure the Web server logs contain the most information. Additionally, the host system should be set properly to log system and security events. Be sure to set the host to log maximum events so you can easily catch all the events possible.

TIP

Often, log files on systems with heavy activity fill up quickly. On a Microsoft host, there are three main event logs: Application, Security, and System. We can easily force these logs to auto-archive when they reach a certain size. We have found that event logs greater than 100MB (approximately 300,000 entries) in size can sometime be difficult to work with. By setting the following registry entries, we ensure the event logs get no larger than 100MB, they do not overwrite any events, and they auto-archive:

```
[HKEY_LOCAL_MACHINE\SYSTEM\CurrentControlSet\Services\Eventlog\
Application]
"MaxSize"=dword:06400000
"Retention"=dword:ffffffff
"AutoBackupLogFiles"=dword:00000001
[HKEY_LOCAL_MACHINE\SYSTEM\CurrentControlSet\Services\Eventlog\
Security]
"MaxSize"=dword:06400000
"Retention"=dword:ffffffff
"AutoBackupLogFiles"=dword:00000001
[HKEY_LOCAL_MACHINE\SYSTEM\CurrentControlSet\Services\Eventlog\
System]
"MaxSize"=dword:06400000
"Retention"=dword:ffffffff
"AutoBackupLogFiles"=dword:00000001
```

Now the host will archive and store the event logs in the default event log directory, using the format Logname-YYYY-MM-DD-HH-MM-SSS-mmm.evt

There are many tools available to extract data from log files. For this chapter, we will be using Microsoft Log Parser, because of it versatility and capability to quickly output reports from large amounts of different types of information. Additionally, Log Parser has the capability to read Apache's NCSA common and combined formats, IIS's W3C log file format, and many other native log file formats. We will also explore Awstats graphical output and charting capabilities. More details on Log Parser can be found in Chapter 7, "Managing Log Files with Log Parser," and Chapter 8, "Investigating Intrusions with Log Parser."

NOTE

Microsoft Log Parser is freely available from Microsoft's Download Center and is part of the IIS Diagnostics toolkit. For an in-depth discussion on the commands and use of Log Parser, see *Microsoft Log Parser Toolkit* (ISBN: 1-93226-652-6), which contains over 200 ready-to-use scripts for everything from monitoring your Web server to investigating intrusions.

Web Server Logs

If we keep patterns of normal activity, unusual activity will stand out. The absence of an adequate logging system for Web applications may result in undetected unauthorized accesses that might blind an organization to security threats and breaches—ignorance is not bliss in the security world. We begin by examining Web server logs for useful information that may identify security incidents. We will explore both IIS and Apache Web logs since these are generally the two most common Web servers used on the Internet. We will switch back and forth between the two log formats, so it is important that we understand the differences between them.

Web logs store a lot of useful information, and being able to sift through that information and find key events is a crucial part of log analysis.

> **NOTE**
>
> For convenience and appearance of this book, we have altered log file information. It is probably unlikely that you would have 10,000 404s all from two IP addresses as shown in Figure 4.3. However, you might have a majority of them from one or two IP addresses. In keeping with the title of this book, *Identifying Patterns in the Chaos*, we are looking for patterns, unusual patterns, something out of the norm, or a repeated sequence.

Recon and Attack Information

If we keep track of daily status codes, it is easy to identify when an unusual amount of errors occur.

We could run the following command on a daily basis:

```
logparser -i:NCSA -o:CHART -chartType:Column3D -legend:ON -
categories:ON -values:ON -view:ON -chartTitle:"Status Code
Count" "SELECT StatusCode, COUNT(*) INTO STATUSCODECOUNT.gif
FROM mylogfile.log GROUP BY StatusCode ORDER BY StatusCode"
```

> **TIP**
>
> If we were viewing an IIS log instead of an Apache log, we would substitute IISW3C for NCSA, and sc-status in all the places StatusCode appears.

As mentioned previously, we are going to output all our information into charts, so we can later pull together a report for senior management.

The previous command outputs a daily chart of status codes by the number of each code that we could use to compare against other daily charts, or present to management for reporting functionality (see Figure 4.1).

Figure 4.1 A Status Code Chart

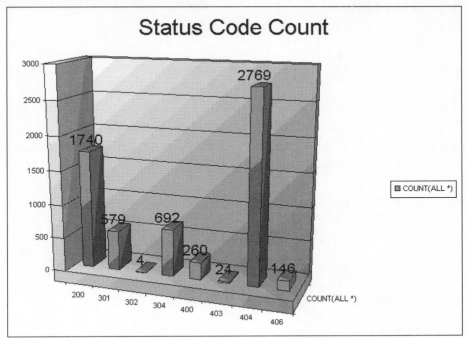

As we can see, Figure 4.1 shows an extremely high amount of 404s; if this is unusual for this particular Web site, it could be a sign of attack. This may warrant further investigation, so we will begin to build a "toolbox" of useful scripts to investigate unusual activity.

Identifying User Agent Types

We need to look further and see if the high number of 404s is a form of recon or an attack.

Possibly, someone could be scanning our Web site with an automated tool, causing the unusually high number of 404s. The following script is useful for discovering the type of User-Agent (browser type). Programs such as Awstats often do not list the actual agent name; they categorize the agent type as Mozilla, MS Internet, Explorer, and so forth. Automated tools such as N-Stalker's N-Stealth, list as a Mozilla compatible User-Agent; however, they may leave an additional signature indicating the actual program name; in the case of N-Stealth, Mozilla/4.0 (compatible; N-Stealth).

By executing the following command, we retrieve a list of User-Agents and their specific names:

```
logparser -i:NCSA -o:CHART -chartType:Column3D -legend:ON -
categories:ON -values:ON -view:ON -chartTitle:"User Agent Type"
"SELECT User-Agent, COUNT(*) As UserAgent INTO UserAgent.gif
FROM mylogfile.log GROUP BY User-Agent"
```

This outputs a chart grouped by the full User-Agent information and the number of hits by each (see Figure 4.2).

Figure 4.2 Tracking Hits by User-Agent Types

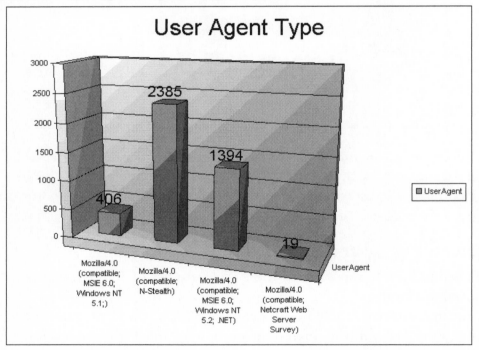

As we can see, there are numerous hits from N-Stealth. This most likely indicates someone performed an automated scan against our Web site, giving us reason to start digging deeper into the pattern we are seeing.

Isolating Attacking IP Addresses

Following our pattern, we have seen an unusually high number of 404s and an automated scan tool in our Web server logs. We will now try to see if there is a pattern in the source IP addresses.

By executing the following command, we can isolate all IPs that have returned a 404 Status Code:

```
logparser -i:NCSA -o:CHART -chartType:Column3D -legend:ON -
categories:ON -values:ON -view:ON -chartTitle:"Hits by IP with
404 Status" "SELECT distinct RemoteHostName AS Client, COUNT(*)
as Hits INTO HitsIP404.gif FROM mylogfile.log WHERE StatusCode IN
(404) GROUP BY RemoteHostName, Client ORDER BY RemoteHostName,
Hits DESC"
```

This outputs a chart that lists each IP address and the number of 404s each IP has returned (see Figure 4.3).

Figure 4.3 Tracking the Number of 404s by IP Address

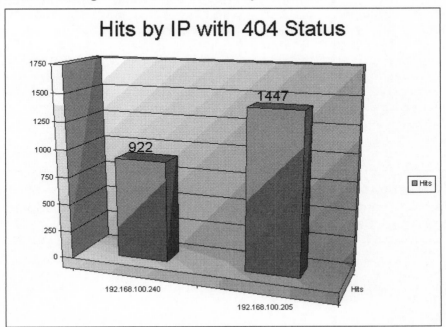

We now can see that all of the 404s from today's log belong to two IP address and probably the same subnet, which is definitely an indication of unusual activity on our Web site. This could be two different people checking for vulnerabilities on our Web server, or it could be the same person switching between different IP addresses.

We should begin to dig deeper into our Web server logs to look for other indications of recon and attacks. Additionally, we should begin to investigate our Web server's host logs for unusual activity.

Correlating Data with the Host System

We will begin by looking at the Host and Hosts event logs to see if we have any unusual activity from those IP addresses.

Did They Try to Get In?

By executing the following command, we will search the Microsoft Hosts Event Log for failed logons:

```
logparser logparser -o:CHART -chartType:Column3D -legend:ON -
categories:ON -values:ON -view:ON -chartTitle:"Host Logon
Failure" "SELECT TO_LOWERCASE(EXTRACT_TOKEN(Strings,11,'|')) AS
SourceAddress, COUNT(EventID) AS TotalLogonFailures INTO
FailLogon.gif FROM Security WHERE (EventID IN (529; 530; 531;
532; 533; 534; 535; 539)) AND (SourceAddress IS NOT NULL) GROUP
BY SourceAddress ORDER BY TotalLogonFailures ASC
```

> **TIP**
>
> Excellent resources for Microsoft EventID information are the Microsoft TechNet Events and Errors Message Center, and the Security Monitoring and Attack Detection Planning Guide.

This will output a chart detailing failed logon events from the host (see Figure 4.4).

Figure 4.4 Tracking Failed Logon Attempts to a Host

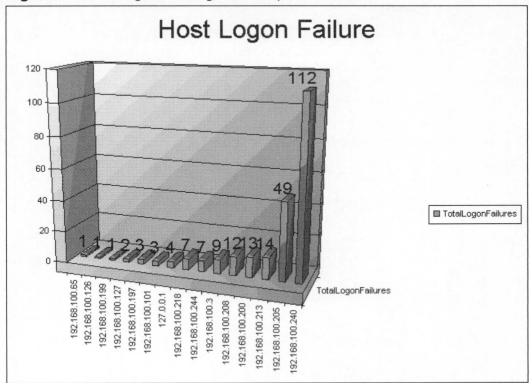

We see an excessive number of failed logon attempts from the IP addresses .205 and .240 that had the excessive 404 errors. Additionally, we see a few failed logon attempts from other IP addresses in the same subnet (assuming this is a /24).

Did They Get In?

The discussion in the preceding section is valuable information in identifying attack and recon information, but perhaps even more valuable is finding successful logon attempts by these IP addresses.

By executing the following command, we will search the Microsoft Hosts Event Log for successful logons from the IP address subnet we discovered in our pattern (see Figure 4.5).

```
logparser -o:CHART -chartType:Column3D -legend:ON -categories:ON
-values:ON -view:ON -chartTitle:"Host Logon Success" "SELECT
TO_LOWERCASE(EXTRACT_TOKEN(Strings,13,'|')) AS SourceAddress,
COUNT(EventID) AS TotalLogonSuccess INTO SuccessLogon.gif FROM
Security WHERE (EventID IN (528; 538; 540; 551; 552)) AND
(IPV4_TO_INT(SourceAddress) BETWEEN IPV4_TO_INT('192.168.100.0')
AND IPV4_TO_INT('192.168.100.255')) GROUP BY SourceAddress ORDER
BY TotalLogonSuccess ASC
```

Figure 4.5 Tracking Successful Logons to a Host

We can see that the .240 IP address has had four successful logons to our Host system.

What Did They Do While They Were In?

Now that we know someone has successfully logged on to the host system, we need to check for unusual activity. Recently created or modified files might be indicative of someone making unauthorized changes to the file system.

By executing the following command, we will search the designated directory for recently modified and created files. In this case, we will search the IIS server Web site directory (see Figure 4.6).

```
logparser -i:FS "SELECT TOP 20 Path, HASHMD5_FILE(Path),
LastWriteTime, CreationTime, LastAccessTime INTO DATAGRID FROM
\SomeDirectory\*.* WHERE (HASHMD5_FILE(Path) IS NOT NULL) ORDER
BY LastWriteTime DESC"
```

Figure 4.6 Using Log Parser to Search for Recently Modified and Created Files

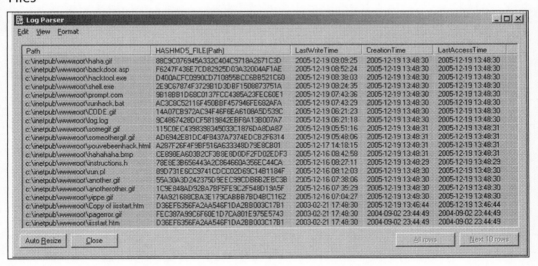

We now see that there are files that have recently been created and/or modified in the root of our Web server.

Are You Owned?

Rapid Response Is the Key

Do you know where to look and what to look for? Taking a proactive and systematic approach to systems and network device reporting can help you efficiently determine if you are owned. Daily auditing is a key component to ensure this is accomplished. With the right tools, this task becomes quick and easy. If you had 500, or even 5000, Web sites to monitor, logging into each host and manually checking its logs would be an overwhelming task. By creating and maintaining a toolbox of scripts, this task becomes easy.

Pulling It All Together

Senior management loves big, pretty reports. Pulling all this information together in one report will probably be beneficial in getting the idea across to the "C" crew.

Awstats Graphical Charting of Web Statistics

Getting useful information out of you web server(s) can sometimes be quite a hassle; however, there are several commercial tools such as WebTrends that could be used to help you parse through these logs. But they have a cost, sometimes expensive, that most organizations won't spend for web servers. In comes an open-source tool called "Awstats" (http://awstats.sourceforge.net). This tool can be used to parse and report web server logs in the form of Apache or IIS, as well as several formats of mail, FTP, and even streaming media server logs. With a quick installation, you can be looking through data such as that shown in Figure 4.7. Figure 4.7 shows an example of Awstats autoupdating hourly.

Figure 4.7 Awstats Main Autoloading Page

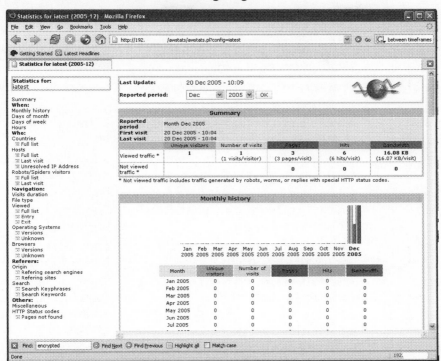

There are a total of 18 different graphs and charts that are all generated on this page! While this level of information may seem like a lot to some, the information in here can be combined with other security projects such as DNS malware blocking or a web honeypot.

For example, if you combined these logs with the Bro http logs for malware hits, you should be able to track all your malware clients. The advantage of the Awstats information is that it shows how much data each malware victim is generating, as can be seen from Figure 4.7. This can help in adding additional DNS blackhole domains or even in determining the highest threat each piece of malware is affecting your web traffic.

It should be noted that each part of the 18 different graphs can be generated individually. These charts and graphs have their own URL keywords, as explained in Table 4.1.

Table 4.1 Awstats Individual Keywords

Keyword	URL Example	Explanation
alldomains	awstats.pl?config=<yoursite>&output=alldomains	Breakdown of all DNS domains
allhosts	awstats.pl?config=<yoursite>&output=allhosts	Breakdown of all IPs
lasthosts	awstats.pl?config=<yoursite>&output=lasthosts	Shows the last several IPs
Unknownip	awstats.pl?config=<yoursite>&output=unknownip	Shows all IPs that don't resolve to DNS name
Alllogins	awstats.pl?config=<yoursite>&output=alllogins	Show all logins (optional)
Lastlogins	awstats.pl?config=<yoursite>&output=lastlogins	Show last several logins (optional)
Allrobots	awstats.pl?config=<yoursite>&output=allrobots	Show all automated searches (search engines such as google or yahoo)
Lastrobots	awstats.pl?config=<yoursite>&output=lastrobots	Show last several automated searches
Urldetail	awstats.pl?config=<yoursite>&output=urldetail	Shows full URI requests (GET/POST statements)
Urlentry	awstats.pl?config=<yoursite>&output=urlentry	Show the page(s) that were first used to get to Web site(s).
Urlexit	awstats.pl?config=<yoursite>&output=urlexit	Show the page(s) that were last used before exiting Web site(s).
Browserdetail	awstats.pl?config=<yoursite>&output=browserdetail	The name and version of Web clients hitting site(s)
Osdetail	awstats.pl?config=<yoursite>&output=osdetail	The OS (based on user-agent string) of the Web clients hitting site(s).

Continued

Table 4.1 continued Awstats Individual Keywords

Keyword	URL Example	Explanation
Unknownbrowser	awstats.pl?config=<yoursite> &output=unknownbrowser	List of Web clients that are not common. Malware shows up here often.
Unknownos	awstats.pl?config=<yoursite> &output=unknownos	Web clients usually malware, that don't give an OS label.
Referrerse	awstats.pl?config=<yoursite> &output=refererse	HTTP referrer field that has a value that came from a search engine
Referrerpages	awstats.pl?config=<yoursite> &output=refererpages	Pages that were touched through HTTP referrer calls
Keyphrases	awstats.pl?config=<yoursite> &output=keyphrases	List of search requests from Web site(s)
Keywords	awstats.pl?config=<yoursite> &output=keywords	List of external Web site(s) requests.
Errors404	awstats.pl?config=<yoursite> &output=errors404	List of HTTP errors that don't fall into the other categories. Also place for malware to show up.

Another useful piece of information that can come out of the Awstats information is the Search options. These tables display the top 10 search keywords that were search requested out of your malware victims, as well as the top 10 search keywords coming from outside your network to those malware clients. This type of information could hopefully be used to help your organization detect the next worm that uses a Google search to find victims.

Top Attacker and Top User for the Web Server

Using the tool Awstats to determine which IPs connected to your Web server and used the most bandwidth is done with the extra URL option &output=allhosts, such as in Figure 4.8.

Figure 4.8 Top IP Utilization with Awstats

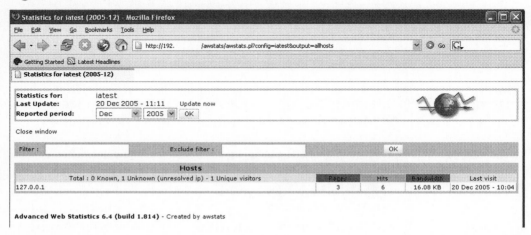

However, as most Web logs are stored for much longer periods of time in order for an organization to perform trending of these usually public-facing services, Awstats can be used to search for longer periods of time. Using another variable for monthly information:

```
"?config=<yoursite>&output=allhosts&month=<2 digit month number>"
```
or even yearly
```
"?config=<yoursite>&output=allhosts&month=<4 digit year>"
```

We can get statistics for these much longer periods of time. These reports can be linked from other applications, such as the portal site in Chapter 1, to provide quick access to this information from a common source. Another option is to take this information and have it output to an external format such as PDF. This format can be used to then distribute this information to other parties via e-mail. There is another Perl script in the tools directory for Awstats directory called awstats_buildstaticpages.pl that is used to create the

PDF files for your time frame. You will have to have the Unix tool htmldoc installed to create the PDF files. In the following example, this was a PDF file that was generated for the 20th of December 2005; that is in the option "build date."

```
perl tools/awstats_buildstaticpages.pl -config=iatest -
dir=/usr/local/awstats/test -builddate=051220 -
buildpdf=/usr/local/bin/htmldoc
```

The PDF file that is generated has a file name in the format of awstats.<your_config_name>.051220.pdf. This file is created in the directory that the script was called from, so be careful where you run the script from or else you won't get a PDF if you don't have permission to write in that directory.

These are some of the examples of what kinds of data you can gather from your Web servers using Awstats. We hope these examples have given you some ideas on how to display and disseminate this information. There are several Web formats and some specific charts available that could easily be integrated into a Web-based "managers" report with all of the graphics, as well as the tabled and full listing of charts that could go into an "analysts" report template.

Finally, if you don't want to or can't give Web access to other groups that need to see this information, you can export it to PDF for dissemination in quick one-table formats, full monthly or yearly reports, and everything in between using several scripts found with the distribution.

Summary

Now that you have been shown a small section of the available tools and types of logs that are available to a security staff to monitor and maintain their hosts and systems from each host's own logs, you should be aware that even something as simple as storing and parsing your Web servers' logs can be used to determine the health and wellness of those systems. These logs can also be viewed from a different angle and show geo-location and common requests to possibly identify attackers. When this type of technology is combined with other defensive measures, such as DNS blackholing or malware redirection, it can be leveraged to create better defenses, such as extending DNS blacklists. Another possibility would be to use these types of logs to help formulate your incident response based on the victims in host or Web logs. These can prove invaluable when trying to determine the number of victims in a large network, and they can also help limit wasted man-hours searching for victims.

Lastly, keep in mind that these components are only one piece of the puzzle when considering your security team's full view of the health and wellness of your network(s). These types of tools are best used when combined with other measures, such as your IDS, VA , and policy team's data. These components can be summed up in the form of an ESM system, but if one is not available, then creating a reporting structure that integrates these tools into it to provide your organization with a cohesive view should be implemented. Again these logs and the data they provide are only as valuable as you make them.

Solutions Fast Track

Web Server Logs

☑ Make sure you Web servers are logging at their fullest. Enable NCSA combined format for the Apache Web servers or W3C extended format for your IIS Web servers.

☑ Make sure all other available logs on your Web servers are turned on and recording adequately. Make sure logs are rotating and that you are keeping enough information to be able to fully investigate your systems.

Recon and Attack Information

☑ Review the status codes returned by your Web servers daily and look for unusual increases in errors. Errors will indicate either problems with the site or potential attacker.

☑ You can identify automated scanners by telltale user agents and high rates of server error codes made by one or a few different IP addresses.

Correlating Data with the Host System

☑ Once you find an indication that a remote host has been attacking your system, you'll need to examine your event logs for related activities. Check for host logon failures and successes.

☑ Examine the file system of the Web server and look for recently created or modified items in the Web root.

Frequently Asked Questions

The following Frequently Asked Questions, answered by the authors of this book, are designed to both measure your understanding of the concepts presented in this chapter and to assist you with real-life implementation of these concepts. To have your questions about this chapter answered by the author, browse to **www.syngress.com/solutions** and click on the **"Ask the Author"** form.

Q: How do I enable NCSA combined format in my Apache configuration?

A: Under default installations, the "combined" tag should already exist in your sample httpd.conf file. Use this nickname after the CustomLog directive in the configuration file.

Q: My Web server has virtually hosts. How should I handle logging for these domains?

A: Although you could configure Apache to add the virtual host name to each log entry. It may be best to enable a separate log file for each virtually hosted server.

Q: How do I enable W3C Extended Format on my IIS Web server?

A: Open the service master properties for your Web server or your entire Web site. Under the website tab, make sure that Enable Logging is checked and choose the W3C Extended Log File Format under the Active log format: pulldown menu. Also, click **Properties** and adjust the rotation schedule according to your needs. Under the Extended Properties tab, make sure that date and time are checked.

Q: How can I tell what all those Web server status codes mean?

A: The W3C Web site has a posting of the relevant parts of RFC 2616 that cover HTTP/1.1 (www.w3.org/Protocols/rfc2616/rfc2616-sec10.html).

Creating a Reporting Infrastructure

Solutions in this chapter:

- **Creating IDS Reports from Snort Logs— Example Report Queries**

- **Creating IDS Reports from Bro Logs— Application Log Information**

☑ **Summary**

☑ **Solutions Fast Track**

☑ **Frequently Asked Questions**

Introduction

Having seen all the different formats and types of data you can gather from your security devices, it is apparent that these reports require a support structure of their own. In addition, your organization and security shop will be best served in gathering the information in these reports and disseminating the right information to the right teams or individuals.

Creating IDS Reports from Snort Logs—Example Report Queries

If your organization is typical, you have mountains of IDS data flowing to somewhere, whether an ESM/SIM or a back-end log server. However, in previous chapters you were shown some examples of culling useful data out of those mountains. One of the keys to using this information is to put it in reports that can be automated or in templates to be filled in when needed. As you think about the reports you can automate, also consider how you can frame these reports and their associated templates into a flexible and scalable resource. One example of such a templated report would be to simply pull all of the snort data for a specific host sorted in some kind of meaningful way such as the report shown in Figure 5.1. Both the screenshot and the script that follows are called when looking at current snort log files. This can be useful if you restart snort every 24 hours to pull a host report only during the specified period. However, this can be easily extended to search dated files, specific days, or timeframes with some minor tweaking. As an added feature using systems commands *host* and *whois*, found on almost every *nix operating system, we added information about our search target. This way, in the initial report we have DNS (if available) and IP information for the host. With the additional information about the target IP, a team might be able to determine if a target should be responding a certain way. For example, with DNS and host information, partner network vulnerability host might be then recognized for performing a risk assessment.

Figure 5.1 Snort Host Report

The code that created the report template in the previous example is a simple Borne shell script heavily commented to help ease of use and modifications specific to your deployments. This script takes the target IP as the first argument such as the following example:

```
#/bin/sh /opt/SCRIPTS/host_report.sh <target IP>
```

This script could be placed in a directory that is accessible from your IDS team and just as easily be added to a menu system. However, in this case, we are simply calling it by itself; later, we will pull it into a larger report.

Here is an example of code for a snort single host report:

```
#!/bin/sh

# Simple single host report for snort data
```

```
# Variables
# This sets the first argument on the command line as the
variable hostlook
hostlook=$1


echo "" > /path/to/logs/SHR_snort.txt
echo "    SNORT DATA FOR HOST $hostlook " >>
/path/to/logs/SHR_snort.txt
echo "" >> /path/to/logs/SHR_snort.txt
echo " DNS INFORMATION: ">> /path/to/logs/SHR_snort.txt
# Unix DNS command host returns an IP's DNS name
/path/to/logs/SHR_snort
host $hostlook > /dev/null 2>&1
if [ $? -eq 0 ] ; then
echo "Host has not been seen before trying DNS lookup" >>
/path/to/logs/SHR_snort.txt
nslookup $hostlook >> /path/to/logs/SHR_snort.txt
else
echo "Host seen before…" >> /path/to/logs/SHR_snort.txt
host $hostlook >> /path/to/logs/SHR_snort.txt
fi
echo "" >> /path/to/logs/SHR_snort.txt


echo "" >> /path/to/logs/SHR_snort.txt
echo "---- ALERT TOTALS ---------" >>
/path/to/logs/SHR_snort.txt
# Using grep we are searching the snort alert file
# 2 lines before the "hostlook" (-B 2 value) , then filtering for
the alert line
# with values of "[**]" and lastly simply counting the results
"uniq -c"
grep -B 2 "$hostlook" alert.old | grep "[[**]]" | uniq -c >>
/path/to/logs/SHR_snort.txt
```

```
echo "" >> /path/to/logs/SHR_snort.txt
echo "---- TCP SESSIONS -------------" >>
/path/to/logs/SHR_snort.txt
echo " Client: " >> /path/to/logs/SHR_snort.txt
# If snort stream4 "keepstats" is turned on.
# outputing the file then filtering on the "Client IP" field (10th
column) and
# counting the resulting lines with our "hostlook" in it.
cat session.log.old | awk '{ print $10 }' | grep -c $hostlook >>
/path/to/logs/SHR_snort.txt
echo " Server: " >> /path/to/logs/SHR_snort.txt
# If snort stream4 "keepstats" is turned on.
# outputing the file then filtering on the "Server IP" field (19th
column) and
# counting the resulting lines with our "hostlook" in it.
cat session.log.old | awk '{ print $19 }' | grep -c $hostlook >>
/path/to/logs/SHR_snort.txt
echo "" >> /path/to/logs/SHR_snort.txt
echo "---- PORTSCANS ----------------" >>
/path/to/logs/SHR_snort.txt
echo " COMMON:------ " >> /path/to/logs/SHR_snort.txt
# If the sfportscan preprocessor is enabled
# Counting for all 10 common scan types
echo "Open Port: `grep "Open Port" sfportscan.log.old | grep -c
$hostlook ` " >> /path/to/logs/SHR_snort.txt
echo "UDP Decoy Portscan: `grep "UDP Decoy Portscan"
sfportscan.log.old | grep -c $hostlook ` " >>
/path/to/logs/SHR_snort.txt
echo "UDP Portscan: `grep "UDP Portscan" sfportscan.log.old |
grep -c $hostlook ` " >> /path/to/logs/SHR_snort.txt
echo "UDP Portsweep: `grep "UDP Portsweep" sfportscan.log.old |
grep -c $hostlook ` " >> /path/to/logs/SHR_snort.txt
echo "TCP Portsweep: `grep "TCP Portsweep" sfportscan.log.old |
grep -c $hostlook ` " >> /path/to/logs/SHR_snort.txt
echo "TCP Portscan: `grep "TCP Portscan" sfportscan.log.old |
grep -c $hostlook ` " >> /path/to/logs/SHR_snort.txt
echo "TCP Decoy Portscan: `grep "TCP Decoy Portscan"
sfportscan.log.old | grep -c $hostlook ` " >>
/path/to/logs/SHR_snort.txt
```

```
echo "IP Protocol Sweep: `grep "IP Protocol Sweep"
sfportscan.log.old | grep -c $hostlook ` " >>
/path/to/logs/SHR_snort.txt
echo "IP Protocol Scan: `grep "IP Protocol Scan"
sfportscan.log.old | grep -c $hostlook ` " >>
/path/to/logs/SHR_snort.txt
echo "ICMP Sweep: `grep "ICMP Sweep" sfportscan.log.old | grep -
c $hostlook ` " >> /path/to/logs/SHR_snort.txt
echo "" >> /path/to/logs/SHR_snort.txt
echo "" >> /path/to/logs/SHR_snort.txt


echo "---------RAW----------------" >>
/path/to/logs/SHR_snort.txt
echo "" >> /path/to/logs/SHR_snort.txt
echo "" >> /path/to/logs/SHR_snort.txt
echo "--------WHOIS--------------" >>
/path/to/logs/SHR_snort.txt
# Using the unix "whois" command getting IP space for the target
whois $hostlook >> /path/to/logs/SHR_snort.txt
echo "" >> /path/to/logs/SHR_snort.txt
echo "---------ALERTS------------" >>
/path/to/logs/SHR_snort.txt
# Same as above but outputting all of the hits in the full
format
# May have to be adjusted for more common output
# gets 2 lines below "-B 2" and 4 lines after "-A 4"  the target
IP
 grep -B 2 -A 4 "$hostlook" alert.old  >>
/path/to/logs/SHR_snort.txt
echo "" >> /path/to/logs/SHR_snort.txt
echo "" >> /path/to/logs/SHR_snort.txt
echo "---------SESSIONS----------" >>
/path/to/logs/SHR_snort.txt
echo "---CLIENT-----" >> /path/to/logs/SHR_snort.txt
# Outputs the full TCP session information for the target IP
with it
# as the client in the connection
```

```
cat session.log.old | grep "Client IP: $hostlook" >>
/path/to/logs/SHR_snort.txt
echo "" >> /path/to/logs/SHR_snort.txt
echo "---SERVER-----" >> /path/to/logs/SHR_snort.txt
# Outputs the full TCP session information for the target IP
with it
# as the Server in the connection
cat session.log.old | grep "Server IP: $hostlook" >>
/path/to/logs/SHR_snort.txt
echo "" >> /path/to/logs/SHR_snort.txt
echo "" >> /path/to/logs/SHR_snort.txt
echo "----------PORTSCANS---------" >>
/path/to/logs/SHR_snort.txt
echo " COMMON:------ " >> /path/to/logs/SHR_snort.txt
echo "Open Port: " >> /path/to/logs/SHR_snort.txt
grep -B 3 -A 3 "Open Port" sfportscan.log.old | grep -B 2 -A 2
$hostlook >> /path/to/logs/SHR_snort.txt
echo "UDP Decoy Portscan: " >> /path/to/logs/SHR_snort.txt
# This one will have to be tweaked once this output is seen
grep -B 3 -A 3 "UDP Decoy Portscan" sfportscan.log.old | grep -B
3 -A 3 $hostlook >> /path/to/logs/SHR_snort.txt
echo "UDP Portscan: " >> /path/to/logs/SHR_snort.txt
grep -B 2 -A 6 "UDP Portscan" sfportscan.log.old | grep -B 2 -A
6 $hostlook >> /path/to/logs/SHR_snort.txt
echo "UDP Portsweep: " >> /path/to/logs/SHR_snort.txt
grep -B 2 -A 6 "UDP Portsweep" sfportscan.log.old | grep -B 2 -A
6 $hostlook >> /path/to/logs/SHR_snort.txt
echo "TCP Portsweep: " >> /path/to/logs/SHR_snort.txt
grep -B 2 -A 6 "TCP Portsweep" sfportscan.log.old | grep -B 2 -A
6 $hostlook >> /path/to/logs/SHR_snort.txt
grep -B 2 -A 6 "TCP Portsweep" sfportscan.log.old | grep -B 2 -A
6 $hostlook >> /path/to/logs/SHR_snort.txt
echo "TCP Portscan: " >> /path/to/logs/SHR_snort.txt
grep -B 2 -A 6 "TCP Portscan" sfportscan.log.old | grep -B 2 -A
6 $hostlook >> /path/to/logs/SHR_snort.txt
echo "TCP Decoy Portscan: " >> /path/to/logs/SHR_snort.txt
# This one will have to be tweaked once this output is seen
grep -B 2 -A 2 "TCP Decoy Portscan" sfportscan.log.old | grep -B
2 -A 2$hostlook >> /path/to/logs/SHR_snort.txt
```

```
echo "IP Protocol Sweep: " >> /path/to/logs/SHR_snort.txt
# This one will have to be tweaked once this output is seen
grep -B 2 -A 2 "IP Protocol Sweep" sfportscan.log.old | grep -B
2 -A 2 $hostlook >> /path/to/logs/SHR_snort.txt
echo "IP Protocol Scan: " >> /path/to/logs/SHR_snort.txt
# This one will have to be tweaked once this output is seen
grep -B 2 -A 2 "IP Protocol Scan" sfportscan.log.old | grep -B 2
-A 2 $hostlook >> /path/to/logs/SHR_snort.txt
echo "ICMP Sweep: " >> /path/to/logs/SHR_snort.txt
# This one will have to be tweaked once this output is seen
grep -B 2 -A 2 "ICMP Sweep" sfportscan.log.old | grep -B 2 -A 2
$hostlook >> /path/to/logs/SHR_snort.txt


#END
echo "---------END---------------" >>
/path/to/logs/SHR_snort.txt


# Feeling Adventurous then add all of these :)


#(portscan) UDP Filtered Portsweep
#(portscan) UDP Filtered Distributed Portscan
#(portscan) UDP Filtered Decoy Portscan
#(portscan) UDP Filtered Portscan
#(portscan) UDP Distributed Portscan
#(portscan) TCP Filtered Portsweep
#(portscan) TCP Filtered Distributed Portscan
#(portscan) TCP Filtered Decoy Portscan
#(portscan) TCP Filtered Portscan
#(portscan) TCP Distributed Portscan
#(portscan) IP Filtered Protocol Sweep
#(portscan) IP Filtered Distributed Protocol Scan
#(portscan) IP Filtered Decoy Protocol Scan
#(portscan) IP Filtered Protocol Scan
#(portscan) IP Distributed Protocol Scan
#(portscan) IP Decoy Protocol Scan
#(portscan) ICMP Filtered Sweep
```

In some organizations, showing trends in the IDS data can be most helpful; for example, after a new anti-spyware product was installed the enterprise showed a drop in the number of spyware-related IDS events…hopefully. Another use of showing trends would be to assist in a network change, such as recommending a DNS and IP filtering ACL be implemented. If your network suffers from things such as malware, porn, and hostile networks, filtering and blocking would make the most sense. However, in most organizations, your security team will have to demonstrate how malware is affecting your network. One way to do so is with a graph such as the one shown in Figure 5.2 to show how many of your IDS events are related to malware over any given time.

Figure 5.2 Snort Malware Events Trend

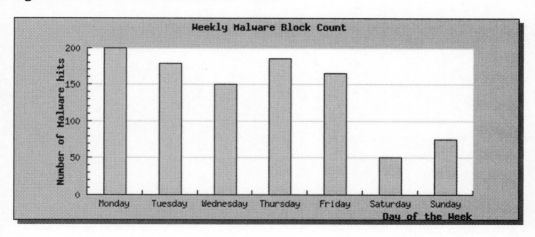

Figure 5.2 can be created if you archive the daily text file from Chapter 2 that shows the total amount of DNS malware traffic. The script in the next example was used to create the graphic shown in Figure 5.2 from static test data. However, to enable the reading of the values from a text file, enable the dynamic data section. This section assumes that you archive the daily malware text file from Chapter 2 into day-of-week files such as Sunday.txt.

```php
<?php

// INCLUDES FOR GRAPH
```

```
include (
"/usr/local/apache2/htdocs/SUPPORT/jpgraph/src/jpgraph.php");
include (
"/usr/local/apache2/htdocs/SUPPORT/jpgraph/src/jpgraph_bar.php")
;

// DATA

// Create blank arrays for place holders
$day = array();
$dnstotal = array();
$malwaretotal = array();

// Dynamic file lookups
// Assumes that you have a file called "t" that is a 1 line file
of the daily totals
// in the format of value,value,value
// read from file
//$f = fopen("t","r");
//while ($array = fgetcsv($f,7,",")) {
//array_push($malwaretotal, $array[0]);
//print "VALUES: $array[0] <br>";
//}
//fclose($f);

//STATIC TESTING
$day = array("Sunday","Monday", "Tuesday", "Wednesday",
"Thursday", "Friday", "Saturday");
$malwaretotal = array("200","178","150","185","165","50","75");


//// CREATE GRAPH SIZING AND FEATURES
$graph = new Graph (600,250,"auto");
$graph->SetScale("textlin");

// Add drop shadow
$graph->SetShadow();
```

```
// Create bar plot
$bplot = new BarPlot($malwaretotal);
$graph->Add($bplot);

// Titles and x/y axis labels
$graph->title->Set("Weekly Malware Block Count");
$graph->xaxis->title->Set("Day of the Week");
$graph->yaxis->title->Set("Number of Malware hits");
$graph->xaxis->SetTickLabels($day);

// Fonts
$graph->title->SetFont(FF_FONT1,FS_BOLD);
$graph->yaxis->title->SetFont(FF_FONT1,FS_BOLD);
$graph->xaxis->title->SetFont(FF_FONT1,FS_BOLD);

// Display the graph
$graph->Stroke();

?>
```

Another example of using snort data to push policy would be to document how much of your traffic is porn or at least triggering on sexually explicit rules. This type of report could be created in graphic format (see Figure 5.3) to help document the need for an Acceptable Use Policy (AUP).

Figure 5.3 Snort Porn Trending

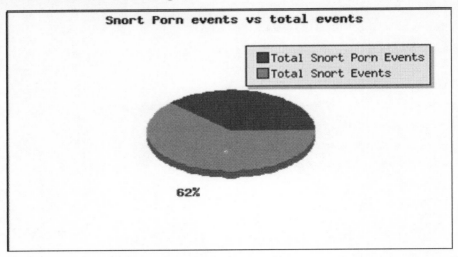

Keeping a count on the number of IPs that show up in the porn report and how many times might be helpful in enforcing the AUP. For example, an attached report in the form of a simple table, such as the data shown in Figure 5.4, could also help to identify repeat offenders.

Figure 5.4 Snort Porn Table

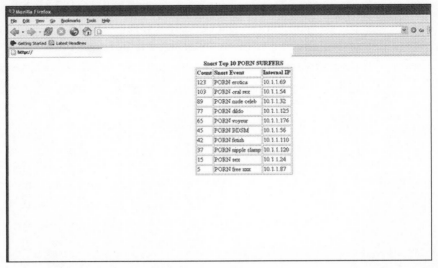

Finally, using several of the preprocessors, we can create a series of "checks and balances" reports that should validate several pieces of operational data, such as:

- Network uptimes and outages—using the snort perfmonitor preprocessor

- Traffic load—using the snort perfmonitor preprocessor

When these tools are front-ended with the newly renamed pmgraph (http://people.su.se/~andreaso/perfmon-graph/), a graphical representation of both reports can be created (see Figure 5.5).

Figure 5.5 Snort Operational Data Report (pmgraph)

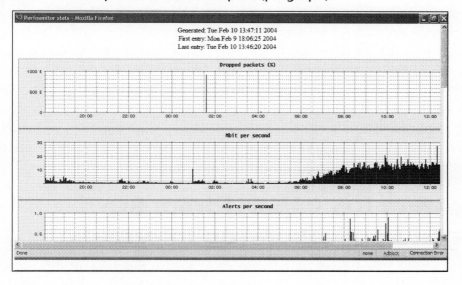

Prepare Different Report Formats—Text, Web, E-mail

The key to this information is to remember where it's going and who will be looking at it. For example, you might push out a daily report for your IDS and security engineering teams that contains detailed information on events over the last 24 hours. The client and project manager might get a simpler report that shows the security teams are doing a good job!

Another key area to focus your reporting on is the report format, in terms of how to get the reports most effectively to others who need access to the data. For example, your security personnel more than likely want to see raw sets of data in a "non-manager friendly" format such as a text-based report directly on a consoled connection. Alternatively, if your organization has an integrated "web portal" such as a security intranet, having the reports populate several key areas might be more beneficial to more groups. When setting up these web reports it is easy to extend the reports and the automation into using third-party tools such as Adobe Reader to generate .pdf files for those reports.

Finally, if you have to send those reports to other organizations or business units, you need to come up with a way to distribute those reports, such as through an e-mail distribution list. However, the data in the e-mail reports is more than likely of a sensitive nature and should be encrypted if possible with S/MIME, PGP, or some other type of encryption to protect the confidentiality of the data. If your reports are created on a *nix platform, for example, using a command-line tool such as GNUPG (www.gnupg.org) will allow you to automatically encrypt the contents of a file and then mail the encoded e-mail with your report as an encrypted attachment.

Creating IDS Reports from Bro Logs—Application Log Information

Bro is an application-level IDS system that can also function as a "protocol anomaly" detection tool. It runs on Linux- or BSD-based systems. Note that especially at higher speeds, the BSD kernels can be helpful in buffering the packets through the kernel.

Tools & Traps…

Adding a BPF Filter to Your Kernel

If you are on a FreeBSD platform for your sensors, 5.4 series for stability, you can give your libpcap-based sensors a boost in performance by setting a kernel option such as:

```
Sysctl -a "debug.bpf_bufsize=10000"
```

This option can be set at boot in the /etc/sysctl.conf file and can be used to adjust the BPF buffer size up to 10MB in the kernel. This provides an extra layer of protection on your sensors from dropping traffic under load.

Tools & Traps…

Linux Can Play, Too

For those organizations set on using the Linux kernel in your sensors, you can patch or modify your platforms to get significant performance increases. For example, if you set up the PF_Ring modification (www.ntop.org/PF_RING.html), you will see an almost 70-percent increase in sniffing performance. However, if you don't want to modify your kernel, you can use Phil Woods' (http://public.lanl.gov/cpw) libpcap library, which has been tweaked with the NAPI (New API) to increase the amount and size of the buffer outside of the kernel to drastically improve the performance of the sniffing library.

As Bro captures and logs application-level traffic such as DNS, HTTP, and others, its logs are quite detailed and can be used to provide almost any view of the data a data miner wants. For example, if you are capturing DNS traffic, several useful pieces of information can be gleaned out of that data:

- Top-10 DNS requesters (users who surf all day)

- Top-10 DNS returns (for example, the number of people requesting the IP for www.playboy.com...)

- Domain breakdowns (how many of your users' DNS queries are .com, .net, etc.)

- Foreign site lookups (for example, how many credit card applications your users want from visa.victim.ru)

- Foreign site users (for example, the number of users going to visa.victim.ru—which could indicate a targeted attack)

While displaying these types of reports in raw text form might be useful, it more than likely won't impress your management. To make these more "manager friendly," changing the format to graphical will help your management understand the high-level information you are trying to get across, such as the importance of patch management (top DNS requests), or the host-level security/anti-virus (foreign sites) and phishing attacks.

The easiest way to get "management friendly" reports is to put a graphical face on the reports. A caveat to that is to make the reports easy to access; one of the easiest ways to do this is with a web-based report. Since Bro data is in a text format that is hard for some people to use, a graphing library already in place for another security tool would be ideal. If you have deployed BASE, a common snort front end, you already have the JPGRAPH library available. This library is used to generate the graphical representation of snort data in BASE, and can be leveraged to form useful reports from Bro text data.

For example, if you want to get a listing of the top-10 Web surfers in a day, using a simple shell script on your sensors to pull the numbers out will work.

```
#!/bin/sh

#

# Simple shell script example that will query the log files of
BRO HTTP for
```

```
# the information we are requesting


# variables

mydate='date'



# Query the http log files if they are in the format

# http.log.<hour><10 minute window><day><month><year>

# For example, 10:00 to 10:10 am on 08 November 2005 would look
like

# http.log.101008112005



# First get the total number of HTTP sessions started

total_queries=`grep "start" /path/to/bro/http/http.log.*$mydate
| cat -n | tail -n 1 | awk '{ print $1 }' `

# Then sort the top ten source IP's into a text file for later
graphical display

grep "start" /path/to/bro/http/http.log.*$mydate | awk '{ print
$4 }' | sort | uniq -c | sort -nr | head -n 10 >
/log/Top10_http.log



# OPTIONAL:

# Perform the same search and sort on the top ten destination
IP's this can be

# later run through a DNS log for better understanding
```

```
grep "start" /path/to/bro/http/http.log.*$mydate | awk '{ print
$6 }' | sort | uniq -c | sort -nr | head -n 10 >
/log/Top10_dst_http.log

# Done
```

Then, by outputting this data to a text file, the file can be queried by a web script that will take the text output and, using PHP, call the JPGRAPH library to generate either a dynamically generated image (this example) or a static .png file format image. The latter would be more likely to be created if your data was going to be called from other remote sites that didn't want to have to re-render the data every time the page was requested. In Figure 5.6, we are assuming that a small script scp's the log files to the proper location on the security web server. Once the file is on the web server box, it is read into the graphical report using PHP and the data is fed into the file in multiple arrays.

Figure 5.6 Graphical Report of Top 10 HTTP Surfers

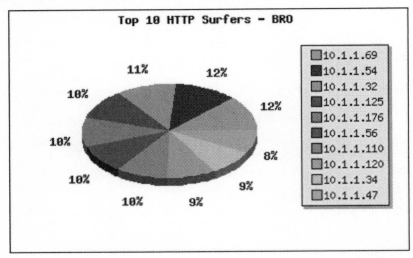

Using the code in the following example, the data about the top HTTP surfers is dynamically fed into a file and then displayed. This code can be easily added to a dynamic daily security report or "portal" page, such as the

one in Chapter 1, which would provide your security team a central place to
look for security information.

```php
<?php

// INCLUDES FOR GRAPH
include ( "/path/to/base/jpgraph/src/jpgraph.php");
include ( "/path/to/base/jpgraph/src/jpgraph_pie.php");
include ( "/path/to/base/jpgraph/src/jpgraph_pie3d.php");

// DATA

// create blank arrays to use

$count = array();
$host = array();

// Should be called from a file for dynamic updates
$totalhttp = 3128;

// read from file
$f = fopen("/log/Top10_http.log","r");
 while ($array = fgetcsv($f,25,";")); {
  $newvalue = $totalhttp - $array[0];
  $array_push($count, $array[0]);
  $array_push($host, $array[1]);
  }
 fclose($f);

$data = $count;
$leg = $host;


// CREATE GRAPH SIZING AND FEATURES
$graph = new PieGraph (450,400,"auto");
$graph->SetShadow();
```

```php
// Set Title
$graph->title->Set("Top 10 HTTP Source IPs");
$graph->title->SetFont(FF_FONT1,FS_BOLD);
// Position of the legend box x and y axis values
$graph->legend->Pos(0.04,0.05);


// Create plots

// First Graph
$p1 = new PiePlot3D($data);
$p1->SetLegends($leg);
$p1->SetSize(.13);
$p1->SetCenter(0.25,0.32);
$p1->value->SetFont(FF_FONT1,FS_BOLD);
$p1->value->SetColor("blue");
$p1->SetTheme('earth');
$p1->title->Set("Top 10 HTTP Surfers");


$graph->Add($p1);
//
$graph->Stroke();

?>
```

This same type of reporting can be extended to other types of Bro data such as DNS, SMTP, FTP, and so forth. Each can provide you with several useful pieces of information about your network(s)—from using the top and bottom of the DNS requests to discover possible malware sites, and odd DNS requests for such things as Trojan sites, to searching through SMTP attachments for sensitive files sales_pipeline.xls sound bad going out?

Some of these searches are not easily displayed in a graphic format; however, they can be useful in some other format such as text or tables.

Prepare Different Report Formats—Text, Web, E-mail

As already seen, some of the security information can be displayed in graphical web format to help disseminate the information clearly, although in some cases, a web format is not possible or sensible, such as locations that rely on e-mail for alarms and events. These could be your remote sites that you don't retain a connection to at all times, or those sites that are slow links. One method for providing useful information over these text-based mediums would be using text tables and simple text. For example, the following example text file could be sent to a security group's mailbox daily to show how effective a malware DNS poisoning policy was working.

```
Generating data for Mon Aug 22 05:15:00 2005 on DNS queries


This is the total DNS queries made yesterday: 155753


This is the UNIQUE DNS queries made yesterday: 20498


This is the Total DNS query that resolved to the Security box:
2896


----------------------ALL DONE!
```

This simple example of converting the Bro DNS information into a useable, readable, and easily distributed format such as e-mail is quite simple to do. The previous example, which displays DNS information that has been recorded from Bro in its "complex" format, has now been distilled to a three-line, easy-to-understand format for distribution to other groups. The first line dates our text file so we can determine when it was run, and the second line counts all DNS "A" record queries made during the previous 24 hours. As this count can pick up duplicates of the records for popular sites such as yahoo.com or google.com, the third line simply counts only the unique records. The last line is a count of all the DNS "A" records that had a domain that was "redirected" to the malware black-hole host IP. This data can be pulled out of the sensors collecting this information using a simple shell script

that culls the data for the requested information and then places it in a text
file ready for mailing or pickup by a log aggregation server with mail capabilities.

Here is an example of the script used to pull the DNS malware
information:

```
#!/bin/sh

####################
#
# Jake Babbin
# 07 July 2004
#
#
# This script is used to gather the DNS queries for malware
# This script assumes that you are poisoning your DNS server
# entries and pointing to a malware collection box.
#
# This script should be used to validate the effects of a DNS
# poisoning initiative
#
#
# Tested on FreeBSD 4.x, and 5.x platforms
#
# This data can be emailed or sent to the portal health report
#
#####################

# Variables
yesdate=`date -v -1d +"%m%d%Y"`
yeslongdate=`date -v -1d +"%c"`
# TEMP
mydate=`date +"%m%d%Y"`
longdate=`date +"%c"`
```

```
# Gather the previous day's total DNS record
yesDNSTOTAL=`grep "?A " /path/to/bro/dns/dns.log.*$yesdate |
grep -v "Xnam" | awk '{ print $6 }' | grep "[.]" | cat -n |
tail -n 1 | awk '{ print $1 }' `
# Gather the previous day's total UNIQUE DNS records
yesDNSUNIQUE=`grep "?A " /path/to/bro/dns/dns.log.*$yesdate |
grep -v "Xnam" | awk '{ print $6 }' | grep "[.]" | sort | uniq
-c | sort -nr | cat -n | tail -n 1 | awk '{ print $1 }' `
# Gather the previous day's count for the total UNIQUE that
resolved to SECURITY
yesDNSSEC=`grep "?A " /path/to/bro/dns/dns.log.*$yesdate | grep
-v "Xnam" | awk '{ print $6 }' | grep "[.]" | sort | uniq -c |
sort -nr | grep "<MALWARE COLLECTION BOX IP>" | awk '{ print $1
}' `


# TEMP
# Gather the day's total DNS record
DNSTOTAL=`grep "?A " /path/to/bro/dns/dns.log.*$mydate | grep -v
"Xnam" | awk '{ print $6 }' | grep "[.]" | cat -n | tail -n 1 |
awk '{ print $1 }' `
# Gather the day's total UNIQUE DNS records
DNSUNIQUE=`grep "?A " /path/to/bro/dns/dns.log.*$mydate | grep -
v "Xnam" | awk '{ print $6 }' | grep "[.]" | sort | uniq -c |
sort -nr | cat -n | tail -n 1 | awk '{ print $1 }' `
# Gather the day's count for the total UNIQUE that resolved to
SECURITY
DNSSEC=`grep "?A " /path/to/bro/dns/dns.log.*$mydate | grep -v
"Xnam" | awk '{ print $6 }' | grep "[.]" | sort | uniq -c |
sort -nr | grep "<MALWARE COLLECTION BOX IP>" | awk '{ print $1
}' `



# MAIN


echo "Generating data for $yeslongdate on DNS queries" >
/LOGS/DAILY_MALWARE.txt
echo "" >> /LOGS/DAILY_MALWARE.txt
```

```
echo "This is the total DNS queries made yesterday: $yesDNSTOTAL
" >> /LOGS/DAILY_MALWARE.txt
echo "" >> /LOGS/DAILY_MALWARE.txt
echo "This is the UNIQUE DNS queries made yesterday:
$yesDNSUNIQUE " >> /LOGS/DAILY_MALWARE.txt
echo ""  >> /LOGS/DAILY_MALWARE.txt
echo "This is the Total DNS queries that resolved to the
Security box: $yesDNSSEC " >> /LOGS/DAILY_MALWARE.txt
echo "" >> /LOGS/DAILY_MALWARE.txt
echo "---------------------ALL DONE!" >>
/LOGS/DAILY_MALWARE.txt
```

After this script is run, a simple log collection script could get the log files from each sensor to provide a central repository for these files. This would serve as the distribution point for these logs, or these files could then be renamed and dated for later use in trending information. Although most shops will want to do both as the script in the following example does, with a little creativity the renamed files could be searched and indexed for graphical representation over time as well. Alternatively, an astute reader could parse and insert this information into a database for scalability and long-term trending.

Here is an example of the script to mail and store malware logs:

```
$!/bin/sh

##
# This script will take the new malware file "DAILY_MALWARE.txt"
# and email it to the proper mailing lists in the organization
# then rename and move the file to an archive directory for later
use
# in trending reports
#
# NEEDED:
# Mail capable machine with mutt installed
#
##
```

```
# Variables
# Date in short format
mydate=`date +"%m%d%Y"`

# Start sending out the daily file
#
mutt -a /logs/DAILY_MALWARE.txt -s "Daily DNS blocking report
for $mydate" DNS_mgrs@organization.com < /dev/null
mutt -a /logs/DAILY_MALWARE.txt -s "Daily DNS blocking report
for $mydate" IDSTEAM@organization.com < /dev/null
mutt -a /logs/DAILY_MALWARE.txt -s "Daily DNS blocking report
for $mydate" IA_mgrs@organization.com < /dev/null

# Once the mailings are complete move the daily file to the
archive
mv /logs/DAILY_MALWARE.txt
/logs/ARCHIVE/DAILY_MALWARE.$mydate.txt

# DONE!
```

These are some quick examples of what can be reported with some of the Bro data and in what formats you can report that information to internal and external groups.

Summary

This chapter further illustrated the depth and breadth your security logs can cover—from using your IDS systems to validate compliance and tracking events in several formats, to using your firewall logs to geolocate threats and attackers. One important point to consider is that the examples presented here are a starting point for your organization. We encourage you to change and extend these solutions to better suit your organization's audit and compliance structures such as for HIPPA, GBL, or SOX, to name a few. Almost all of these solutions were from open source tools and reporting applications to illustrate that anyone can do these reports with a little help.

Solutions Fast Track

Creating IDS Reports from Snort Logs—Example Report Queries

☑ Using simple scripts, a host report can be created for IPs you are investigating.

☑ Using snort rules and JPGRAPH, reports can be generated to show everything from unapproved network use such as porn browsing to tracking malware.

Creating IDS Reports from Bro Logs—Application Log Information

☑ Bro information can be used to show detailed tracking of malware infection victims.

☑ Bro information can be used to illustrate malware effects on a network through DNS, SMTP, or even HTTP traffic logs.

Frequently Asked Questions

The following Frequently Asked Questions, answered by the authors of this book, are designed to both measure your understanding of the concepts presented in this chapter and to assist you with real-life implementation of these concepts. To have your questions about this chapter answered by the author, browse to **www.syngress.com/solutions** and click on the **"Ask the Author"** form.

Q: Are there other tools available to get host information from snort events?

A: Yes, there are several. OpenAanval (www.aanval.com) is one GUI for searching through snort events. This GUI is built more for use as a single console from detection to incident response than for single host queries.

Q: Can you perform trending of malware for longer than a week?

A: If you offload the search data to a database, you can easily search for longer periods of time, such as a month.

Q: Is there any more documentation on using the snort perfmonitor preprocessor?

A: Yes, on the snort.org site under documentation there is an entire section on the preprocessor.

Q: Are there other tools or hardware available to help capture traffic on higher speed networks?

A: Yes, a company called endace (http://www.endace.com) is one of several that sell a libpcap on the card, a network device that links via programming an API to the most common IDS tools, such as snort and tcpdump.

Q: Where can I learn more about malware detection and mitigation solutions such as DNS blackholing?

A: A good resource for quick and easy solutions is the bleedingsnort spyware listening post found at http://www.bleedingsnort.com/staticpages/index.php?page=listeningpost. This Web site provides a wealth of information. For example, it has links to ISC BIND and MS DNS Server configurations to use as blackholing servers.

Scalable Enterprise Solutions (ESM Deployments)

Solutions in this chapter:

- **What Is ESM?**

- **When Deploying ESM Makes Sense**

- **Which Security Reporting Tools to Aggregate into ESM**

- **Using ESM Reporting for Maximum Performance**

- **Special Considerations for Using ESM**

- **Lessons Learned Implementing ESM**

- ☑ **Summary**

- ☑ **Solutions Fast Track**

- ☑ **Frequently Asked Questions**

Introduction

Early in the history of enterprise applications, all management of those applications was controlled and monitored through mainframes. This system allowed for automatic consolidation and correlation of data from multiple sources and provided a single place to look when something went wrong. All aspects of the system as a whole—including network connectivity, system stability, and application functionality—could be ascertained by looking in one place.

Time has moved on and distributed systems have become the norm. No longer do we have a default single point of information regarding systems in our environments. Now, instead of a "central computer," we have heterogeneous systems distributed in multiple locations connected by multiple networked systems and secured by multiple security devices. This increase in distribution has given us a plethora of information sources regarding the functional aspects of the systems we are responsible for maintaining.

Aside from there being different sources for the information we need, the information is often in different formats. Data gathered from a Windows 2003 server will differ from that gathered from a Cisco switch, which in turn will be in an entirely different format from the data you pull from an AIX server. This has led to a great deal of specialization where experts on specific systems can understand and translate the retrieved data, but technical people fluent in other platforms may not be able to understand it. This adds an additional challenge to managing the systems within an enterprise.

With varying sources of information gathered in different formats and only readable by specialists on specific platforms, there is a huge challenge in understanding what is happening within an enterprise. The simple question of, "Why am I unable to run the financial application?" has changed from a quick glance at the mainframe monitors to a consolidated effort across multiple technical teams dealing with a wide variety of systems. This has caused the mean time to repair (MTTR) of systems and the level of expertise required to fix problems to increase.

The same problem has also become apparent in the world of information technology security. We are responsible for ensuring that security policies are created, implemented, and enforced in environments that are constantly growing and changing. The log files we looked at yesterday are gone today, having been replaced with something entirely different. This will change tomorrow, of course, and we will have to be able to move with the technology.

The number and variety of information sources we work with in the security field are now just as varied as they are for systems administrators. We have data available on network equipment, client and server systems, intrusion detection systems (IDSes), firewalls, and so forth. Most of this data differs in format and retrieval methods as well as quantity. Some systems provide much more data than others do, and typically there are more individual sources of some types of data. For example, most enterprises will have many more server systems than they have firewalls, and we need to be able to handle this quantity appropriately.

With all this data, how is it possible to effectively manage the security of our enterprise? How can we possibly go through all of this data and extract the information we need to find problems in our security? Depending on the number of information sources we are dealing with, this problem becomes increasingly difficult to solve. Bringing on more people to analyze data could help, but then we risk losing correlation of some data since multiple people would be analyzing it. We could use sampling techniques to look through portions of the data to show trends, but we could easily miss crucial individual events.

As we consider the challenges apparent in this scenario, we look back in time for the solution. The efficiency and correlation available on the mainframe systems certainly seem to be better suited for our needs. However, how can we gain the advantages of a centralized system when working with distributed systems? The answer is Enterprise Security Management (ESM).

ESM is defined simply as *the process of controlling configuration, deployment, and monitoring of security policies across heterogeneous platforms and disparate security products.* This simple definition describes both the problems we have discussed and the concept of a solution similar to how this was done in the centralized computing world.

In this chapter, we will be exploring what ESM is, how it works, and when and where it should be used. In some cases, ESM is not necessary, and in others, it is mandatory. In addition, we will go over some features of ESM and how it can make your job easier and your work more effective. Lastly, we will discuss some ESM tools currently available on the market.

What Is ESM?

The question of what Enterprise Security Management is should be fairly simple, but the answer is somewhat complex. Some people consider ESM the standard day-to-day practices of implementing enterprise security. Others consider ESM the process of ensuring that the enterprise security policies are current and contain the appropriate information to support legal and regulatory requirements. Still others feel that ESM is a tool used to consolidate all of their enterprise security data and provide a single information source for security data. The real answer is that all of these are correct. ESM is a multi-faceted concept, which allows for it to mean all these different concepts to different people.

Based on the previous definition, we will be looking at ESM from a process perspective. We will of course be looking at tools and the technical aspects of ESM processes, but our focus should be directed from a process standpoint. It is from this direction that ESM becomes the most all-encompassing and useful tool available to enterprise information technology security professionals.

The most common cause for the need of ESM is the existence of security problems and threats. The need to protect an organization and its assets drive the need for security in general. As the organizations we protect grow, our toolsets must grow to compensate. You cannot expect to gain a full understanding of how effective your security policies are by looking at a single system in your enterprise, so examining multiple systems is necessary. Eventually, this need grows to state that examining *all* systems in the enterprise is necessary. Any time you follow this path and start viewing data from multiple systems, you are starting to practice the foundation of ESM.

Keep in mind that the process of ESM includes more than just examining data from systems. Again, ESM is *the process of controlling configuration, deployment, and monitoring of security policies across heterogeneous platforms and disparate security products*. In this section, we will examine each component of ESM and work to define exactly what is involved in this process.

TIP

We really can't stress this enough... ESM is a process, not a specific tool or action. You will need to think of ESM from the process perspective as we discuss it throughout this chapter. By taking this perspective, you will be able to separate the process of ESM from the tools that can help you in implementing the ESM process.

Security Policy

The first thing that must be in place for any security implementation is your security policy. Remember one of the tenets of IT security: No security device provides security; it simply enforces your security policy. The same concept applies to ESM. Before embarking on a full ESM solution, you should first have a well-defined and approved security policy in place. From there, it is the purpose of ESM to control configuration, deployment, and monitoring of the policy.

It is beyond the scope of this book to tell you how to create a good security policy. However, there are some important components you should include within your security policy that will help in the implementation of ESM:

- Access control
- Accountability
- Authentication
- Availability
- Confidentiality and privacy
- System and network maintenance

Each of these components and more are required to have a useful security policy. What is special about these components is that each of them can be rolled in to your ESM solution. In most cases, they can be configured, deployed, and monitored through ESM. This allows you to have a single solution that enforces the key areas of your security policy as you have defined it.

The most important thing to remember is that ESM cannot help you unless you already have this policy defined. ESM is not meant to build your policy, but rather to control the configuration, deployment, and monitoring of the systems that enforce the policy.

Controlling Configuration

With a security policy in place, the next step is to configure the devices and systems in your enterprise to comply with the policy. This can involve many distinct tasks, such as configuring:

- Access control lists (ACLs) on network devices
- Password expiration and change policies for directory services
- Password expiration and change policies for databases
- Password lockout processes for directory services and databases
- Multifactor authentication for sensitive systems
- Applications to use centralized authentication systems
- Servers and workstations to be hardened
- Firewalls
- IDSes
- VPN systems
- Load balancing systems
- Physical security systems

This is just a short list of some of the configuration-related items you may have to consider after defining a security policy. All devices and systems across the entire enterprise must be configured to support the rules defined for them in the security policy. Depending on the number of devices and systems, this can be a very large undertaking.

What is worse is that the configuration of these systems is usually not just done once; the entire process must be repeated each time the security policy is updated. For example, assume that you have a security policy in place stating that the minimum length for passwords is seven characters. Within your organization, a disgruntled employee used brute-force techniques to determine another user's password. Because of this, a decision is made to increase the minimum password length and to lock out accounts after three failed authentication attempts. To apply this policy, every system and device must be reconfigured to support the change. If the environment you are working in has hundreds of servers, thousands of workstations, and dozens of network devices, this simple change could take months to implement manually.

This is where the controlling configuration aspect of ESM comes into play. Rather than make each of these configuration changes manually on all devices, wouldn't it be much more convenient to have this work done for you? Imagine having a single system where you type in these two changes and it determines which systems the changes need to go to, how to make the changes on the systems based on what they are, and then makes the changes for you. This is the power of ESM. While different ESM tools have different capabilities, this is the direction all of them are headed.

Automatic configuration of systems and devices to support your security policy is a wonderful feature and can help you in many ways. Not only do you avoid having to do the manual work to implement configuration changes, you are also protected from making human errors. Any time a large number of changes must be made manually, the risk of errors increases. Depending on what changes are occurring, these errors can cause anything from ineffective security to system failures. This is mitigated with the use of automation in the area of configuration.

A fortunate side effect from the automation of device and system configuration is systematic configuration change management. Change management is one of the more critical aspects of maintaining an enterprise system, and ESM can help you in this as well. By forcing all changes to be done through ESM, you now have created a repository showing all changes done to a device or system. If a change is made outside of this process, it would be considered unauthorized and a violation of your change management system. Additionally, if a device or system is functioning poorly, the first thing to do when troubleshooting is to find out what changed since it last functioned properly. ESM can help with that by giving you a single point of reference for all changes made.

Controlling Deployment

Deployment is another important aspect of systems security. This refers to the implementation of security policies into devices and systems. While deployment by this definition may seem similar to configuration, it is quite different. Whereas configuration deals with the changing of individual parameters, deployment is concerned with the publication of larger quantities of data. Some examples of deployable objects are static routing tables, firmware upgrades, software upgrades, intrusion detection signatures, and virus signatures. All of these objects and others must be deployed to various devices and systems within your enterprise.

In most cases, deployments are done by sending the deployable object to the device or system and executing a specific procedure causing the device or system to accept the new object. These procedures can range from executing a program through the operating system to modifying code stored on a memory chip. Regardless, a specific set of commands or processes must be used to deploy an object. Due to the nature of these deployments, it is critical that these procedures are executed precisely and without error; otherwise, they could have very detrimental effects.

Another aspect of deployments is the requirement to verify that the deployment was successful. It isn't enough to simply push out a new object; verification that the object was successfully pushed and accepted is important, too. This increases the time required to deploy objects because you are now spending the initial time required to deploy and then going through yet another procedure to ensure the object arrived successfully. Then, you must ensure that the object was accepted by the device or system using it and moved into an active state, which in many cases can take more time than the deployment of the object!

Examples of this can be found with ACL updates for routers or INI file changes for running applications. In both of these cases, you must take some sort of action in order to make the changes take effect. With the router, a specific command must be issued in order to store the ACL to the active router configuration. For the INI file change, the application may need to be restarted or a command issued to reload its INI file. With these types of systems and others, additional actions beyond simply making a change are certainly required in order to cause the systems to note that a change has been made.

This is yet another area where ESM shows its usefulness. Through the task of controlling deployment, ESM tools can automate and simplify the processes used to deploy objects to devices or systems. Many tools exist outside of the ESM realm for accomplishing these tasks for specific systems. For example, there are tools available that monitor the release of Microsoft operating system patches and then deploy the patches to your systems when they are released. Similar tools also exist for Linux systems. The idea of ESM, however, requires that these system-specific tools be rolled into one central tool to accomplish deployments across a heterogeneous enterprise.

With ESM technology expanding, tools now exist that can keep a record of the devices and systems in your environment and deploy new patches, files, or signatures to them in the manner appropriate for the device or system. This gives you a centralized point of control where all deployments are managed across your enterprise automatically. Verifications are done after the deployment to ensure it was successful and you have visibility into reports showing the deployment status at any point in time. Again, ESM provides time savings as well as prevention of human error.

Tools & Traps…

The Differences between Tools

As we discuss ESM, we will be going over a huge number of possible functions that ESM tools can perform. Not all tools perform all of these functions, and many tools offer more than what we will discuss. With all of the ESM tools that have been developed, there is certainly no perfect tool that will work for all organizations. Prior to choosing a tool, develop your organizations' requirements. Then, carefully examine the options that are available and choose the tool that best fits the needs of your specific organization.

Monitoring

The process of monitoring your security policy is, in our opinion, one of the most important parts of performing IT security, and what we consider the most exciting and time-consuming part as well. After you have done all the configuration and deployment associated with devices and systems used in implementing your security policy, you'll need to focus on making sure the policy is working. This involves monitoring for exceptions to the policy that occur, and monitoring for unexpected activity not originally considered by the policy. With this in mind, monitoring requires the active and constant watching of system activities, log files, events, and external factors.

The performance of systems is an excellent indication as to what the system is doing. If, for example, a file server in a finance department is using a large amount of memory and processor, it could indicate that someone is using a financial application. However, if the same system is showing an unusually high amount of disk and network I/O, it could indicate that someone is pulling a large amount of data off the system. One of these should trigger an alert just to make sure everything is okay, whereas the other could probably be considered innocuous. We'll leave it to you to determine which is which, but the point is the granularity of system information that should be included as part of your security monitoring.

Most devices and systems generate log files detailing what is going on with them. The level of detail provided and the format of these log files differ depending on how the system or application was designed. Some systems may also have multiple log files being generated simultaneously. For example, a Windows system operating as an application server may have a security log, application log, and system log from the operating system as well as log files generated from the application being served. This common example shows four distinct log files for a single system. Depending on the level of detail for the logs, this can be a huge amount of information, much of which may be unnecessary from a security standpoint. However, if a single entry in one of these logs indicates a security problem, you should know about it, which means they all must be monitored and the data must all be reviewed.

System events encompass all activities that occur on a device or system. This could be the act of accessing a file or the removal of a USB memory stick. Anything that happens to a device or system is considered an event.

Many systems record events that occur to a log file of some type; however, not all events are considered important enough to log. For example, the default configuration of many systems does not log a successful file access attempt. The reason for this is the sheer amount of data that would be generated if this were done.

On the other hand, consider the scenario of a successful system intrusion. An attacker has successfully accessed a system and has full control over it. You know the attacker has downloaded some sensitive files and you must act to limit the damage caused by this. Which files did the attacker download? How can you tell if the system is not logging file access events? In many cases, there is no need to send all of this data to log files that can quickly fill up the drive space on a system. However, there may be times when the data could be useful and it might be wise to retain it, at least for a little while. The event of a successful file access and other systems events can serve a useful purpose obviously, so this should be considered when you are thinking about monitoring the security in your enterprise.

All of the monitored items we have discussed so far relate back to internal devices or systems and internal data. The need also exists to monitor external factors, which can range from the current stock price of the company you work for on the stock market to reports of new spamming techniques. This is the part of IT security work that is less systematically driven and typically requires more of the "human touch." While most other monitored factors can be considered digital, external factors can be either digital or analog depending on the factor you are monitoring. It is important not to ignore this aspect of security monitoring, as it can often lead you to knowledge you would not otherwise have. Some examples of external factors and what they can mean are listed in Table 6.1.

Table 6.1 External Factors

External Factor	Impact to Your Enterprise
A tremendous increase in the cost of oil causes diesel prices to soar.	Your backup generators rely on diesel to operate. Due to the cost increase, the facilities department decides to only fill the tanks halfway, reducing the duration that your systems can remain operational.
NOAA reports increased sunspot activities.	Wireless communications can be affected by this. When a mobile device user of your company calls in to report that he thinks someone is attacking his mobile device, you know that while this is possible, it is more likely that solar activity is simply causing interference.
A security organization starts to see many intruders attempting to attack a specific port and posts a newsgroup message stating this.	You have an application in your organization that uses this specific port. Chances are good that a vulnerability has been found in that application or another application using the same port.
NOAA reports an increase in tornado activity near the Kansas border.	This is where your backup datacenter is located. While the tornadoes may not affect your primary datacenter, you may have decreased redundancy while this is occurring.
A news bulletin is released stating that some hackers have found a way to quickly crack encryption using 1024-bit keys.	Your security policy states that the use of 1024-bit keys is sufficient for the encryption of sensitive information emailed out of the company. Now, any information being transmitted is vulnerable to being decrypted and read.

These factors all may seem fairly common and unimportant as far as IT security is related, but by examining the impact, it quickly becomes obvious how important they can be. To provide full enterprise security, it is important to monitor external factors that can have an effect on your security policy enforcement. Often, the monitoring of external factors can give you indications of future problems before you would see the problems using internal data alone.

Obviously, monitoring is a very large part of enterprise security and involves many individual factors. Manually monitoring all of this incoming data is almost impossible, so tools have been created that simplify these efforts. Some tools will allow for the monitoring of entries going into log files as they occur, while others allow for the monitoring of overall system perfor-mance. Still others watch for specific system events and send out e-mail alerts when these events occur. All of these tools simplify the effort of monitoring the implementation of your security policy, but we run into the same problem where different tools use different formats and display data in dif-ferent places.

This is yet another area where ESM can help you to provide an overall enterprise security solution. ESM by definition includes the monitoring of heterogeneous distributed systems, including security systems. ESM isn't a security system, but a process that allows you to make more effective use of your security systems. Many ESM tools focus on the area of monitoring. They allow for a centralized view of data from monitored devices and systems with the ability to drill down into more detail or generate reports based on the data. Simply having a single point of reference for monitoring data across your enterprise is a huge advantage provided by ESM and one of the primary reasons for its existence.

When Deploying ESM Makes Sense

So far, we've discussed what ESM is and some of the challenges it can help you solve. In most cases, these challenges only become unbearable within large enterprises. When working with smaller subsets of devices and systems, it is certainly possible to manage them successfully without using the concepts put forth in ESM. Just as there are reasons to implement ESM in your envi-ronment, there may be reasons not to.

You must remember that with every change in information technology, there is some form of cost involved, be it monetary or systematic. As far as ESM is concerned, in some cases the costs may outweigh the benefits. Remember that the purpose of ESM is to *control configuration, deployment, and monitoring of security policies across heterogeneous platforms and disparate security products.* If ESM is controlling all of these things, the control is completely automated and does not have the "human touch." This creates a cost: the loss of human intervention and intuition. Patterns that may be recognized by experienced security engineers may be missed by ESM if it is not programmed to note the patterns. Zero-day exploits may not be caught by ESM if ESM itself is not carefully monitored. The cost of automation can be very expensive if not done correctly.

On top of this is the cost of ESM tools. There are many tools available for performing security actions, but they tend not to integrate well. To perform day-to-day tasks, most security engineers have a toolkit containing over 40 different tools. These are just for day-to-day tasks and do not include specialized tools for performing unusual or infrequent tasks. With that in mind, how can one tool combine the features of all of these individual tools used by a security engineer? Simply, it can't. However, what an ESM tool *can* do is combine the management of the individual tools into a single point of reference.

The technology required to do this is not cheap in most cases. Since ESM tools must be aware of changes in all the tools they work with, constant maintenance is required. ESM tools cannot simply be sold as-is and considered complete; they must constantly be revised to encompass more information sources and changes to existing information sources. Often when purchasing an ESM tool, you are paying more for the service behind the tool than the tool itself. This is where the ongoing cost for the companies providing these tools is, and those costs are reflected in the cost of the products and services being offered.

The goal of ESM is not to replace your existing tools, but rather to combine them so they are easier to use and the output from each is easier to analyze. You may use snort as an intrusion detection tool and a Cisco PIX firewall in your environment. To get a good view of your enterprise security, it would be wise to examine the logs of both of these tools simultaneously to see if there is a correlation that might be important. Certainly, this can be done manually, and if you have the time and bandwidth to do so, chances are you don't have a pressing need to use ESM. However, if you are attempting to do security work like this in a large enterprise and have more data than you can deal with, ESM might be a fit.

The point of this is that ESM is not for every organization. Some organizations can be more secure by manually performing actions that ESM automates. Some organizations feel that their money is better spent on hiring qualified individuals than buying tools or external services. Others may think that the technology behind automation of security management is not mature enough to entrust their information technology assets to that technology. The choice of whether to use ESM is an individual one for every organization and should be carefully considered.

TIP

ESM makes sense for many large organizations, but not for everyone. Even if it turns out that a full ESM implementation does not make sense for your organization, it is a good idea to understand ESM and the benefits this process provides. You may find that you can implement individual parts of ESM just to make your organization a little more efficient.

Questions Your Organization Should Be Asking

So, how can your organization go about making the decision as to whether to use ESM? The first step is to analyze whether ESM is right for your organization. This can be done by asking a series of questions and examining the answers in the context of how ESM can help you. Again, ESM is not for every organization, and careful thought should be put into the decision on whether it should be used. Once this decision is made, the more difficult questions then come into play on how the tool should and should not be used in your enterprise.

In this section, we're going to go through a little quiz and think about some questions your organization should consider when thinking about ESM. Our hope is that by the time we finish, you will have a good idea of the questions organizations should ask and what to do with the answers. With that in mind, let's begin our quiz.

What Problem Are You Trying to Solve?

Ah, the big question that should always be asked first in information technology! Before implementing any technology, you should ask yourself or your organization what problem is being solved. Many organizations forget this and implement technology simply because it exists. New technology must be better, so it should be implemented as soon as possible, right? Perhaps not.

This leads to the question of what problem needs to be solved in the organization that needs new technology.

In the development world, the answer to this question leads to project requirements. The same thing should happen in IT security. By carefully defining the problem, you can ensure that the best solution is put in place rather than the solution that has a better salesperson but doesn't quite fit your problem. Another way to look at this is considering the problem you are addressing as a lock that needs to be opened. The right solution serves as the key and will open the lock, whereas an incomplete or incorrect solution will not fit properly and the problem will remain as it currently exists.

Earlier in this chapter, we addressed some of the problems ESM can solve. As we look now into the problems of your enterprise, we can examine the problem and see whether ESM fits as a solution. For example, one problem you could be experiencing is a flood of log file data. Too much information from too many devices and systems is coming in and you are unable to properly analyze all of the data to find security problems. Is ESM a fit for this problem? The answer is, maybe. If this is the only problem you are dealing with, other products that just do log file analysis and do not perform all of the additional functions of ESM might be best for your organization.

On the other hand, if you have more than one problem, all of them must be addressed if possible. Assuming you have the problem of too much information, plus additional problems of too many devices and systems to patch, plus problems with trying to keep virus definitions current on too many systems, ESM might be an even better fit here. The choice is based on the problem or problems you are trying to solve. The more problems that can be solved with this single solution, the better the case for using ESM. Just make sure that you understand the problems you are trying to solve and how ESM can be the solution rather than just implementing ESM because it exists.

How Many Information Sources Are Manageable?

In your organization, how much information is too much? In some organizations, input from hundreds or thousands of devices is considered a manageable flow of data due to the way they have structured their processes. Sometimes, a huge amount of information is not too much of a problem within an organization. This goes back to the first question of what problem you are trying to solve. If your organization is built to handle a large number of information sources and you have not exceeded that capacity, there is no problem to solve.

Other organizations are designed with more of an operational perspective and spend the majority of their time just keeping things running rather than analyzing data coming in from devices or systems that are not "down." This reactive approach is very common, and while not as effective as a proactive approach, it does work. An organization in this state may derive some benefit from having some system automate the analysis of incoming data so they can focus on the problems as they are detected rather than manually spending time trying to detect future problems.

This is of course dependent on the enterprise. There may be a high-water mark that once exceeded justifies the use of ESM to manage the incoming data from a number of information sources. Determining what this threshold is requires some analysis and certainly intimate knowledge as to what the organization can and can not manage manually.

TIP

It is important to note that too much information can cripple your use of ESM. Limit the information to that fine line between too little and too much. That will be the "right" amount of data for your implementation. Determining what level of input you should allow into ESM is a very difficult decision and may take some trial and error to get right.

What Benefits Do I Gain from ESM?

The primary benefit of ESM is very simple: you gain the solution to the problems you have identified in all cases where ESM is the right answer. This all goes back to identifying the problems you are attempting to solve. If ESM really is the correct solution to the problem you have identified, implementing ESM obviously provides the benefit of solving your problem.

Other than this simple answer, what other benefits can be gained from using ESM? A huge benefit is time savings. Once ESM is implemented properly and in use, you can save a great deal of time and effort by automating routine tasks. Simple things such as applying the latest security patch to a system can be very time consuming when it must be done to hundreds of systems. The time savings provided by automating this process can be immense.

Other tasks that can be automated using ESM include the parsing of log file data, gathering data from multiple sources for consolidation and correlation, deployment of various files and data, and alarming on identified security problems. Each of these tasks can and often are done manually, but can be automated by ESM tools. This is a huge benefit of ESM and is incredibly useful.

Another rather large benefit of ESM is quality assurance. It is a fact that people make mistakes. Systems generally only make mistakes if a person made a mistake in programming them. The same logic applies to ESM. ESM tools can help eliminate the possibility of human error in tasks that are routine and able to be automated. This can result in reduced downtime and increased efficiency by eliminating the need to double-check work or redo work done by someone else.

Reporting on incoming data is a very tedious and difficult task given to many security administrators. To develop understandable reports, administrators must pull data together from many different sources, simplify them to provide data points, and then chart out these data points with a brief summary. In some cases, this can take hours or days. With ESM, even if you do not use ESM tools for automating administrative tasks, you can use the single point of information ESM provides as the data source for your reports. This eliminates the need to gather the data from all of the sources manually, as this would have already have been done by ESM. Consequently, simplification of reporting is yet another benefit of ESM.

When dealing with IT security issues, one of the most important parts of our work is responding rapidly to problems. In many cases, this may be as simple as needing to reset a user's password, or as complex as determining what data an intruder has obtained. Regardless, we always need to work quickly to resolve issues. This is another area where ESM provides benefits. By automating specific response tasks, we can use ESM to aid us in responding more quickly when an event occurs. For example, if you have a specific procedure you follow when a system's security has been compromised, you may be able to script this procedure into a process that an ESM tool can perform for you and speed up the execution of the process tremendously. Standard procedures such as changing important administrative account passwords when key personnel are terminated can also be automated to ensure that this work is done quickly and effectively.

All these benefits are very useful, but again, it is important to ensure that ESM solves the problems you are experiencing before you consider implementing it. ESM is a solution geared toward solving specific problems. If you are not experiencing these problems, you do not have a valid use of ESM. Always remember to solve problems rather than spending time and resources on solutions you may not need.

What Is the Return on Investment for ESM Tools?

What is the return the organization receives if they spend resources on a product? This is a question that all organizations must ask before purchasing any product. Typically, the return can be numerically calculated and presented as a value versus the cost of the product. To determine what this value is takes some research and a great deal of knowledge about your organization.

The first factor as always is to list the problems you are trying to solve. This is obviously becoming a very common theme, but this is as it should be. Each problem has a specific cost associated with it, whether lost time, efficiency, or money. If the cost is lost time or efficiency, a dollar figure can be associated with the loss to help determine the monetary cost of the problem. For example, if two security engineers are spending half their time developing reports, it can be assumed that at least 40 hours a week are being spent developing reports. Multiply this value by the hourly cost of your average security engineer and you have the weekly cost of developing reports. To provide a good estimate of investment versus return, calculate this for a year's worth of report generation.

Add together the values you developed for a year's cost for every problem you are trying to solve. This will give you the amount of loss you currently suffer due to these problems. Next, calculate how many resources will be spent on these same tasks *after* you implement an ESM solution. It is a given that the tasks won't go away completely, but the amount of resources they consume may be reduced. For example, it may now take only five hours a week for a security engineer to develop the reports your organization needs, rather than the 40 hours a week previously being spent. Adding together these new values will give you a post-implementation cost of operations. We will refer to this in our calculations as the "remaining cost of problem" in order to show that the tasks associated with the problem are not gone, simply reduced in scope.

The next step is to calculate how much the ESM implementation will cost over a year. This value should include the cost of software, updates, software maintenance, implementation, hardware, and software administration. Typically, the total is several times more than the cost of the software alone. This calculation gives you a true year's cost of the ESM implementation and can be used to develop your return on investment values.

With all this data in hand, it is time to calculate the return on investment for the ESM implementation. The result of a return on investment can be given as either a dollar figure or a time frame. The dollar figure result typically shows how much money can result after an investment is made. Normally, this type of result does not work well for services organizations such as IT departments. The time-frame result is a little different in that it shows how much time it will take for the investment to break even and then start providing cost savings. This is a much more accurate figure for services organizations.

Assuming that we have chosen to provide a time-frame result, we would use the following formula to determine the return on investment for our ESM implementation:

(Cost of Problem + Cost of Solution) / (Cost of Problem − Remaining Cost of Problem) = Years to ROI

For example, assume we use the values shown in Table 6.2.

Table 6.2 ROI Values

Variable	Value
Cost of problem	$1,000,000
Cost of solution	$1,500,000
Remaining cost of problem	$250,000

By plugging these values into our formula, we end up with this math equation: $(1000000+1500000) / (1000000-250000) = X$. Solving the equation leaves us with a value of 3.33 years, which means that in 3.33 years, we will have broken even on the cost of the solution and will begin to see the benefits of cost savings. This may seem like a long time to see results, but three years is a pretty normal ROI time frame.

WARNING

!

Be very careful when advertising the return on investment for your implementation and make sure your numbers are as accurate as possible! If you are wrong, it is likely that you will be held accountable for your mistake. Work with your accounting department if possible to obtain their assistance in generating an accurate ROI figure.

What Type of Reports Do I Expect from ESM?

As we have discussed, one of the areas in which ESM can benefit an organization is reporting. ESM can assist with both the simplification of data gathering for reports and generation of the reports themselves. This capability is one of the selling points of ESM and is known as its most visible benefit to upper management. To make the most of this capability, an organization must determine exactly what reports it is looking for. Some reports are simply not possible in any reporting tools, and others can be easily generated using an ESM tool. It is wise to be realistic and understand what your ESM tools can and cannot do for you in the way of reporting.

The first step in answering this question can be very simple. What reports are you generating today? If the reports you are currently generating are considered useful by your organization, they should be continued and potentially enhanced. Make a list of your current reports and the data source for them. It is realistic to assume that any data source that is digital in nature should be able to be gathered by an ESM tool. If this is the case, the list of reports you have already generated is a realistic expectation for ESM.

The next step is to define new reports you do not currently generate that would be useful for your organization. Developing this list requires that you understand what your organization needs in the way of reports and the type of data that can help you in your job. Keep in mind that reports are not necessarily just used for statistical presentations to management, they can also be used to provide the information you need to do your job. When developing your list of new reports, keep this in mind and make sure the list of reports includes those that will assist you in your own job as well as those required by upper management for statistical purposes.

Some of the more common reports are listed here:

- Account Lockouts
- Number of Spam E-mails Blocked
- Number of Viruses Caught
- Inactive Users
- Terminated Users
- Expired and Unchanged Passwords
- Blocked Intrusion Attempts
- Number of Patches Deployed
- Systems with Unconfirmed Patch Deployments
- Number of New User Accounts Created
- Unusual System Activity
- Financials Accessed

These types of reports may or may not need to be on your list. Every organization is unique and has unique reporting needs. Developing a comprehensive list of reports prior to implementing ESM will help you to ensure that the reporting capabilities of your ESM solution fit your needs.

With your list of reports in hand, compare them to the capabilities of your ESM solution. Remember that ESM reporting is only as good as the data it has access to. If you expect reports of a specific type out of ESM but do not provide accurate and meaningful data, you are setting yourself up for failure. Also, ESM can generate reports showing correlation between many different sources of data, which should be considered as well. ESM can generate the report you want, and may also be able to correlate the data on that report with data from another to provide an even more comprehensive view of the data with which you are working.

Monitoring and Managing versus Reporting

When you are determining the viability of ESM, remember that it does offer a plethora of features, some of which you may or may not need in your organization. One large area where this comes in to play is the difference between monitoring and managing of systems and the reporting of data. ESM tools have the capability to accomplish both tasks, but that may not necessarily be what you want for your organization.

Monitoring and managing of systems is one capability of ESM. This involves configuration and deployment of your security policy as well as monitoring for adherence to the policy. This aspect of ESM is intended to reduce the effort required to perform these tasks manually and save time for security administrators. The problem with performing these tasks with ESM is that many people feel that the hands-on approach is more effective. With the use of automated tools, you lose the human touch as we've talked about before and introduce some risk of missing critical data.

For organizations that feel the risk far outweighs the benefits, ESM can still provide some value. Security administrators can manually handle management and monitoring of security policy deployments while using the resource of ESM to help with reporting. Again, ESM can help in correlating data from many different sources and use this data to generate reports. These reports can then be used by administrators in performing their daily functions or by management to show the effectiveness of your organization's IT security department.

If this is the route your organization chooses to go, perform the same analysis of ESM we did earlier in this chapter, but limit it to reporting capabilities. Ensure that the ROI exists for the tools if they are used exclusively for reporting. Chances are good, however, that once the capabilities of your ESM tool become well known, more reliance will be put on the tool and its use will expand beyond reporting.

ESM is a process where you can choose the benefits you want without using features you don't. It is possible to just use the reporting capabilities of ESM and nothing else, which can still provide benefits to some organizations. Expanding the features you use can of course provide more benefits, but keep in mind that they may not be necessary if they are not solving a problem you currently have. All of the discussions we have had on the usefulness of ESM tie back into the simple concept of identifying problems and the solutions. If ESM matches as a solution, it fits like a key into a lock.

Which Security Reporting Tools to Aggregate into ESM

ESM has the potential to be of immense benefit to your organization if used correctly. To provide this benefit, ESM must be able to have a full enterprise view of your environment. By limiting the amount of information ESM tools have to work with, you limit the effectiveness of those tools. The concept of enterprise security management includes the combination of heterogeneous systems and diverse security devices into a single point of reference. To operate at its best, an ESM tool must have data from a variety of sources and be used to correlate data.

With this in mind, which data sources should ESM look to for information in your enterprise? The answer to this of course is as many as possible. The more data ESM tools have to work with, the better results they can give you. Some examples of data sources are listed here:

- Routers
- Switches
- Firewalls
- Intrusion detection systems
- Intrusion prevention systems
- Windows servers and workstations
- *NIX servers and workstations
- PBXs
- Physical security devices (card readers)
- Virus scanners
- Content filters
- E-mail systems
- Application logs
- Backup systems
- Data center physical environment monitors

While this list is somewhat extensive, it by no means shows all of the relevant data sources you should consider for inclusion into ESM. In many implementations, security engineers feel that if a device or system generates operational data, that data should go into ESM. This of course generates a huge amount of data that no human could possibly parse through. The idea is to use ESM tools to parse through the data and find important events whether individually or through correlation to other events.

Does this mean that every single device and system in your enterprise should report data back to ESM tools? Perhaps. Again, this depends on your organization. Some organizations feel that the additional bandwidth used by the systems to perform this action is not worth the results and they throttle the amount of data going into ESM. This can be done by limiting the incoming data to a sampling of devices and systems throughout the enterprise. Additionally, data can also be limited by only sending significant events and filtering out common or innocuous events.

This approach is worthwhile in some organizations to reduce the amount of data going into ESM, but there is a trade-off. With less data, ESM is less effective and some crucial events could be missed. Other organizations take a slightly different approach. They may deploy ESM to each of their sites to collect data specific to that site. ESM tools are used to analyze that data exclusively and items of significance are then passed on to a central ESM that is responsible for correlating specific data from across the entire enterprise. Figure 6.1 shows a diagram demonstrating how this can be done.

Figure 6.1 Distributed ESM Diagram

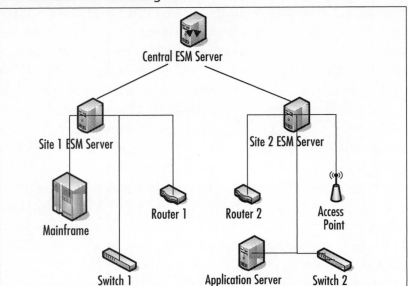

The approach of a distributed ESM is effective for some organizations as well. While the central ESM server is certainly not given the full amount of data necessary to correlate all events, it may have enough to correlate true enterprise-affecting events. This leaves the responsibility and the data collection of site-wide events to the site-specific ESM servers.

Another way of looking at data collection from the ESM perspective is by understanding how you plan to use ESM. If you don't plan to do anything with some specific type of data, there is no need to send this data to your ESM tool. For example, if you have technology in place that deploys patches to your client desktops and you have no monitoring or reporting needs associated with this action, there is no need to send the results of deployments to ESM. Alternatively, if system backup and recovery processes for the enterprise are handled by a completely different team in IT outside of the security team and IT management sees no need to roll these results into the security team, you may not even have the data available to bring in.

Overall, the choice of ESM architecture and the data sources given to ESM is up to the organization implementing the technology. Much benefit can be derived by providing ESM with sufficient data, but there can be some obvious detriments as well, such as increased network utilization and more required storage capacity for ESM. Weighing these benefits and detriments can only be done by someone with good knowledge of the organization and the operations for which ESM will be used.

Determining How Much Data Is Too Much

The possibility certainly exists that too much data can be sent into ESM. There are several problems associated with doing so, and you need to be aware of these. The first is simple system overload. The servers your ESM tools run on are limited by processor, memory, and I/O constraints the same as any system. If you are unable to analyze all the data coming in fast enough, you end up with a bottleneck in the ESM system itself. If this happens, ESM is no longer providing useful data to you and the benefits of the system are gone.

ESM tools require a great deal of processing power to perform their functions. To analyze and correlate data from a large number of disparate data sources, ESM tools must process data fast and cross reference it with previously processed data fast as well. To do this, ESM tools also require a large amount of memory to store results of analyses so they can reference the information quickly. In addition, for the incoming data feed a great deal of network capacity may be necessary. This is dependent on the number of data sources and how frequently they send data. With this in mind, your ESM system should be well thought out, but regardless of how large it is, limitations can still be reached.

Another limitation for ESM systems is that of storage. Depending on the amount of data coming into the system and the length of time you plan to maintain that data, a large amount of storage capacity may be necessary. We have seen this data storage reach into the terabytes in some organizations, so be prepared for the amount of data you really want to keep. Purging of unnecessary data is certainly necessary and should be considered when implementing your ESM.

Another problem you can run into if too much data is sent into ESM is a loss of correlation capability. Mathematically, the more data you have over a given time period, the more likely it is that there will be some correlation shown between the data points, whether this correlation is real or imaginary. This is based on simple statistics that show that the more data points there are, the easier it is to envision links between the data points that are not really there.

For example, let's assume that you have data points that show that every time Bob opens his car door, his overhead light turns on. This conclusion would be reached by correlating the factors of Bob having a car, Bob opening the door, and the active status of the overhead light. In all, three data points are analyzed in this example. Now, what if you add in some more data points? Add the data point of grass growing one-half millimeter per day. If you factor this into the same correlation, you can now come up with three statements about poor Bob. First, his overhead light turns on every time he opens the door. Second, his overhead light turns on every day the grass grew one-half millimeter. Third, Bob opens his car door every day the grass grows one-half millimeter.

Obviously, two of these statements are erroneous assumptions. However, they are assumptions that a machine could make if fed all this data and asked to correlate it. Consequently, too much data is not necessarily a good thing when using automated correlation. Inaccurate results could potentially result if your ESM has too much information to deal with, which is something you should consider when deciding how to implement your ESM correlation activities.

Using ESM Reporting for Maximum Performance

One of the major benefits of ESM we've discussed is reporting. This is a key function of ESM and one that many organizations really need. Most organizations have a large amount of data, and they report on this data to the best of their abilities. However, they are limited by various factors such as the source of the data and the format in which it is provided. Consequently, it is difficult to create a comprehensive view of the enterprise's security environment without a lot of manual effort.

In some cases, reporting is the only reason why organizations purchase ESM tools. They may be happy with their current method of configuring, deploying, and managing their security policy, but feel they do not have an accurate all-encompassing view of their enterprise security. If this is the case, ESM can fill that need and provide a reporting infrastructure to your organization.

Most ESM tools accomplish this in one of two ways; they allow you to report on data that is collected in real time from the devices and systems you are reporting on, or poll the devices and systems for data at regular intervals and store the data for reporting and historical purposes. Both methods can accomplish the same reporting goals, but each has its own benefits and detriments.

Real-Time Reporting

To provide real-time reporting, ESM tools must know what data you need and from which systems and devices you need it. In most cases, the amount of data you need is a small subset of the data the device or system could potentially provide. Subsetting the data in this manner reduces the amount of data that must be sent "over the wire" to the ESM system. In addition, real-time reporting gives you data that is very current with minimal latency. This allows for your reports to be very accurate and contain up-to-the-minute information.

Of course, there are detriments to this method of reporting. Since the data is gathered in real time, there may or may not be historical data that can be included in the report. In some cases, reports need some trend analysis to be effective, and this simply may not be possible with some real-time reporting mechanisms. Where historical data is kept on some devices and systems, and the length of time this data is maintained may vary, which could give you inaccurate historical trending. In some cases, this is worse than having no trending at all.

Another detriment of real-time reporting is the length of time it takes to generate the report. Since all the data is being pulled as the report is being generated, it may take some time to do so. Even after the data is completely gathered, analysis may still need to be done—which can take even more time. The generation of the report comes next, which can also be time consuming. All together, this process can take quite a bit of time to generate a single report.

The last detriment of real-time reporting that we'll discuss is the impact on the environment when these reports are generated. All this data is gathered at one time, which causes an immediate impact on the overall environment. All the systems are now using processor, hard disk, memory, and network bandwidth to transfer data to the ESM reporting tool. With many systems doing this simultaneously, the impact on your enterprise can be quite large.

Environment utilization should be kept in mind when considering the impact real-time reporting has.

With that said, there are cases where real-time reporting is certainly worth the detriments. If you are in the middle of being attacked, there is no centralized reporting method that can keep up with the changes occurring within your environment faster than a real-time solution. If you need up-to-date information immediately from multiple sources, the fastest method to obtain this information may be through a real-time ESM reporting tool. Seeing data from multiple viewpoints simultaneously can be a great weapon when trying to track down and reduce the impact of an intruder into your systems.

Centralized Repository Reporting

The alternative to real-time reporting is centralized repository reporting. This method is based on the concept of having a central repository of all data used by ESM and generating reports based on data stored in the repository. With this method, immediate pull of data across the enterprise is unnecessary, as all of the needed data is already available in the repository. Additionally, report generation can run much faster than in a real-time reporting scenario since the only steps necessary are those of analyzing the data and generating the report. The data-gathering step is effectively eliminated from a timing perspective. Lastly, depending on how long you choose to maintain the data in your repository, historical data for trending purposes should be available. This can help in determining long-term trends over time and also find anomalies in those trends. More correlation can be done by using this historical data as well, since all data from the devices and systems is available rather than just subsets.

As with real-time reporting, there are also detriments to doing centralized repository reporting, the largest of which is the benefit of real-time reporting; current data. To reduce the load on the environment, most centralized repositories poll data on a specific interval. This interval can range anywhere from five seconds to 60 minutes depending on the general needs for the data. The longer the interval, the less of an impact is generally felt on the environment, but this also means that your data is just that much older. If the age of the data is not important to you, this is not as much of a detriment. However, in the security industry, current data is one of our most valuable assets.

Another detriment associated with centralized repository reporting is the amount of storage space required. Whereas real-time reporting allows the devices and systems it is reporting on to host its data in a distributed manner, centralized repository reporting requires that all of that data be stored in a single location. This can drive up the data storage needs for the ESM repository tremendously. As mentioned previously, we've seen this data store size range into the terabytes of data. If you have no real storage limitations, this can still cause a problem. As reports are generated against a larger and larger data repository, it will begin to take an increasing amount of time to generate the reports. Any database or storage system decreases in performance as more data is added to the system. This can cause difficulties for report generation using the centralized repository reporting method, although it should theoretically still be faster than pulling the data in real time.

To conclude the discussion of detriments of centralized repository reporting, we will discuss system reliability. When dealing with this type of reporting mechanism, you are heavily dependant on the central data repository. Without this data store, you are completely unable to generate reports from the system. This can obviously cause some serious impacts to your enterprise if you need the data quickly. In the event of failure of this repository, you are out of luck until the problem is repaired. Real-time reporting lacks this reliance on a central data store as it pulls the data from individual devices and systems. If a failure occurs, data from the failed device or system is simply unavailable, but the rest of the report can still be generated. This level of reliability is sometimes preferred over that of a centralized repository reporting system.

You should also be aware that these reporting methodologies are not mutually exclusive. They can be used together in various manners in order to make use of the benefits of each. One method of doing so is to use real-time reporting to handle day-to-day operations while regularly pulling reports to store them into a data repository. This repository can later be used for historical trending information without actively polling the systems in your enterprise. By using combinations like this one, the benefits of each methodology can be gained while mitigating some of the detriments.

Obviously, there are many benefits and detriments to both reporting methodologies. Determining the best choice for your enterprise is a decision that will need to weigh many factors. Be aware that there is no single "right" solution that fits every scenario. In your particular case, one methodology may fit better than another, or a combination of both may be in order. This is a decision that will be different for every organization. Just be certain to examine both possibilities thoroughly and consider the possibility of combining aspects of both methodologies.

ESM Reporting as a Single Point of View

A major benefit of using ESM is that it functions as a single point of reference for security-related data. This allows IT security groups and other groups to base their decisions off a single source of information. Regardless of whether the reports are generated in real time or based on a central repository, ESM provides one reporting source for information. This can be very useful when work needs to be done that requires cross-discipline coordination.

A great example of this is system patching. Due to internal policies or audit requirements, the IT security team in your organization may be responsible for determining the security patch levels that exist on systems in your enterprise. It may also be the job of the systems administrator for those systems to install the patches as necessary in such a way that the impact is minimized. In this case, it is important for both groups to operate off the same information. The list of systems to be patched as determined by the IT security group should match the list that the system admin group is working off. In a case like this, using ESM to provide a single point of reference for the teams is wise and in some cases necessary based on regulatory requirements.

This "single point of view" concept can make work easier for many groups by allowing them to focus on the actual function of their job rather than data collection. For example, development groups need to ensure that they are aware of current security concerns so they can address them in their development efforts. This includes things that have now turned in to development best practices such as confirming the size of a variable before passing it to another function to prevent stack overflows. To get this information, the development group can work on gathering it, but it would be more productive to use their time for actual development. The answer to this can be found through ESM. Sending the developers a report showing the latest signature updates to your intrusion detection systems and data from internal sources can provide them with what they need and prevent them from having to search it out themselves.

This same technique can work for many groups. Within your own organization, there are surely needs that other groups have that can be satiated with data from ESM. Another example would be a listing of terminated employees being sent to application management groups for applications that do not use central authentication. This single point of information can provide them with the information they need to terminate unused accounts. Another example might be a notification sent to multiple IT teams when an intrusion is detected so they can quickly start analyzing the systems they are responsible for to determine the impact of the intrusion. Many examples like these can be found in organizations where a single source of data shared between teams increases effectiveness.

One of the rapidly growing functions of IT security is auditing. As more and more regulatory and legal requirements are implemented within organizations, there is a greater need for internal auditing of the organization's compliance with these rules or laws. Many of these requirements are around security of information technology data and assets. As such, it is important to be able to quickly and easily show proof that you are following the appropriate requirements within your organization to external auditors. To do so, you could potentially spend thousands of man hours compiling data and developing reports for the auditors. Or, using ESM, you could simply point them in the direction of the reports they need and send them on their way. While the choice is certainly yours, our preference would be to give them the information they need and get back to our work on enforcing security policies.

NOTE

The alternative to having a single point of view is that of each group reporting based on self-gathered data. When this occurs, there can often be discrepancies when results between the groups are compared, which makes the entire organization appear inefficient and unprofessional. Using a single point of view for report generation alleviates this and helps to ensure that everyone is using the same data.

Automation of ESM Reporting

How much time do you or your team spend in generating reports? Chances are that it is probably more than it could be using ESM. One of the best features of ESM is obviously its reporting capability; the second best is arguably its report automation functions. Many organizations require reports to be generated that contain data or roll-ups of data from a large number of devices and systems. Combining this data is often a manual effort and requires gathering the data, getting it into the right format, and making sure the results make sense when you are done. It doesn't do much good to show the number of patches deployed to client systems and the number of hits on a firewall in the same graph.

Automating this process would obviously provide some time-saving benefits to an organization. In many cases, ESM tools can generate the reports you need and automate their generation in the future. Once a report template is designed, it simply remains to plug in new data each time when using ESM. With this in mind, it is a simple leap of logic to go to the next step of automation by scheduling the report you need to be regenerated and published when you need it next.

Some reports may need to be generated hourly, while others may only be needed once a week. The scheduling flexibility provided by most ESM tools allows you to schedule these reports to be generated when you need them. In some cases, you can even schedule the reports to be generated at night when system utilization is low and publish them during the day, a feature especially important for real-time report generation tools.

Automating the generation of reports can also have an impact on security audits. Whether you are performing the audit yourself or it is being performed by an external third-party, showing that you have access to the data necessary to protect your environment and regularly report on it can help in demonstrating your organization is doing what it should. As regulatory and legal requirements continue to expand, we can expect this to be a requirement for many organizations. Automatic report generation shows the level of an organization's technological maturity; it also shows that the security policies implemented are monitored and that the organization does pay attention to its security needs. What people do with the reports after they are generated might be another story, but at least the data is made available to the people who need it when they need it.

Special Considerations for Using ESM

So far, we have discussed a number of aspects of ESM. We've gone over what ESM is and isn't, what it does, how it works, and how it can help your organization. Next, we need to discuss some special considerations you should keep in mind when implementing ESM. We have discussed some of these already, so some of the topics may not seem new, but our goal is to provide you with a different point of view as you move toward using ESM in your environment.

In this section, we will be talking about ESM as a service in your organization. The assumption at this point is that you have decided to implement ESM and want to do it the right way. To accomplish this, you should consider aspects of security, reliability, and scalability of your ESM environment. This can affect the way you architect and implement ESM, so each factor should be carefully considered.

Security

When using ESM, it is important to remember that it is simply another process your organization uses to help secure the information technology enterprise. However, the ESM process requires specific tools and systems to be functional. These systems must also fall under the general security practices you employ within your organization and be protected. Your security policy applies to these systems just as they do for any other system and should be rigorously enforced.

Why is it so important to consider this when implementing ESM? Theoretically, you would apply the same policies to your ESM systems as you do to any other system in your enterprise, and therefore no special consideration is necessary. However, consider the impact on your enterprise if an intruder were to gain access to your ESM data repository. Not only would he be able to cover his tracks, he would be able to see what attacks have and have not been successful on your enterprise in the past. The intruder would be able to see which systems have which patches and use that to determine their specific vulnerabilities. He could see what it is you watch for and make sure to avoid setting off those alarms.

Based on this, it is safe to say that security of your ESM systems is paramount to the security of your environment. You should take extra measures to ensure you do everything in your power to ensure these systems are as secure as possible. Put them at the top of your production environment patch cycle list and make sure they are monitored by yet another system to maintain their own integrity. While ESM does provide a single point of reference for you and the people who need security-related information for your enterprise, it is critical that it does not become the single point of reference intruders use to determine information about your environment and how you secure it.

Notes from the Underground…

ESM Security

Why is ESM security so important that it deserves its own section in this chapter? Because we have seen these exact scenarios occur in a large corporation. In one implementation we were asked to analyze, there were no visible signs of an intrusion, but all the facts showed that someone was inside their systems. It turned out that one of the systems the intruders had obtained access to was the ESM system. They determined what the system was and how to change the data within it. Using this knowledge, they were able to cover their tracks and gain information allowing them to have access to other systems in the organization. Since the ESM system had connections to other devices and systems on the network for deployment and monitoring purposes, the intruders were able to use these connections to further their penetration efforts. This is a very important area to keep in mind and certainly should not be overlooked.

Reliability

Any time you create a single source of information in an enterprise, you also create a single point of failure. It is important to remember that with ESM, all devices and systems are reliant on your centralized system for the configuration, deployment, and monitoring of your security policy. System failures within your ESM can cause gaping security holes in your environment and prevent you from being able to perform your job functions. This could lead to an unmonitored security environment.

Building a highly available environment for ESM is a wise idea if you plan to use your ESM systems as a focal point for your security information. Using redundant disk arrays, clustered server technologies, and multiple-power supply systems are some of the ways this can be done. Building a system in this manner will help mitigate the risks involved in the event your ESM system does experience a failure.

Of course, nothing replaces the tried-and-true method of ensuring system availability: regular system backups. To ensure that the time to repair your ESM system is minimized, it is a good idea to have regular system backups and test the restores regularly to ensure your system works as expected. This, too, will help increase the reliability of your ESM system.

Aside from systematic failures, reliability in your ESM system also requires that it be used properly. ESM will not help you manage your enterprise if it is not used correctly. This means that all of the teams within your organization that should be sending data to ESM must do so. Additionally, there should be no one-off operations where ESM is used sometimes but not always. To be effective and reliable, ESM should function as the *single* point of reference and control for your environment. If multiple systems are in place to perform this function, you can lose reliability in the system and it will not be able to perform the functions it was implemented for.

Scalability

We discussed some scalability issues when we looked at reporting methodologies. This is one area where scalability of your ESM system does play a part, but there are others that should be considered as well. To recap, reporting within ESM can be done in either a real-time or a centralized repository manner. Scalability factors associated with these are bandwidth and storage, respectively. When your ESM structure is built out, scalability should be considered a primary factor and used to determine the architecture and the overall design of your ESM solution.

As shown in Figure 6.1, you can use a distributed method of implementing ESM to mitigate some scalability problems. Doing so allows you to do site- or segment-specific ESM functions with some systems and then roll that data up to a centralized system. Scaling out your architecture in this manner can help overcome some of the general limitations that exist in IT systems.

When exploring ESM tools, ensure that you keep scalability in mind when weighing the benefits of each. The tool you purchase should be able to effectively manage your enterprise. Whatever size that enterprise may be, ensure you have buy-in from the tool vendor that their tool will be able to support you now and in the future. Planning for growth should be included in your thoughts at this point, and any increase in scale should be considered during your evaluation.

The concept of ESM is very scalable by design, but you may run into limitation of software or hardware when attempting to work with larger enterprises. Most ESM tool vendors have experience with this and should be able to help you overcome any issues you encounter. Make sure they understand your purpose and what you are trying to do within your enterprise, and leverage their expertise to ensure you implement a solution that is scalable enough to fit your organization's needs.

Lessons Learned Implementing ESM

As we all know, theory is quite a bit different from actual practice. Discussing the concepts behind ESM is great for gaining an understanding as to what ESM is and what it can do for you and for your organization, but the real trial is installing, configuring, and using ESM in the real world. ESM is one of the largest implementations you can consider deploying because it literally touches every existing device and system in your environment if implemented in its entirety. This involves a tremendous effort and must be done correctly to prevent unexpected problems.

Whenever you implement anything new into your environment, always make sure you follow the IT best practice of testing it first. This may seem obvious, but it needs to be said. Many people consider a "monitoring application" innocuous and may think that testing outside of the production environment may not need to be done. We assure you that this is certainly not the case. Any time you plan to implement something new into your production environment, you must ensure it is tested and truly production-ready before allowing it to enter the environment.

The deployment actions of ESM should also be very well tested. Any time you plan to deploy something to your production environment, deploy it to your test environment first. As you are aware, all patches and data changes come with their own risks, and they sometimes don't work the way you may expect them to. ESM allows you to deploy data easily, but it cannot compensate for failures in the patches or data it is deploying. Again, always test before introducing something to your production environment even if it is just a patch or a new data file.

With that said, there are several other lessons learned that we would like to share with you to help ensure your implementation is successful. These lessons are in some cases rather general and coincide with general best practices, but each relates to ESM specifically and has special considerations you should keep in mind. Implementing ESM is not the easiest task, but it is our hope that these tips can help you avoid the larger costly mistakes that can be made when implementing this process.

Knowing Your Environment

Throughout this chapter, we've discussed a lot of information regarding ESM implementations. While exploring this subject, we mentioned that the decisions you make are specific to your organization or to your environment. This is very true for ESM in many phases of the process. To make these decisions correctly, you must understand your environment very well. You or your team should be experts on the design and structure of your environment and know the way all parts of the enterprise work together.

You should have a good understanding of the scale of your enterprise and what amount of data you should expect to be going across the wire. From both a deployment and a monitoring standpoint, a very large amount of data can be generated. You need to ensure your environment is able to handle this load, or redesign either that portion of the environment or the manner in which you choose to implement ESM. Knowing this before you implement is critical to your success.

You should also have a good understanding of what management is looking for from your implementation. You must be able to demonstrate the usefulness of ESM to management to justify the expenditure that was put into the implementation. While early on we discussed developing a return on investment value, you must be able to prove that you received this value or more to show that the project really was worth what was put into it.

ESM can also become a political problem due to the reach the process has. Whenever you are working on a project that crosses multiple teams, there is a political aspect. In the IT security field, we typically enjoy the luxury of being able to enforce policy throughout all of IT due to the nature of our work. This should be done without stepping on toes whenever possible, of course, so coordination with the teams we are working with is important. Educate them on the benefits of ESM and how this process can help make their jobs easier. Help them to understand what it is you are trying to do and how ESM can help reduce the efforts they have to put into handling audits of the overall IT environment.

Another important factor you should be aware of in your environment is the expected growth over time. This plays a part in the scalability of ESM as we have already discussed and is important environmental knowledge to have before beginning your project. You should be aware of the expected growth in number of systems over time, and the number of network and security devices. Even the number of additional sites your enterprise may add is important and should be considered when implementing ESM. Network bandwidth over a WAN is precious, and you may need to re-architect ESM to make more efficient use of WAN links in the event of an expansion. Planning for this in the beginning can help eliminate the need of doing so in the future.

Overall, you should have a very good understanding of your environment and the devices and systems in it. You should also have a good awareness of the organizational structure and political aspect of your organization. Lastly, know what growth is planned and ensure you keep these plans in mind when constructing your ESM solution. Planning for the future is generally better than reacting to the past. Understanding your environment can help your ESM implementation be a success.

Implementing at the Right Pace

Remember the phrase, "slow and steady wins the race." This concept applies very well to ESM. To implement ESM in the best way possible, it is wise to slowly implement the process piece by piece, ensuring that everything works together properly as you progress through the implementation. By taking a phased approach and performing a slow and steady implementation, you are able to leverage the knowledge you gained while implementing the previous phase and perhaps avoid making the same mistakes twice.

While ESM can certainly be implemented in one large step, this is not the recommended approach. Implementing too quickly can cause small problems found in the system to quickly escalate into large problems. Additionally, confidence in the process can wane if it doesn't appear to be successful. While some portions of the process may be working as expected, the failures will be the most visible. Eliminating this problem can help in the positive acceptance of the new process.

Another benefit of using a phased approach is that changes to the scope and needs of the project are more flexible. If you need to change direction while implementing ESM, it is much easier to do so if you are working in small phases rather than try to reorient an entire project. Always use small changes rather than sweeping changes whenever possible. This will help ease the pain of supporting changes as you move along your implementation.

The concept of ESM is one that *requires* a long implementation time to do right. We are concerned with the security of an entire enterprise and every facet of that enterprise. If your organization is large, this can take years to do correctly and sometimes even up to a year or more to get started. Just putting together a detailed plan of how you will implement ESM and which systems will be impacted can take a large amount of time. One of the more difficult tasks for many organizations is simply taking an inventory of their systems. If this is problematic, imagine taking that inventory and then trying to determine how to fit it in to a new ESM implementation. This can be a daunting and a time-consuming task.

On the other hand, it should be noted that taking a more lengthy phased approach to this implementation can cause it to take longer before positive results are seen. This can also have an effect on the return on investment timeline. You should be aware of this as well before choosing how you will implement ESM. There are benefits and detriments to both approaches, and as always, making this decision requires you to have a good understanding of your organization and environment.

Obtaining Vendor Support

When you purchase and implement ESM tools, you are looking at a substantial investment. This may be just the purchase of software or the purchase of software and services. Among the services could be ongoing support or implementation services. All these have a price associated and those are generally not small price tags. When you go through the process of purchasing ESM tools, make sure you do your research and get the best benefits that you can for every dollar you spend. We guarantee that this additional effort will serve you well when the project is complete.

After choosing a vendor and purchasing your product and services, make sure you use the resources provided with that purchase to the fullest. When you make this purchase, you are buying the time and assets of your vendor. You are paying their bills, and they are obligated to provide you with the best support possible to ensure your success. In some cases, this is even spelled out in the purchase contracts to the degree that the vendor isn't paid until the project meets specific success criteria. When this is done, you have a guarantee that the vendor will do everything in their power to ensure your implementation is a full success based on the criteria outlined.

Again, remember that the vendor is there to support you and help you achieve success. They cannot do this if you do not work with them closely. Engage your vendor in all phases of your implementation and work with them to solve any problems that arise along the way. Their support is crucial to your success, and you must make use of this support to the greatest degree possible.

In some cases, the vendor may not feel the same way you do regarding support. At these times, it is important to remind them of the need for customer service and the potential for future referrals or purchases that is dependent on your success. Their goal from a business perspective is to make money, and the best way to do so is by supporting your implementation. While it may cost them a little up front to provide this support, the benefit they receive in positive publicity is worth every penny. In some cases, your organization may allow the vendor to use your implementation as a case study or as a reference to use when attempting to sell their products to other companies. This is an arrangement that frequently benefits both parties and allows both organizations to gain some positive publicity.

Always remember your support structure and make sure you make appropriate use of your vendor relationship. This can be a mutually beneficial relationship if you work together well. They are there to support you, and you should make use of this resource when you need it. Your success is a success for your organization, and for your vendor.

NOTE

Always remember that when you are paying the bills, the vendor works for you. Make good use of this relationship and make sure they understand where you are coming from. They must help you to achieve success for them to be successful in their own goals.

Ensuring Usability

An ESM implementation is worth nothing if it is not used. Make sure that when this process is implemented, it fits the needs of its users. Whether those users are you and your team or other groups within your organization, the usability needs of those individuals should be taken into account when preparing an ESM implementation.

Usability in this case refers to the ability to effectively use a tool to accomplish your goals and requirements. This means that the problems you are trying to resolve with the tool should be able to be easily solved by using the tool as it is intended. A great way to test the effectiveness of any project implementation is to examine the workaround that was used to solve a problem previously versus the process of your new implementation. The new implementation should be faster, easier, and more effective in general than the previous method of accomplishing the task.

As far as reporting goes, ESM should be able to provide *at a minimum* all the data that was previously being reported. If you begin to generate reports out of ESM and they do not meet the criteria specified when planning the project, it is not meeting its goals and is not usable. The reports generated from ESM should present similar if not more accurate reports to those that were previously generated manually. If this is not the case, something is wrong and you will need to quickly discover what the problem is and how to rectify it to ensure your ESM implementation achieves its goals.

A good way to ensure that ESM tools do what they are supposed to in your organization is to put together use cases on what you expect to do with the tool. A use case is a detailed, step-by-step example of a task being executed using a system. Most testing is done based on scenarios derived from these use cases. By defining a use case for what you will be doing with the ESM tool, you will have a baseline of functionality that should be in the tool. This allows you to run tests against the system utilizing the use case as a test scenario to ensure that the system usability is as it should be.

Again, ESM is a process that can help in configuring, deploying, and monitoring your security policy implementation. To be considered a success, ESM must be usable and accomplish this goal easier and more effectively than it was previously done. The usability of the ESM tools you implement will play a large part in the success of your ESM implementation and should be considered as you perform your testing and implement your ESM tools.

Summary

In this chapter, we discussed a great deal of information about enterprise security management. We began with a discussion of what ESM is and what it means to you. We defined ESM as *the process of controlling configuration, deployment, and monitoring of security policies across heterogeneous platforms and disparate security products.* This description leads us to consider ESM a process rather than a specific tool or type of software.

We also discussed the process to follow when implementing ESM. The prerequisites include having a security policy in place before attempting to implement ESM. Following this were the individual steps of ESM itself. Those are configuration, deployment, and monitoring aspects of the implementation and should be implemented in your environment as needed.

Remember that ESM is not for every organization. You can determine whether ESM can benefit your organization by asking a series of questions and answering them to the best of your abilities. The answers to these questions will help lead you to making the right decision for your specific organization as to whether ESM is a worthwhile investment based on your specific needs and requirements.

Setting up an ESM implementation requires a great deal of planning and effort. You must determine how you need to implement the process, and what functions you expect out of it. There is a difference between using the ESM process for monitoring and management versus reporting. Additionally, decisions need to be made as to which security tools should report back to ESM. This involves determining what information you need and how much of it you can handle. There is the possibility of sending too much data into ESM, and this potential needs to be considered.

On the subject of reporting, we discussed a couple different methods that can be used for generating reports out of ESM. We discussed real-time reporting and centralized repository reporting and the benefits and detriments of each. We also discussed the major benefit of reporting from ESM, which is the creation of a single point of view for enterprise security data organization-wide. Automation of reports is also another important feature of ESM tools and can help ease the pain most organizations feel when trying to maintain report generation.

Lastly, we discussed special consideration and lessons learned when implementing ESM. The thoughts and tips we presented can help ease the pain of implementing ESM into your organization. Following many industry best practices and performing the right steps while planning your implementation can help you avoid many problems.

ESM is a great process that can be used to simplify management of security policies in your environment. Properly understanding this process and its implementation can help you in leveraging its capabilities into your own organization to gain the benefits ESM provides. The information we presented in this chapter should be able to help you decide whether ESM is a fit for your organization and help you to plan a successful implementation of this incredible process.

Solutions Fast Track

What Is ESM?

- ☑ ESM is a process, not a tool or specific action. The definition of ESM is "the process of controlling configuration, deployment, and monitoring of security policies across heterogeneous platforms and disparate security products."

- ☑ ESM is intended to help in managing security policies in enterprises where manual management becomes difficult or error prone.

- ☑ The process of implementing ESM requires that a security policy is in place first, and then the elements of configuration, deployment, and monitoring can be implemented.

When Deploying ESM Makes Sense

- ☑ An organization must ask itself a series of questions to determine whether ESM is really necessary for the organization.

- ☑ ESM can be implemented in many different ways both architecturally and organizationally, and the way it is implemented will vary based on your needs.

☑ You can use ESM for monitoring and management of your security policies, or you can use it simply for reporting purposes. Both are valid uses of ESM.

Which Security Reporting Tools to Aggregate into ESM

☑ Determining which tools to aggregate into ESM involves ensuring that you are feeding in enough data on enough systems to allow for successful correlation of data.

☑ Whenever possible, as many different types of devices and systems as possible should be fed into ESM so a complete picture of the environment is available.

☑ Be careful of sending too much data into ESM, however. It is possible to overload the capacity and usefulness of the ESM tools, and this should be considered when determining the amount of data you wish to aggregate.

Using ESM Reporting for Maximum Performance

☑ ESM allows for two primary types of reporting: real-time reporting and centralized repository reporting.

☑ Providing a single point of view for generating reports is a very useful function of ESM and can help cut down on the confusion that is inherent when multiple groups provide differing data.

☑ You can automate the generation and publication of reports using many ESM tools. This feature can save a great deal of time and effort when the need exists to rerun specific reports on a regular basis.

Special Considerations for Using ESM

☑ Security of the ESM system and tools is a critical aspect of your ESM implementation and should be considered during the initial phases of the project.

☑ When using ESM, you begin to rely on it as the single point of reference for your environment, which also makes it the single point of failure. Ensure that a great deal of reliability is built into the implementation.

☑ ESM should be implemented in such a way that it is able to scale to your current and future growth. This scalability should also be considered during the initial phases of the project.

Lessons Learned Implementing ESM

☑ Ensure that you understand all aspects of your environment, both political and systematic. You should understand the various goals your organization has and ensure your implementation is in line with those goals.

☑ Implementing ESM at the right pace and properly using the support offered by your ESM tool vendor is crucial to a successful implementation.

☑ Your ESM implementation must be useful as determined by the end users of the ESM tools to be considered successful. Consider usability as a very important factor when designing and implementing your ESM solution.

Frequently Asked Questions

The following Frequently Asked Questions, answered by the authors of this book, are designed to both measure your understanding of the concepts presented in this chapter and to assist you with real-life implementation of these concepts. To have your questions about this chapter answered by the author, browse to **www.syngress.com/solutions** and click on the **"Ask the Author"** form.

Q: If ESM is so useful, why doesn't every large organization use it?

A: Many organizations are slowly moving in the direction of using ESM. It takes a long time to implement sweeping changes to the way business is done in larger organizations. In addition, ESM isn't right for every organization. Some organizations have examined their options and decided that ESM is simply not the right process for their needs.

Q: What reporting capabilities does ESM offer, and why is this better than the way we are doing reports today?

A: ESM may not offer anything over your current reporting methods depending on how you are generating reports. The reporting function of ESM is based on having a single point of reference for all reporting data. This allows an organization to have a reliable source of data and use the same dataset across the entire organization.

Q: You said that a security policy must exist before implementing ESM. I don't have a security policy yet, so does that mean I can't use ESM?

A: Not necessarily, but it does mean that it will not be as effective as it could be. If you don't have a security policy, we would consider the creation of this policy your top priority.

Q: If I purchase ESM tools, can I save money by eliminating some of my current tools?

A: Possibly, but that is not the purpose of ESM. ESM does not exist to replace your current tools, but rather provides a comprehensive solution to consolidate the information provided by and capabilities of the current tools.

Managing Log Files with Microsoft Log Parser

Solutions in this chapter:

- **Log File Conversion**
- **Log Rotation and Archival**
- **Separating Logs**

☑ **Summary**

☑ **Solutions Fast Track**

☑ **Frequently Asked Questions**

Introduction

Log files are the most critical source of data for most of your information technology systems. As such, they need to be properly managed. There are several areas to focus on when managing log files including conversion, rotation, archival, and separation. In this chapter we will be going over each of these primary areas of focus and showing you some techniques you can use to best manage your log files.

Log File Conversion

When managing log files from various systems, it quickly becomes apparent that just about every vendor of software or hardware wants to use their own format for log file data. Some log files are stored in plain text and some in binary format. Some include tab-separated data and others simply drop whatever information comes in next to the next line in the file. In order to work with all of these files, most technical professionals must learn the formats used for the log files of each application or piece of hardware that they work with regularly.

With Log Parser, there is a new way to work with log file data. Rather than dealing with several different formats of log data, Log Parser allows you to convert log file data to another format. This conversion process goes a long way to making log file data accessible to more people because you can convert the log data into a format that they are familiar with. Throughout this section, we will be going over some conversion techniques and show you some techniques you can use after the conversion to perform better analysis.

Standardizing Log Formats

The first step in log file conversion is to decide on a standard format of log file that will work best for you and the other technical people you work with regularly. Log parser supports many different formats including CSV, TSV, XML, DATAGRID, CHART, SYSLOG, NAT, W3C, IIS, SQL, and TPL. Some of these formats such as DATAGRID, CHART, and NAT are intended for immediate display or presenting a graph and are not appropriate for conversion or standardization efforts. Each of the other formats presents some value in standardization.

Choosing the format that is right for you is completely dependant on your needs and the formats that you understand the easiest. For example, if you are well versed in working with the SYSLOG format, then it would be best for you to standardize on that specific format. Each of the available formats store the data in a slightly different way and some are better for specific purposes than others. For example, you could easily open up a CSV file in Excel and work with the data whereas a W3C file wouldn't give you that option.

All of the specific syntax for each Log Parser output file is included in the program itself and in our quick reference guide so we won't be going through every option for every format in this chapter. However, we will go over a quick overview of each format and give some examples of how to perform these conversions in a couple different ways.

First up are the CSV and TSV formats. These are the *comma-separated values* and *tab-separated values* formats, respectively. Each of these formats will output a plain text file that separates the values for each column with either a comma or a tab. The TSV format will also let you use more than just tabs for the separator. You can actually use tabs, spaces, or any specific string in this format by specifying what separator you'd like to use in the Log Parser command line. This allows for a great deal of flexibility in your TSV format.

XML is a very powerful format that Log Parser supports for output. XML allows you a huge amount of flexibility in both the output of your specific data as well as the format that the data is displayed in when you later display the results. Log Parser allows you to use multiple XML structures, specify the schema for the XML, and even use a UNICODE or non-UNICODE codepage. Many applications are moving to XML as a standard for data output and data conversion and Log Parser's support of this format is very well implemented.

The SYSLOG format is incredibly useful for enterprises that are moving towards using Syslog servers for monitoring log and informational data from all pieces of the corporate infrastructure. When using a Syslog server, you have a single point of reference for everything that is happening in your environment and Log Parser supports the use of this type of monitoring. By using the SYSLOG format, Log Parser will send your converted log file data directly to a Syslog server and format it in a method that the server will understand.

The W3C format is the same format that IIS (Internet Information Server) now uses by default for its log files and many applications have been written to read and interpret this log file format. Log Parser allows you to convert log data into the W3C Extended Format File specification and subsequent programs that support this format can then read data that has been converted from other sources. This would allow you to perform standardization of log files and use existing log utilities to read the result.

Log Parser's IIS Log Format supports the older format that Internet Information Server used to use for its logging. This format has been mostly replaced with the W3C format, but some companies still prefer to use the original IIS format so that existing third-party programs supporting this format can remain in use. Consequently, Log Parser supports this format and will allow you to convert your log file data to IIS Log Format if you so choose.

The SQL format allows you to convert your log file data into a SQL table and store it in a relational database. This capability is a huge step forward in the concepts of log file storage and correlation.

Finally, File Template Output Format, or TPL, allows you to output the format of your converted data based on a specific user-defined template. By specifying a template file for the output, you can generate reports and reformat log file data to fit a specific need. While this isn't typically used for standardization of the actual data, it can be used for standardization of your data output.

All of the formats we've gone over can be used as your own standard format to convert your log files to. Whichever format you choose, Log Parser will allow you to take existing log file data from many sources and convert it over to your standard format to be viewed and analyzed. This capability will help you a great deal in simplifying the task of viewing data from multiple log sources and give you a single formatting style to work with.

To see how this is done, let's go through a quick example. Let's assume that you have some data stored in the W3C format from IIS that you wish to standardize to correspond with some of your other log file data. To standardize the format of your log files, you want to convert the W3C format to XML. This is done through the use of a couple simple commands with Log Parser. To convert the W3C data, we simply use the following command:

```
Logparser.exe file:Ch07ConvertW3CtoXML.sql -i:W3C


--- Ch07ConvertW3CtoXML.sql ---
SELECT
    *
INTO ex041008.xml
FROM ex041008.log
--- Ch07ConvertW3CtoXML.sql ---
```

When you run this command (against valid log files), you will end up with a new XML file that contains all of the data from your original W3C file. The SQL used for this can be further refined to only include records that show errors for example. If we want a list of all errors converted to XML, we could use this code instead:

```
Logparser.exe file:Ch07ConvertW3CErrorstoXML.sql -i:W3C


--- Ch07ConvertW3CErrorstoXML.sql ---
SELECT
    *
INTO ex041008.xml
FROM ex041008.log
WHERE sc-status >= 400
--- Ch07ConvertW3CErrorstoXML.sql ---
```

After running this conversion, you will have a file named ex041008.xml that contains only the errors from your original W3C log file. If you open this file in Internet Explorer, it should look similar to the screenshot shown in Figure 7.1.

Figure 7.1 W3C File Converted to XML

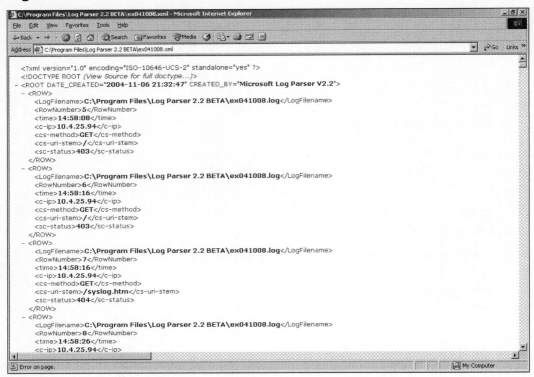

Using XML for Reporting

XML is a very versatile format that can easily be used to generate report data. By using an XSL template when you convert your logs to XML, you can change the result from the standard XML display to something more readable. Figure 7.1 shows an XML file that has had no additional formatting applied to it. While it contains all the data you need and provides an excellent standardized format for your data, it's not easily readable.

In order to apply formatting to your XML file, Log Parser allows you to define an XSL template. This template will be applied by any XSL-enabled XML browser to the resulting XML output and will change the format of the resulting data file. An excellent sample XSL template, included with Log Parser, formats incoming data into a table view. This sample is shown in the following example:

```
--- Ch07Table.xsl ---
<?xml version="1.0"?>
<xsl:stylesheet xmlns:xsl="http://www.w3.org/TR/WD-xsl">

 <xsl:template match="/">
  <xsl:for-each select="ROOT">
   <HTML>
    <HEAD><TITLE><xsl:value-of select="@CREATED_BY"/> Generated
Log</TITLE></HEAD>
    <BODY>


     <CENTER><H1><xsl:value-of select="@CREATED_BY"/> Generated
Log</H1></CENTER>
     <CENTER><H2>Generated on <xsl:value-of
select="@DATE_CREATED"/></H2></CENTER>

     <CENTER>
      <TABLE BORDER="0" BGCOLOR="#E0E0E0" CELLPADDING="5">
       <xsl:apply-templates select="ROW"/>
      </TABLE>
     </CENTER>

    </BODY>
   </HTML>
  </xsl:for-each>
 </xsl:template>

<xsl:template match="ROW">
     <TR BGCOLOR="#F0F0F0">
     <xsl:for-each select="*">
      <TD>
       <xsl:value-of select="."/>
      </TD>
     </xsl:for-each>
     </TR>
</xsl:template>
```

```
</xsl:stylesheet>
--- Ch07Table.xsl ---
```

In order to use this XSL file, we simply add it to the command line we use to run Log Parser. For example, to use this formatting option with the query we used previously to output W3C log file errors, we would use the following command:

```
Logparser.exe file:Ch07ConvertW3CErrorstoXML.sql -i:W3C -
xslLink:Ch07table.xsl
```

After running this command, you will have generated a new file named ex041008.xml. This file will contain a link referencing the XSL file you specified for formatting the data. When the new XML file is opened in an XSL-enabled browser, the browser will follow the link, load the XSL, and format the XML document as specified. Figure 7.2 shows the difference in formatting when our new file is displayed in Internet Explorer.

Notes from the Underground…

Using XSL Files

Using XSL files is a very powerful way of formatting XML to be very readable and easy to understand. Along with the sample that comes with Log Parser, you can find a large number of samples and information about XSL on the Web. Using these template files with XML will allow to you take any XML file that you create with Log Parser and present it in a more understandable format than the standard XML display. Make sure that you utilize these XSL files to their full potential and format your Log Parser XML files in the manner that best suits your needs.

Figure 7.2 XML File Formatted with XSL

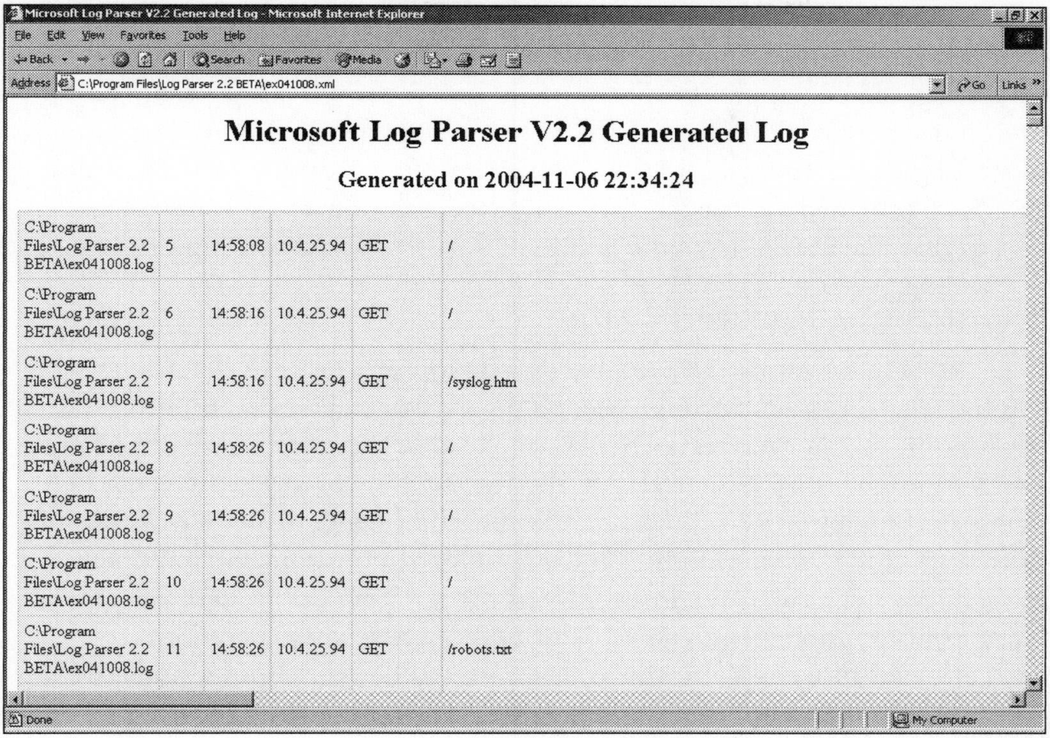

Correlating Log File Data

One of the more difficult tasks any systems administrator faces is the correlation of log file data from multiple sources. This problem is very apparent in the area of security administration when log files from many different systems, devices, and applications must be parsed through to find information that might relate to a specific event. However, even in normal systems administration work, you may have to correlate data from multiple sources in order to track down the root cause for a failure or events that led up to a system crash

Log Parser can help a great deal in this area with both the extensive queries that can be created as well as the conversion capabilities of the utility. Since Log Parser accepts so many possible input types and supports a large number of standard output types, it is the obvious choice of tool for correlating log file data from all of your source systems or applications.

The greatest benefit of correlating log file data using Log Parser is the speed and ease in which this work can be done. Using traditional troubleshooting methodologies, an admin may look at a system log, then a Web server log, then an application server log, then some other log simply to try and find where a failure actually occurred in the chain of interlinked systems. With Log Parser, the data from each of these sources can be combined and queries performed against the data as if it were from a single source. This means that it will take less time and less effort to track down important data.

Identifying Related Data

The first step in setting up a log file correlation process is to determine which log file data is related. For example, if you are working with a multi-tiered application with a Web server tier, an application server tier, and a database tier, you might consider correlating the log data from all systems in the hierarchy as a single source of log data. On the other hand, if you're only dealing with a specific tier, you might want only information from the multiple systems in the tier that you're involved with. Identifying the related data that you need is fairly simple once you've determined where your focus lies.

Let's take an example where you want to gather data from a single web server and a single application server. From the Web server, you will probably want the operating system event logs and the Web server logs. From the application server, you will want the operating system logs and the individual log files from the specific application that you're working with. Collecting these logs and combining them will give you a well-rounded picture of the events within your environment.

On the other hand, what if the problem you're working with appears to be network or security related? You might want to also add in log data from routers or switches as well as any network security equipment that is installed on your network. The idea is to correlate all data from point A to point B in order to get a complete view of the environment you're working in.

From these examples, you should have a pretty good idea on how to identify related data. Always go with the premise that the more data you have, the better results you'll get when trying to use correlated data to solve a problem. Since Log Parser is so versatile in the log file formats it can use, it's very easy to gather data from all the sources in an environment and use their related data.

Converting Related Log Files

Step two in correlating log file data using Log Parser is to convert the log files that you're working with into a standardized format. Typically you will be gathering data from a number of sources and each will be coming to you in a slightly different format. As we've already discussed, Log Parser is very capable of converting from a multitude of formats and storing the result in a single, standardized format for your future use.

In the example listed above, we discussed an environment where you want to gather W3C logs from a Web server's IIS installation as well as operating system event logs. To correlate the data from these two sources, it is easiest to convert them to a format such as XML. For the purposes of this example, we'll do just that and convert these log files into a single XML document.

First, we'll need to design the SQL for Log Parser to use for the conversion. We'll have to do the conversion in two distinct steps, as Log Parser does not currently support converting from multiple formats simultaneously. Therefore our first query will be to gather the data from the W3C log file and convert it into an XML document that uses the same fields that an event log uses. Using the following command and query will accomplish this:

```
Logparser.exe file:Ch07ConvertW3CtoCombinedXML.sql -i:W3C -o:XML
```

```
--- Ch07ConvertW3CtoCombinedXML.sql ---
SELECT
    LogFilename AS EventLog,
    RowNumber AS RecordNumber,
    to_timestamp( SYSTEM_DATE(), time) AS TimeGenerated,
    time AS TimeWritten,
    sc-status AS EventID,
    cs-method AS EventType,
    cs-method AS EventTypeName,
    cs-method AS EventCateagory,
    c-ip AS SourceName,
    cs-uri-stem AS Strings,
    c-ip AS ComputerName,
    c-ip AS SID,
    cs-uri-stem AS Message,
```

```
    cs-uri-stem AS Data
INTO combined.xml
FROM ex041008.log
--- Ch07ConvertW3CtoCombinedXML.sql ---
```

After running this code, we now have an XML file called combined.xml, which contains the W3C log file data in a new format. In order to properly combine the data from the W3C with the event log data, we must make the format of the XML match. To see a better view of how the fields are mapped in this XML file, refer to Table 7.1.

Table 7.1 W3C to XML Field Mappings

W3C Data Field	XML Data Field
LogFilename	EventLog
RowNumber	RecordNumber
to_timestamp (SYSTEM_DATE(), time)	TimeGenerated
time	TimeWritten
sc-status	EventID
cs-method	EventType
cs-method	EventTypeName
cs-method	EventCategory
c-ip	SourceName
cs-uri-stem	Strings
c-ip	ComputerName
c-ip	SID
cs-uri-stem	Message
cs-uri-stem	Data

Notes from the Underground…

Conversion Mapping

As you can see in Table 7.1, we've mapped out the columns between the W3C format and the EventLog format as it fit our needs for this example. Whenever you start a conversion process, you should always map out your fields first. If you're converting to a standard format of your own, then you already have a pretty good idea of which fields in the source should convert to which fields in the destination. However if you're converting from one standard format to another, a little guesswork is involved. Regardless, mapping out your fields in a table similar to that shown will make your conversion effort go a lot smoothly and give you accurate documentation on how to repeat the process in the future.

The next step in our task of converting this data is to add the appropriate operating system event logs to the combined.xml file. Log parser can easily add in all three event logs for the same date as the W3C log at once using the following command:

```
Logparser.exe file:Ch07ConvertEVTtoCombinedXML.sql -i:EVT -o:XML
-filemode:0
```

```
--- Ch07ConvertEVTtoCombinedXML.sql ---
SELECT
    *
INTO combined.xml
FROM system,
    security,
    application
WHERE TO_DATE(timegenerated) = TIMESTAMP('2004-11-06', 'yyyy-MM-
dd')
--- Ch07ConvertEVTtoCombinedXML.sql ---
```

Make sure you note the *filemode* parameter for the Log Parser command line. This parameter instructs Log Parser to append the output to an existing

XML file rather than overwrite it. After running this code, the combined.xml file now contains the event log data from all three event logs as well as the log data from the W3C log in a standardized format using the same field names.

There is one final step in completing this task. When we added in the event log data, we simply appended the data to the existing XML file. When doing so, Log Parser automatically added in the XML header prior to the new data. This problem wouldn't occur when using a CSV, TSV, or SQL database, but must be fixed when using XML. To do so, simply open up the combined.xml file using a text editor such as notepad and remove the second header. In our example, the header that should be removed looks like this:

```
</ROOT>?<?xml version="1.0" encoding="ISO-10646-UCS-2"
standalone="yes" ?>
<!DOCTYPE ROOT[
 <!ATTLIST ROOT DATE_CREATED CDATA #REQUIRED>
 <!ATTLIST ROOT CREATED_BY CDATA #REQUIRED>
 <!ELEMENT EventLog (#PCDATA)>
 <!ELEMENT RecordNumber (#PCDATA)>
 <!ELEMENT TimeGenerated (#PCDATA)>
 <!ELEMENT TimeWritten (#PCDATA)>
 <!ELEMENT EventID (#PCDATA)>
 <!ELEMENT EventType (#PCDATA)>
 <!ELEMENT EventTypeName (#PCDATA)>
 <!ELEMENT EventCategory (#PCDATA)>
 <!ELEMENT SourceName (#PCDATA)>
 <!ELEMENT Strings (#PCDATA)>
 <!ELEMENT ComputerName (#PCDATA)>
 <!ELEMENT SID (#PCDATA)>
 <!ELEMENT Message (#PCDATA)>
 <!ELEMENT Data (#PCDATA)>
 <!ELEMENT ROW (EventLog, RecordNumber, TimeGenerated,
TimeWritten, EventID, EventType, EventTypeName, EventCategory,
SourceName, Strings, ComputerName, SID, Message, Data)>
 <!ELEMENT ROOT (ROW*)>
]>
<ROOT DATE_CREATED="2004-11-07 04:18:44" CREATED_BY="Microsoft
Log Parser V2.2">
```

Basically, you'll need to remove all the data from the last </ROW> of your first XML segment to the first <ROW> of your second XML segment. This manual data change is required to change the file to a valid XML file and must be done before you can run any queries against the new XML file that you've created. In this manner, we now have converted four log files into a single standardized log file format and can query against the new XML file to correlate the log data.

Analyzing Related Log File Data

In the previous sections we have gone through the process of identifying related data and converting the related data into a standardized format. Now it's time to do something with the data we've gathered. Performing a query against the combined.xml file that we created in the last section is the same as performing a query against any standard XML file. To identify fields for your query, simply use the fields specified in Table 7.1.

As an example, let's say that we want to find all the events that occurred at around 1:00 P.M. from the combined log set. To do this, we could use the following command and query:

```
Logparser.exe file:Ch07EventsWithinanHour.sql -i:XML -o:XML -
xslLink:ch07table.xsl


--- Ch07EventsWithinanHour.sql ---
SELECT
    *
INTO 1pmEvents.xml
FROM combined.xml
WHERE TO_STRING(timegenerated, 'yyyy-MM-dd HH') = '2004-11-06
15'
ORDER BY timegenerated
--- Ch07EventsWithinanHour.sql ---
```

Using this code will parse through the XML file that we created by combining a W3C log file with three event log files and identify all events that occurred at 3:00 P.M. It will then take this data and output it to another XML file while formatting it according to the format specified in the XSL file we used previously. The end result is an easily read XML file that contains all of the data for the hour that we're interested in. Viewing the resulting XML file in Internet Explorer should give you a result similar to that shown in Figure 7.3.

Figure 7.3 Formatted, Limited, and Combined XML

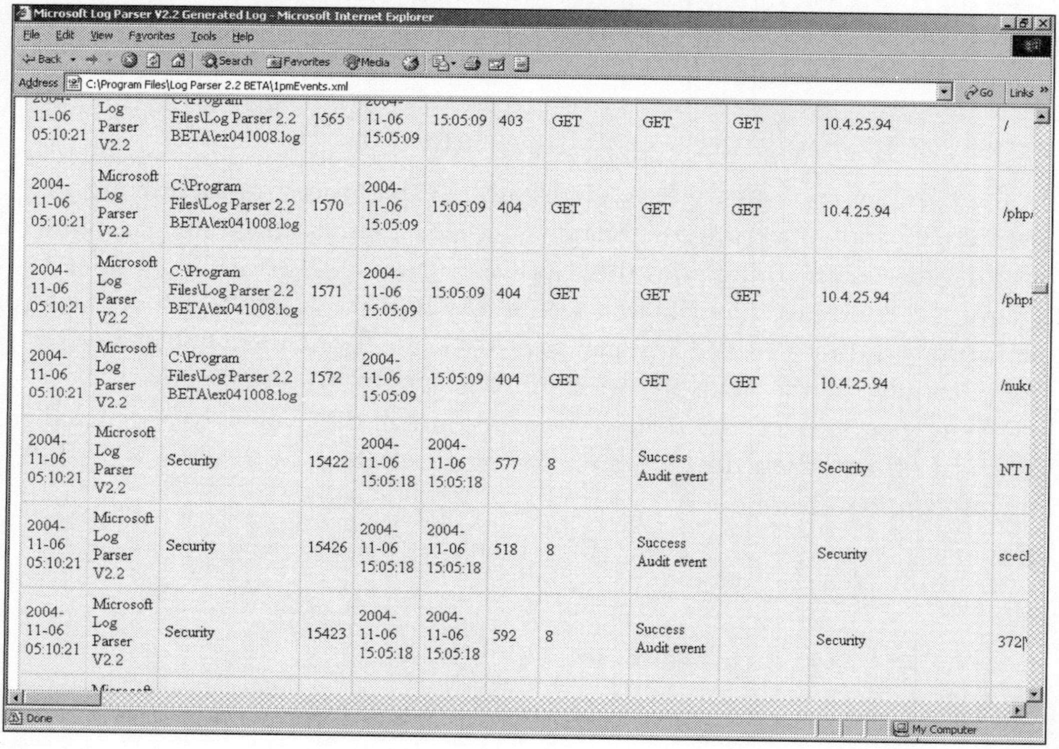

2004-11-06 05:10:21	Log Parser V2.2	C:\Program Files\Log Parser 2.2 BETA\ex041008.log	1565	2004-11-06 15:05:09	15:05:09	403	GET	GET	GET	10.4.25.94	/
2004-11-06 05:10:21	Microsoft Log Parser V2.2	C:\Program Files\Log Parser 2.2 BETA\ex041008.log	1570	2004-11-06 15:05:09	15:05:09	404	GET	GET	GET	10.4.25.94	/php
2004-11-06 05:10:21	Microsoft Log Parser V2.2	C:\Program Files\Log Parser 2.2 BETA\ex041008.log	1571	2004-11-06 15:05:09	15:05:09	404	GET	GET	GET	10.4.25.94	/php
2004-11-06 05:10:21	Microsoft Log Parser V2.2	C:\Program Files\Log Parser 2.2 BETA\ex041008.log	1572	2004-11-06 15:05:09	15:05:09	404	GET	GET	GET	10.4.25.94	/nuk
2004-11-06 05:10:21	Microsoft Log Parser V2.2	Security	15422	2004-11-06 15:05:18	2004-11-06 15:05:18	577	8	Success Audit event		Security	NT I
2004-11-06 05:10:21	Microsoft Log Parser V2.2	Security	15426	2004-11-06 15:05:18	2004-11-06 15:05:18	518	8	Success Audit event		Security	scecl
2004-11-06 05:10:21	Microsoft Log Parser V2.2	Security	15423	2004-11-06 15:05:18	2004-11-06 15:05:18	592	8	Success Audit event		Security	372

Further queries and analysis can be done on your combined log file to use the correlated data in a way that best fits your needs. As previously mentioned, you can run any query against this combined XML file that you can against a standard event log file as they use the same field names.

You can see by this example that it's relatively simple to combine multiple log files as well as multiple log files from multiple sources into the same final log file. This process will help you a great deal with correlating log file data and using Log Parser to further analyze the resulting data. Keep in mind that while I used an XML file for this example, you can also use almost any format that Log Parser supports for output to combine your data.

Log Rotation and Archival

We all realize that log files are a critical part of tracking system functionality and ensuring that everything within your enterprise is functioning up to spec. There is one overwhelming problem with all the logging that occurs to create these files, however; it never stops. Therefore the log files just keep getting larger and larger to the point that if not properly taken care of, they can fill up system drives.

This becomes more and more apparent in larger enterprises where disk space is critical and hundreds or thousands of systems must be monitored to ensure that the various log files stored on the systems are not growing too large. Some applications provide specific logging features to allow for log rotation and archival, but you as an administrator must decide upon the strategy you wish to use and ensure that it is consistent across multiple systems and multiple applications.

In this section, we're going to cover some basic techniques of log file rotation and log file archiving that will help you accomplish two main goals. The first goal is to keep your systems clean and prevent log files from filling up the drives. Second, you want to ensure that you have an adequate amount of historical log data retained for reporting or tracking of ongoing system problems.

Rotating Log Files

One method of keeping log files from piling up on any given system is to rotate the log files out. This basically involves specifying at what point the log file is considered full or complete and moving to a new log file when that point is reached.

There are two major methods used to determine when a log file is complete. First, you can base your completion criteria on the size of the log file itself. Second, you can base your completion criteria on a specific date or time match, for example, rotate log files hourly or daily.

While log file rotation may initially seem the same as log file archival, there are some differences and we'll discuss those as we go along. Remember, the primary goal of a log file rotation is to stop writing to a log file that is deemed complete and to start writing a new log file. No movement of the log files is necessarily done in a straight log file rotation method.

Rotating Log Files Based on Size

When working with log files, you'll find that every operating system or application looks at logging in a different way. Some actually allow you to modify the way the application does its logging and define a specific rotation strategy, but most require some form of manual intervention in order to accomplish any log file rotations.

For example, Windows 2000 allows you to set a maximum log file size, but does not allow you to specify a way to rotate out the log files themselves. It simply allows you to choose whether or not you wish to overwrite previous entries. This feature is better than many applications, however, because at least you have some options to help you eliminate the possibility of log files filling up the system drives.

To further refine this process, you'll want to implement some form of archival. We'll explain how that is done later in the chapter. In the meantime, let's look at an application that has no default log file rotation mechanism. For the purposes of this example, we'll use the iPass Connect VPN solution. iPass stores its log file as C:\Program Files\iPass\iPassConnect\log\connection.log. It does not rotate the log files and simply appends any new data at the bottom of the existing file. This is pretty standard for most applications.

In order to create your own log rotation process for these log files manually, you simply need to rename the old file to something useful and create a new blank file for storing future data. However, since you want to rotate the log files based on size, you only want to do this for files that are above the size that you specify. There are some methods you can use to automate this process, and we'll cover those a little later in this section.

Rotating Log Files Based on Date

Another method of handling log file rotation is to rotate log files based on the file date or time. Some applications create so much logging data that you'll want to rotate the log files on an hourly basis to keep the log files from growing too large. In order to perform this type of rotation, you'll need to determine, on average, how much data is being placed in your log files during a specific timeframe. When you have this information, you will be able to determine what frequency you'll need to use in rotating out the log files.

Similar to the example above with an iPass Connect log file, any log file can be rotated out based on a date structure and typically this is easier than relying on file size. By implementing a log file rotation schedule based on date, you'll have specific times that your automated log rotation process will need to run in order to rotate the log file out. An example of a program that does this by default is Microsoft IIS. IIS rotates out its logs every night and stores one day's worth of data in each log file. While this process does not automatically archive the data, it does rotate the logs so that they can be more easily archived by using another process.

Automating Log File Rotation

Our discussion of log file rotation so far has given you the basic methods and methodologies of log file rotation. Now you should understand the purpose and benefits of rotating log files and have a pretty clear idea of how this process is accomplished. But how do you actually implement this in a real-world environment in such a way that it is easily managed? The answer is automated log file rotation.

The method you choose to automate your log file rotation will vary depending on the specific applications that you're working with. Every application is different, but you can apply the same reasoning regardless of the way the application works and apply some sort of log rotation. Let's go through a couple examples on how to set this up.

First, let's look at doing an automatic log file rotation of the Windows 2000 application log. Let's assume that you want to set this up to only occur when the log file reaches 500k. The best way to set up something along those lines is to create a visual basic script file or a batch file that checks the size of the application event log and starts Log Parser to grab out the data if the file is larger than 500k. You then use the Microsoft Task Scheduler to schedule this file to execute on a regular basis. An appropriate command line to use with Log Parser would be:

```
Logparser.exe file:Ch07RotateApplicationLog.sql -i:EVT -o:XML
--- Ch07RotateApplicationLog.sql ---
SELECT
    *
```

```
INTO AppLog.xml
FROM application
--- Ch07RotateApplicationLog.sql ---
```

   You would then follow this up with a purge of the application event log using a third-party utility. Using this method of log rotation isn't necessarily the cleanest, but it gets the job done. It's usually very difficult to set up a good log rotation system when the applications that you're working with don't natively support a function such as this.

   For another example, let's do something similar with the system event log, but this time base it on date instead of log file size. This is much easier to set up than a file size-based log rotation because you simply schedule the automated run of Log Parser followed by an event log purge utility on the specific dates or times that you want the process to run. There's no need to check for file size, etc. So to use Log Parser in this manner, you might use the following command and query:

```
Logparser.exe file:Ch07RotateSystemLog.sql -i:EVT -o:XML
--- Ch07RotateSystemLog.sql ---
SELECT
     *
INTO SysLog.xml
FROM system
--- Ch07RotateSystemLog.sql ---
```

Determining an Archiving Methodology

Throughout this section, we've discussed log file rotation and extracting data from log files for storage and future analysis. But where should all those log files go? You certainly don't want to create and retain gigs upon gigs of log file data on every system in your enterprise. The answer to this is log file archival.

   There are several reasons for archiving logs. First is the obvious space savings on individual servers, but there are other reasons that are sometimes even more important. First, in the event of a security breach, you should try to have as much data as possible available to parse through in search of clues to the security problem. Setting up a log file rotation is the first step of this, but you want to move those log files to a secure location regularly so they aren't compromised when the system itself is.

Second, there are sometimes legal or policy requirements that force you to retain logs of important data for several years. Typically the best way to meet this need is to archive the files off of the system where they were generated and store them with other data that has a long-term retention need.

You may also need to archive log files to protect yourself or your company. This sometimes falls under legal requirements, but even if the situation you're in isn't being viewed from a legal perspective, it may be wise to protect yourself.

Whatever the most pressing reason is, there is always some justification that proves log archiving to be necessary. Through the remainder of this section we will be going over some of the reasons why you might want to archive logs and specific methodologies to use based on your reasoning. We'll also go over some industry best practices as they relate to log archival and storage.

Meeting Legal or Policy Requirements

Often there are legal or policy requirements around log retention. In order to comply with several corporate audit standards such as Sarbanes-Oxley, ISO-9000, and VISA CISP you must have a corporate policy in place that covers the subject of critical system log archive retention. Depending on the standards, the retention duration and other requirements vary. However, they all require some specific duration that you must keep log files.

In order to meet these requirements, many companies are quickly implementing corporate policies around log file archiving and retention. Some are using Syslog servers and storing the data on their Syslog server for the specified duration. Others are simply doing a file copy and storing the log files on a centralized file share. Another option is writing log files to one exclusive backup tape system so they are stored long-term on tape.

Regardless of which methodology is chosen, the best base concept behind all of them is centralized storage in one manner or another. Using this type of system moves the responsibility of the log file retention and archival from the individual systems and to a centralized system or set of systems. This allows for easier purging when the storage duration has been exceeded as well as a single place to look for log files regardless of which system or application generated them.

One major benefit of this centralized storage scheme is that you have a single place to look for information from all of your systems. Using Log Parser, you can easily look through multiple logs simultaneously and cut down on the amount of time necessary to query for data. For example, if you wanted to gather all system startup events from a series of logs in the same directory, you might use the following command and query:

```
Logparser.exe file:Ch07MultipleFileStartupEvents.sql -i:EVT
-o:datagrid
```

```
--- Ch07MultipleFileStartupEvents.sql ---
SELECT
    timegenerated AS EventTime,
    message AS Message
FROM *.evt
WHERE eventid= '6005'
--- Ch07MultipleFileStartupEvents.sql ---
```

Archiving Logs for Non-Repudiation

Another reason many companies require log file archival is for non-repudiation. The purpose of this is for proof that a transaction happened so it cannot be refuted later. One example of this is digitally signing e-mail messages. If you digitally sign a message, the receiver knows that you sent this message and you cannot deny it later.

The same thing applies to system logs. If an event is captured in a system log and later this log is to be used for legal purposes, you need to ensure that the log files are archived and protected. In many situations, you may actually be required to encrypt the files as well, but usually placing them on a secure system on the network or even an out-of-band system will suffice.

WARNING

Whenever you're working with non-repudiation, make sure that you coordinate with your company's Legal department prior to changing any existing processes. There may be a specific reason for storing files in a particular manner based on state or local law. Always make sure that a company attorney is aware of your efforts and helps you to ensure that you have complied appropriately with any legal requirements.

Regardless of where the log files go, you need to have a policy in place to cover this situation in the event that it occurs. By coupling this policy with your standard log file archival and retention policy, you can cut down on the number of documents that have to be maintained and use a single point of reference for your logging requirements.

Log Parser can help you with this effort by automatically sending the data from log files on individual systems over to a storage location on a centralized system in a standard format. For example, in order to copy security event log data to a central server you could use the following command and query:

```
Logparser.exe file:Ch07RemoteServerSecurityLog.sql -i:EVT -o:XML
```

```
--- Ch07RemoteServerSecurityLog.sql ---
SELECT
    *
INTO \\server1\log$\server23.xml
FROM security
--- Ch07RemoteServerSecurityLog.sql ---
```

Notes from the Underground…

Using Remote Systems

When you're working on remote systems with Log Parser, remember that with the exception of a Syslog server, you're simply using UNC shares to perform your work. With that in mind, if you want to use a share on a remote system to store all of your log files, simply create it, assign appropriate permissions, and use Log Parser to send the data over as you're converting it. Rather than coping the files over after they're converted, you can use Log Parser to combine these steps and save yourself some time.

Building a Hierarchical Logging Directory Structure

When you begin to use a centralized server to store your enterprise log files, you'll quickly learn that the system becomes unmanageable without using good naming conventions and file structures. If all of the event logs or application logs from multiple systems are simply dumped into a single directory, you risk overwriting existing files or not being able to identify which system a specific log file originated from. This can cause a great deal of confusion or even make the entire process of log archiving useless.

To prevent this, there are two key steps you must take. First, name your log files in an accurate and easy to understand naming convention. Be consistent on this because as with most services offered in IT, once this is available its use will grow. You want to ensure that you have a solid standard in place from the beginning.

Second, you should use a hierarchical directory structure to store the log files. The way you set this up will differ depending on your specific needs. Some administrators prefer to use the system names as the top level in their hierarchy. Others prefer to base them on what the system is used for and put the name on the next level. Another method I've seen is to use the application name as the top level, followed by system function, followed by name. It's all a matter of preference. Whichever you choose, just be consistent. If you set up the log file storage differently for different systems then you will run into problems locating files and retrieving data later.

Figures 7.4, 7.5, and 7.6 show three examples of how this can be done. Again, don't use multiple methods on a single system. Choose the hierarchy that works best for you and stick with it.

Figure 7.4 Sample Hierarchical Logging Directory Structures – Application-Based

Figure 7.5 Sample Hierarchical Logging Directory Structures – Function-Based

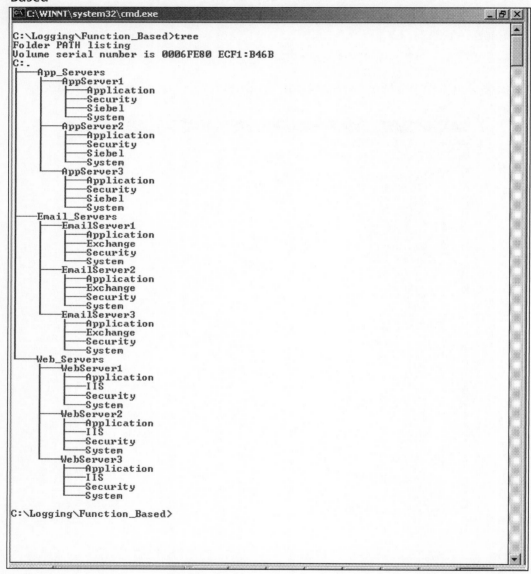

Figure 7.6 Sample Hierarchical Logging Directory Structures – System-Based

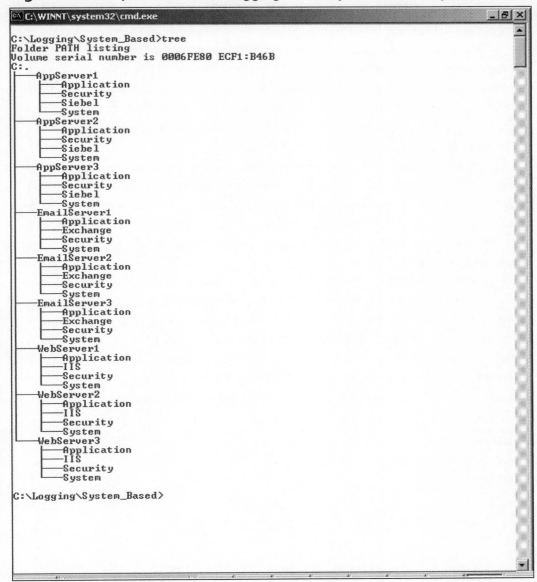

Using a Syslog Server

Many corporations make use of a Syslog server to centralize storage of their log files. Syslog messaging was originally used on UNIX systems for application, network, and operating-system logging. Many network devices can now also be configured to generate Syslog messages. These Syslog messages are then transmitted via UDP to a server configured with a Syslog daemon to accept the messages.

As more and more devices support Syslog messages, many enterprises are moving toward using a Syslog server as their primary archival location of event messages from across the enterprise. Syslog servers can also be set up to do automatic notifications if specific critical events are sent to it. This feature allows for a faster response time from IT personnel to system outages and helps to reduce the overall amount of downtime.

By using a Syslog server, you have a centralized point on your network to receive, alert on, and archive log files. However, many systems don't yet support this method of sending log files and this leads many enterprises to having both a hierarchical logging system and a Syslog server. Log Parser can help alleviate the pain of keeping two logging points on your network by sending log messages to a Syslog server.

Log Parser natively supports the use of a Syslog server as an output type and can use this function to convert and forward your log files to your enterprise's corporate Syslog server regardless of the support of individual applications. To use this feature, you must know the server and port (optional) to which you need to send the Syslog messages. In addition, there are a number of features specific to Syslog servers that Log Parser supports. A quick example follows that shows the conversion and transmission of event logs to a Syslog server:

```
Logparser.exe file:Ch07EventlogtoSyslog.sql -i:EVT -o:SYSLOG
--- Ch07EventlogtoSyslog.sql ---
SELECT
    *
INTO @syslogserver:514
FROM system,
    application,
    security
--- Ch07EventlogtoSyslog.sql ---
```

Separating Logs

Throughout this chapter we've been discussing the conversion and centralization of enterprise log files. The processes and methods we've discussed serve several very useful purposes including drive space utilization reduction, centralized log data for reference and correlation, and centralized archival for legal or policy needs. However, there are occasions when you need to use a slightly different method for working with your log files.

Log file separation is the process by which centralized files are broken down into specific categories and referenced based on their category. If you have a centralized system in place using a hierarchical directory structure, you may need to gather files from multiple places in the structure in order to correlate them for a specific purpose. For example, if a specific set of systems and hardware devices were involved in a security breach of the enterprise, you may want to gather a subset of the log files consisting of the log files specific to those systems and devices.

Another reason for log file separation is to separate a single log file into categories. An occasion where you may need to do this is when you have a very large log file containing multiple days of data and you want to break up this log file by date. Doing so can make the log more meaningful or be a first step in preparing the file for inclusion with other log files from the same individual dates so that it fits properly into your hierarchical structure.

In this section we'll be going over some of the strategies and methods of using separated logs. You'll find at times that this seems in direct contradiction to the strategies we discussed in the section on log file correlation, but as we go along you'll see how log file separation and correlation/consolidation can go hand in hand.

Determining Log File Separation Strategies

The first step in putting a log separation process in place is to determine your strategy behind the process. There are many different reasons for setting up log file separation. As I've mentioned, you may be separating log files for ease of use, correlation with other like files, or as a preparation task for centralizing the files in a hierarchical structure. All of these are valid reasons for implementing log file separation and all fall into specific strategies.

The three main strategies of log file separation are separation by date, separation by type, and separation by system. Using one of these strategies will help break your log files down to more manageable chunks for analysis. We'll go through each strategy in detail and discuss how each one is implemented.

Separating by Date

The first log separation strategy we'll discuss is separating by date. This is probably the most common form of log file separation and one of the most frequently implemented. The basic premise behind separating by date is pretty obvious; you want to separate out a log file based on the date that the event occurred and was logged. This is usually used in cases where an application continues writing within a single large log file regardless of date until some criteria is filled, such as an application restart.

When considering this strategy, you need to determine the type of log file you're dealing with and the way the application handles logging. Based on the way the application works, you may need to answer the following questions:

- Does the application start overwriting the log file after it reaches a specific size?

- How does the application store time stamps in the logs? Since date is your primary criteria here, this is critical.

- Are there specific criteria that the application uses to determine that it should rotate to another log file?

- Do the log files from multiple systems have to be recombined after the individual system logs have been separated by date?

Answering these questions based on your specific environment will help you to determine the best way to separate your log files by date. Many administrators find that it is helpful to extract out the previous day's worth of data out of a log file and store that in a hierarchical structure similar to the structures discussed previously. This is one of the major ways that log file separation by date is used.

Separating by Event Type

Another form of log file separation is separation by type. This strategy basically involves separating out log file messages based on the type of message.

An example is the separation of error messages from benign messages. This form of separation is primarily used to limit the amount of data that an administrator must go through in order to find important information about the ongoing operation of a system, device, or application.

While Log Parser can easily parse through a log file and output the results of a query for this information on the fly, it's sometimes necessary to actually maintain a constant output of this data on a daily basis. One reason that this is done is to support an automated reporting or statistics gathering tool. When this is the case, it makes more sense to separate out the events of interest and store them in another file.

To use this strategy, you'll probably want to set up an automated process through Windows Task Scheduler or some other means in order to start up Log Parser. The parameters and query that you use for Log Parser would be similar to that used earlier in this chapter to convert the log file data to another format gathering only the data matching your specific criteria. These new files can then be used for any automated or manual evaluation process.

Separating by System

Some administrators are more concerned about the overall operations of individual servers, rather than each specific application running on those servers. In this case, an administrator may want to separate out all log file data for all applications on a system and look though this data independently from the data retrieved from other systems.

In the event that you are doing centralized storage and archival of log data, you may need to extract data out of the central store to serve this need. This form of separation is what is considered separation by system. Typically this strategy is used to either fill the need mentioned above or to help consolidate logs by system for future review. Figure 7.7 shows a breakdown of this process and should make it a little more understandable.

Figure 7.7 Log File Separation by System

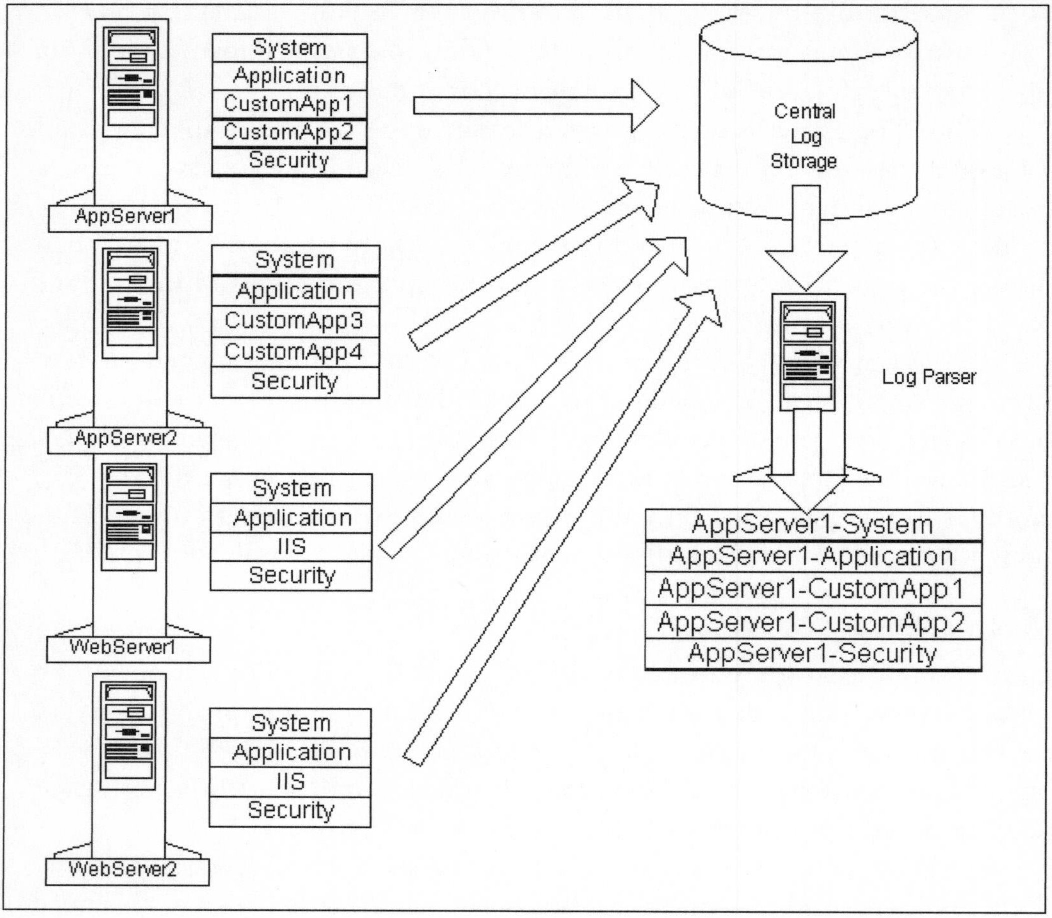

As you can see, all of the application and Web servers in this environment are sending their system, application, and security logs to a centralized store in addition to any log from other software on the system. To illustrate this example, an administrator uses Log Parser to pull all data related to AppServer1 from the centralized store for a full system analysis.

While the administrator could have simply gathered this information directly from the server, using the centralized store allows the administrator to get more historical information than what would be available on the server. In addition, the use of the centralized store makes it easy for the administrator to also run a query that looks at applications across multiple servers, etc. depending on their needs.

Using Separated Log Files

Now that we've examined the various log file separation strategies, it's time to learn how to use them. So far we've covered the three main strategies that are used with log file separation and learned how each can benefit you as an administrator depending on your specific needs. Before going forward and implementing any one strategy, make sure that you thoroughly understand your enterprise and choose the strategy that best suits the needs of your organization.

There are three steps to using separated log files. First, you must create them. Throughout this book, we've gone over various ways to use Log Parser to query against log files of various types. In this chapter, we've covered how to convert and centralize log files within an enterprise. Using all of this information together is all you need to know on how to create separated log files. Basically, you are simply extracting the log data that you want from the centrally stored log files using Log Parser queries and storing the newly separated log file in a format of your choosing.

Second, since you have now created separated log files, you have to store them somewhere to make them useful. This doesn't necessarily have to be the same storage location as your central log archive, but you do need some method of keeping the separated log files organized.

Finally, you must make use of the data within the separated log files. This means using Log Parser to query against one or more of your separated log files to find information or display data. Since your separated log files are a subset of your centralized log files, querying against them should be slightly faster and you can be sure that any data you receive is directly related to the subset of data you requested when creating the separated log file.

Now we'll go over a method you can use to store your separated log files. Using this suggestion in combination with everything else you've learned in this chapter and a well-thought-out log file strategy will allow you to leverage the power of Log Parser and use this tool to help you troubleshoot or understand your enterprise better.

Developing a Separated Log File Hierarchy

In order to utilize the separated log files that you create, you need to ensure that they are stored in a logical manner. This is where a separated log file hierarchy comes into place. Similar to the hierarchical logging directory structure that we discussed earlier in the chapter, a separated log file hierarchy allows you to logically separate out separated log files so that they are easy to find and use.

Refer to Figures 7.4, 7.5, and 7.6 earlier in this chapter for some sample hierarchical structures. These same structures apply to separated logs as well as your centralized log storage location. The primary difference is that you don't necessarily need to store the separated log files at the same location. In this case the log file hierarchy is simply used for organizing the files for your personal temporary use, not to position them for log time archival.

You'll find that if your centralized log storage hierarchy is set up in such a manner that it really fits the needs of your enterprise, you may be able to simply use the same hierarchy for your separated log files as well. While this may seem to mean that you're duplicating data, in reality you're simplifying the use of the data by making a temporary duplicate.

Summary

Throughout this chapter, we have covered several of the more administrative aspects of using Log Parser. We went over using Log Parser to convert multiple types of log files into standard formats for easy future reference as well as consolidation. In addition, we went over some methods you can use to store your log files in a logical hierarchical manner so that they are very easy to access and use at a future time. Finally, we went over how to work backwards and separate the consolidated log files in order to run queries faster and limit the data to exactly what you need a little easier.

As we've gone over each section within this chapter, you should have mastered performing conversion efforts using Log Parser. Using this powerful tool, it's very quick and easy to convert data from the plethora of formats that Log Parser supports. In addition, you should have a good understanding of how and why log files should be consolidated as well as when you should separate them back out for ease of use. Mastering these techniques and understanding these procedures will help you to be more effective in your ongoing use of Log Parser.

Solutions Fast Track

Log File Conversion

☑ Many organizations know to collect logs, but don't know what to do with them. Take the first step beyond identifying that logs are a critical resource.

☑ Log conversion is necessary to standardize all of the different vendor "standards" that are out there. Using Log Parser you can convert all of your existing logs into a common format that will fit your needs.

☑ Deciding on a log file format is heavily dependent on your needs and requirements. Large enterprises may want to consider sylog or XML formats because of their extensibility and scalability. Smaller shops may want to consider W3C or csv formats for ease of manipulation through common desktop applications. Users familiar with databases might want to try the SQL format.

☑ XML is very flexible and somewhat standard file format. When used with XSL templates you can create XML-based log repots that are formatted for human readability.

☑ Syslog format is widely used in enterprise environments where centralization and standardization are critical.

☑ Automating the correlation of disparate log files is a powerful analyst tool. However, the analyst will need to plan carefully on what data sources from which to draw. You'll need to decide on your area of focus (one server or multiple), you format log standard, and map log column fields from source formats into your standard.

Log Rotation and Archival

☑ Collecting and using logs can result in massive amounts of data. You'll need to plan carefully to keep you systems disks from filling up and at the same to retain enough historical data to be able to provide relevant reports.

☑ Use scheduling utilities available in your systems' OS to automate your log rotation either by file size or by time.

☑ Archiving requirements may be driven by disk space availability, system admin needs, policy, and legal obligations. In all cases, centralization may be the best solution for relaxing requirements on log sources.

☑ If you identify that you will need to retain logs for legal purposes, you will want to check with you legal department for guidelines regarding nonrepudiation, storage, and other requirements will want. Getting buy off from them may pay off when data from logs is used in any kind of legal event.

Separating Logs

☑ Log file separation will allow you to organize your data by source or function. For example, you can separate logs by date, source, or message severity. Careful log file separation will help keep you organized so that you can conduct quick investigations.

☑ Centralizing your logs and then separating them by function (for instance all web servers) will allow you to monitor your environment with more efficiency.

☑ Developing a log file storage hierarchy makes sense for an enterprise network or any network environment that maintains a large number of logs.

Frequently Asked Questions

The following Frequently Asked Questions, answered by the authors of this book, are designed to both measure your understanding of the concepts presented in this chapter and to assist you with real-life implementation of these concepts. To have your questions about this chapter answered by the author, browse to **www.syngress.com/solutions** and click on the **"Ask the Author"** form. You will also gain access to thousands of other FAQs at ITFAQnet.com.

Q: What log format is fastest?

A: This will depend heavily on your needs and environment. For low-volume systems, you may find that Syslog or CSV format works very well for the purposes of centralization and reporting. For scalability, you may want to stay with Syslog, or you might want to consider moving to SQL-based storage. Ultimately, Log Parser has enough flexibility for you to produce reports using any csource format.

Q: How can I send Windows logs to my UNIX syslog server?

A: You'll definitely need to get a third-party program to send logs from your Windows server to your syslog server. Products vary in price (from free to shareware to costly) and functionality.

Q: How long should I keep my logs?

A: You should check with your legal department and present your legal advisers the different kinds of logs that are available and ask them for requirements. Depending on your business type, there might be some legal needs that have to be met. You should also carefully think about what kind of information you want available to you when you are investigating an incident.

Q: My logs don't seem to sync up with respect to time. What's going on?

A: You'll need to make sure that all your systems are getting their time synchronized. Consider using NTP in your environment and set up your own internal set of time servers. Have your systems pull time from these sources. It's critical that data and time stamps on all our systems match.

Q: Can I send my logs to any kind of database server?

A: With Log Parser you can output your data to any database that supports SQL.

Q: My logs have gotten very big. I don't have any disk space left, and I determined I need to keep what I have. What should I do?

A: Consider using compression such as bzip2. Compression can be scripted in using many common tools.

Investigating Intrusions with Microsoft Log Parser

Solutions in this chapter:

- **Locating Intrusions**
- **Monitoring IIS**

☑ **Summary**

☑ **Solutions Fast Track**

☑ **Frequently Asked Questions**

Introduction

Investigating intrusions is usually a difficult and tedious task. Faced with megabytes and sometimes gigabytes of log file data, it is easy to overlook some of the most critical evidence. Often it is difficult to determine that a security incident has even occurred.

But Log Parser changes that. Log Parser can combine, sort, and parse through log files to give you a unique perspective of your data. With the right queries, important evidence tends to float into view. Our goal in this chapter is to build a toolbox of queries that we will have ready to use as needed. Here you will learn powerful features and capabilities of Log Parser that will help you track down almost any intrusion.

Locating Intrusions

To locate intruders, you must first detect the intrusion. Fortunately, most attacks leave some kind of trail. The trick is in knowing how to find these intrusions among thousands of normal log entries. The secret is to start with high-level queries then work your way down to more and more specific conditions in your WHERE clause. In this chapter, we will focus on the most common and the most obvious threats.

TIP

If you anticipate prosecuting an intruder with the information you gather, you should take careful steps to preserve the original evidence, and only run these queries on copies of log data. If you expect legal proceedings, you should always consult a forensics expert on how to best preserve evidence for use in court.

Suspicious behavior is usually abnormal behavior. Knowing this, it is usually possible to identify an intrusion just by measuring normal behavior. Suspicious log entries often show up on top 10 lists or cluster around specific pieces of information. For example, you can often identify SQL injection attacks by watching for unusually high hits to one page, especially from a single IP (Internet Protocol) address. However, you must also be creative.

For example, sometimes an attacker will not show much activity in any single day, but if you do a top 10 list for six months, the attacker's IP address will show up.

The key is to look at your data in many different ways. By doing this you will find that suspicious data tends to bring itself to your attention.

Monitoring Logons

The most basic element of a security system is user account access. Many security mechanisms rely upon authenticating a user and then authorizing that user to take actions or access resources on a server. If properly configured to audit logon events, a Windows server records account activity in the Security Event Log. When you browse through the Security Event Log, it is difficult to identify anything suspicious, but when you use Log Parser to summarize the data, it is very easy to spot malicious activity. Monitoring account logon activity is an essential element of intrusion detection.

Excessive Failed Logons

One common sign of intrusion is excessive failed logins, either for a single user or across your domain. Although login failures are common, abnormally high login failures are a good indication of attack. The query Ch08UserLogins.sql will list the total number of failed and successful logons for each user account, with the highest number of logins listed first. This query looks for all events with an EventCategory of 2, which is any logon/logoff event. It also filters results to only include those events with an EventID less than 541 and where the username is not blank.

Run this query with the following command:

```
LogParser file:Ch08UserLogins.sql
```

```
--- Ch08UserLogins.sql---
SELECT
    TO_LOWERCASE(EXTRACT_TOKEN(Strings,0,'|')) AS Account,
    SUM(CASE EventType WHEN 16 THEN 1 ELSE 0 END) AS Failed,
    SUM(CASE EventType WHEN 8 THEN 1 ELSE 0 END) AS Success,
    COUNT(*) AS Total
FROM m1Security.evt
```

```
WHERE EventCategory=2
    AND EventID < 541
    AND User<>''
GROUP BY User
ORDER BY Total DESC
--- Ch08UserLogins.sql---
```

The query should return something like this:

```
Account         Failed Success Total
--------------- ------ ------- ------
PCW204$             0     218    218
PCW218$             0     114    114
administrator      27     103    130
anonymous logon 0        108    108
awest              12      86     98
network service 0         87     87
local service   0         67     67
cnorth             19      24     43
PCW205$             0      28     28
```

Review these results for users with abnormally high failed logins, high total number of failed logins, or failed logins for invalid accounts.

Note that failed logins and successful logins are separate records in the event log, but here we want to see the totals for each account on a single line. I accomplished that with these two lines:

```
SUM(CASE EventType WHEN 16 THEN 1 ELSE 0 END) AS Failed,
SUM(CASE EventType WHEN 8 THEN 1 ELSE 0 END) AS Success,
```

These lines use the CASE statement to check for the values of 16 and 8 and if they exist, change the field value to 1. The SUM statement then totals these 1's for each user as specified in the GROUP BY clause.

Terminal Services Logons

Because Terminal Services allows for remote console access to a server, it is an attractive target for hackers. If you have a Terminal Server exposed to the Internet, it is critical that you monitor the logins to this server. If you are investigating an intrusion, it is important that you check logins to all public

Terminal Servers. The query Ch08TSLogins.sql lists all failed logins to
Windows 2003 Terminal Services along with the originating IP address.

```
--- Ch08TSFailedLogins.sql---
SELECT
    Count(*) AS Failed,
    EXTRACT_TOKEN(Strings,1,'|') AS Domain,
    EXTRACT_TOKEN(Strings,0,'|') AS User,
    EXTRACT_TOKEN(Strings,11,'|') AS Source
USING EXTRACT_TOKEN(Strings,2,'|') AS Type
FROM Security
WHERE EventID=529
    AND Type='10'
GROUP BY Domain, User, Source
ORDER BY Logins DESC
--- Ch08TSFailedLogins.sql---
```

Although failed logins are interesting, perhaps more interesting is checking
for successful logins from unrecognized IP addresses. Ch08TSLogins.sql is
similar to the previous query, except that this time it lists all successful logins.

```
--- Ch08TSLogins.sql---
SELECT
    Count(*) AS Logins,
    EXTRACT_TOKEN(Strings,1,'|') AS Domain,
    EXTRACT_TOKEN(Strings,0,'|') AS User,
    EXTRACT_TOKEN(Strings,13,'|') AS Source
USING EXTRACT_TOKEN(Strings,3,'|') AS Type
FROM Security
WHERE EventID=528
    AND Type='10'
GROUP BY Domain, User, Source
ORDER BY Logins DESC
--- Ch08TSLogins.sql---
```

Notes from the Underground…

Terminal Services Logins with Windows 2000

Microsoft introduced the login type 10 with Windows XP and Windows 2003 to indicate a Terminal Services login. This event, therefore, is not available in Windows 2000. Instead, Windows 2000 uses type 2, which is the same as a console login. Furthermore, Windows 2000 does not record the IP address of the remote system.

Windows 2000 does, however, record the IP address when a user disconnects from or reconnects to a session. Windows records session disconnects with event 683 and session reconnects with event 682. Although this information is by no means complete, it nevertheless might prove useful when investigating an intrusion. To list the IP addresses from Terminal Services disconnects and reconnects, use the Ch08Win2kTSConnectsDisconnects.sql query.

```
--- Ch08Win2kTSConnectsDisconnects.sql ---
SELECT
    Count(*) AS Events,
    EXTRACT_TOKEN(Strings,0,'|') AS User,
    EXTRACT_TOKEN(Strings,5,'|') AS Source,
    CASE Event
        WHEN '682' THEN 'Reconnect'
        WHEN '683' THEN 'Disconnect'
    END AS Reason
USING TO_STRING(EventID) AS Event
FROM Security
WHERE EventID=682
    OR EventID=683
GROUP BY User, Source, Reason
ORDER BY Events DESC
--- Ch08Win2kTSConnectsDisconnects.sql ---
```

Monitoring IIS

Having a Web presence is a critical business strategy for many companies, sometimes providing the only storefront for their business. However, because they are exposed to the world and their complexity often provides a large attack surface, IIS (Internet Information Server) logs are often the most obvious place to look for signs of an intrusion. Fortunately, web-based attacks usually leave enough evidence to identify the attack and help track down the attacker.

Identifying Suspicious Files

A quick and easy way to identify an attack is to check your web directories for suspicious files. A suspicious file might be an unidentified executable or a recently modified server side script. Although this query might not reveal anything suspicious, if it does turn up something this will significantly reduce your effort to identify an intrusion and is therefore a good place to start.

The query Ch08NewWebFiles.sql identifies the twenty files most recently modified or created in your web directories. Run the query with this command:

```
Logparser.exe -i:fs file:Ch08NewWebFiles.sql -rtp:-1
--- Ch08NewWebFiles.sql ---
SELECT TOP 20
    Path,

COALESCE(REPLACE_IF_NOT_NULL(TO_STRING(LastWrite,'yyyy'),'Modifie
d'),'Created') AS Action,
        COALESCE(LastWrite,CreationTime) AS TimeStamp

USING

TO_TIMESTAMP(REPLACE_IF_NOT_NULL(TO_STRING(INDEX_OF(TO_STRING(SU
B(TO_INT(CreationTime),TO_INT(LastWriteTime)),'yy'),'-
')),TO_STRING(LastWriteTime,'yyyy-MM-dd hh:mm:ss')),'yyyy-MM-dd
hh:mm:ss') As LastWrite

FROM c:\*.* /* put your path here */
ORDER BY TimeStamp DESC
```

```
--- Ch08NewWebFiles.sql ---
```

The query should output results such as this:

```
Name                                    Action   TimeStamp
--------------------------------------- -------- ----------------------
-
c:\inetpub\wwwroot\global.asa           Modified 2004-10-18 20:20:14.0
c:\inetpub\wwwroot\default.asp          Modified 2004-10-18 20:20:13.0
c:\inetpub\wwwroot\database.asp         Created  2004-10-14
13:50:58.853
c:\inetpub\wwwroot\orders.asp           Modified 2004-10-08 10:51:50.0
c:\inetpub\wwwroot\download             Modified 2004-09-24 21:27:07.0
c:\inetpub\wwwroot\about.asp            Modified 2004-09-03 11:37:52.0
```

This query is particularly interesting because it demonstrates both the weaknesses and strengths of Log Parser. Its weakness is that it does not support SQL joins or unions, making it difficult to combine data into a single column. However, its strength is that with a little creativity, it is surprisingly capable of compensating for its weaknesses.

In this case, I wanted to combine the file modification time and file creation time in a single list and sort by the time of the action taken. The value of the Action column will be either *Modified* or *Created* and the TimeStamp column will contain the date of that action. The key to accomplishing this is the LastWrite field, which consists of numerous nested functions. Here is a breakdown of how I built that field:

1. Log Parser subtracts the integer value of LastWriteTime from the integer value of CreationTime and converts the result to a string.

2. If the LastWriteTime is later than the CreationTime, then the result will be a negative timestamp, so I use the INDEX_OF function to look for a minus sign (-). I convert this value to a string so the next function can use it.

3. At this point, the value is either a zero if it found a minus sign, or null if it didn't. I use the REPLACE_IF_NOT_NULL to replace all zeros with the actual LastWriteTime, which I first have to convert to a string for use with the REPLACE_IF_NOT_NULL function.

4. Finally, I take the result and convert it back to a timestamp.

At this point, the LastWrite field contains the LastWriteTime value if that is the latest date, otherwise it will contain a null. I finish the process when defining the TimeStamp field: I use the COALESCE function to take the first non-null value of either the LastWrite or the CreationTime field. In other words, if the LastWrite field contains a null, Log Parser will instead use the value of the CreationTime. The result is the greater of the creation and modified dates in a single column.

The Action field works similar to the TimeStamp field, but in this case I use the REPLACE_IF_NOT_NULL function to convert all non-null dates to the word *Modified*. The COALESCE function then uses either this value, or if it is null, the constant *Created*. The result is a column that indicates which date we are using in that row.

Finding Modification Dates

Unfortunately, some hackers are smart enough to change file dates, which is by no means difficult to do. Fortunately, if you know that someone modified a file on your Web site and you want to determine when this happened, there is a trick you can use to narrow it down. First, you must understand something about IIS status codes.

When a user requests a file from your website, the server will send the file and record a status code of 200 in the IIS logs. The user's web browser will usually store this file in a local disk cache to speed up subsequent requests. So the second time the user requests the file, the web browser will make a quick check on the server to make sure the file has not changed. If the file has not changed since the last request, the web server will return a 304 status code. The web browser will then return the locally cached file to the user.

Now suppose that a hacker is somehow able to remotely modify files on your website. Chances are the hacker will visit the page before and after modifying the file to verify the change. This might result in a scenario such as this:

1. The hacker visits a page and IIS records a 200 entry in the website logs.
2. The hacker browses the site, looking for a file to target.
3. The hacker returns to one page, and IIS returns a 304 because is has not changed.

4. The hacker modifies the file, planting some malicious code.

5. The hacker returns to the page, and since it has changed, once again logs a 200 status code.

Therefore, by looking for a 200-304-200 combination from a single IP address, you have a good chance of identifying when the file contents changed. You can do this with Ch08IISFileModified.sql using the following command:

```
Logparser.exe file:Ch08IISFileModified.sql?Source=ex*.log
```

```
--- Ch08IISFileModified.sql ---
SELECT DISTINCT
    date,
    time,
    c-ip,
    cs-uri-stem,
    sc-status
FROM %Source%
WHERE c-ip in
    (
    SELECT DISTINCT
        c-ip
    FROM %Source%
    WHERE sc-status=304
    )
    AND
    (
        sc-status=200
        OR sc-status=304
    )
ORDER BY date,
    c-ip
--- Ch08IISFileModified.sql ---
```

Reconstructing Intrusions

When you investigate an intrusion, you usually have several goals:

- Identify the hole that let the intruder in.
- Identify the intruder for possible prosecution
- Determine the scope of the intrusion and damage assessment.

We have investigated many small intrusions where the victim is not so much interested in finding and prosecuting the intruder as they are assessing the damage and patching the holes. To accomplish any of this, it is helpful to determine exactly what the intruder did to your system. This section will help you reconstruct the intruder's actions.

Most Recently Used Lists

Many users express concern about privacy and the numerous ways that Windows tracks your actions. Fortunately, we can use this same information to track an intruder.

Many Windows applications track your most recently used files so that you can later access them quickly. Here are some examples of most recently used lists found in Windows:

- Internet Explorer's history of recently visited sites.
- The Recent Documents selection on the Start Menu.
- The My Recent Documents button in the Open File dialog box of Microsoft Office applications.
- The list of recently executed programs in the Run dialog box launched from the Start Menu.

All of this information is extremely valuable to an investigation and because there are so many different recently used lists, it is very difficult for an intruder to effectively clean all traces.

The following query, Ch08ListRegistryMRU.sql, searches the Windows Registry for any entries that either look like recently used lists or that might contain information such as last access times. Because this information can be extensive, it saves the lists to a CSV file named RegistryMRU.csv that you can easily open with Microsoft Excel.

Execute this query with the following command:

```
Logparser.exe file:Ch08ListRegistryMRU.sql
--- Ch08ListRegistryMRU.sql ---
SELECT
    Path,
    ValueName,
    Value,
    HEX_TO_ASC(Value) AS Value2
INTO RegistryMRU.csv
FROM \HKCU
WHERE  Path LIKE '%MRU%'
    OR Path LIKE '%recent%'
    OR Path LIKE '%Used%'
    OR Path LIKE '%Usage%'
    OR Path LIKE '%Time%'
    OR Path LIKE '%Date%'
    OR Path LIKE '%Last%'
    OR Path LIKE '%Updated%'
    OR Path LIKE '%History%'
    OR Path LIKE '%Accessed%'
    OR Path LIKE '%Last%'
    OR ValueName LIKE '%MRU%'
    OR ValueName LIKE '%recent%'
    OR ValueName LIKE '%Used%'
    OR ValueName LIKE '%Usage%'
    OR ValueName LIKE '%Time%'
    OR ValueName LIKE '%Date%'
    OR ValueName LIKE '%Last%'
    OR ValueName LIKE '%Updated%'
    OR ValueName LIKE '%History%'
    OR ValueName LIKE '%Accessed%'
    OR ValueName LIKE '%Last%'
ORDER BY Path, ValueName
--- Ch08ListRegistryMRU.sql ---
```

You might be surprised by the number of records returned with this query, but in an effort to be complete, you will get many unrelated results. If your results are very large, you might want to adjust the query to further constrain the data or run the results through another Log Parser query to further mine this data.

Some applications store recent file lists as shortcuts in a directory. This is the case with Windows Explorer, Internet Explorer, and Microsoft Office. To view these and other lists, execute the query Ch08FileMRU.sql with the following command:

```
Logparser.exe file:Ch08FileMRU.sql -i:fs
```

```
--- Ch08FileMRU.sql ---
SELECT
    LastWriteTime,
    CreationTime,
    Path
INTO FileMRU.csv
FROM '%SystemDrive%\documents and settings\*.*'
WHERE Path LIKE '%recent%'
    AND Path NOT LIKE '%.'
ORDER BY LastWriteTime DESC
--- Ch08FileMRU.sql ---
```

Downloading Stolen Data

Usually when someone breaks into a system, he or she has some goal in mind. It might be a malicious attempt to damage the system or to use the system as a launching pad for other attacks. Often the motivation is to steal something such as private databases, sensitive files, software, or intellectual property. Somehow, the intruder has to move this information off the system and IIS is a good way to accomplish this.

It might be a long shot, but it is worth checking the IIS logs for any large file transfers. The query Ch08TopIISDownloadBytes.sql lists all web files, along with the average, maximum, and minimum number of bytes sent to the client. Run the query with the following command:

```
Logparser.exe file:Ch08TopIISDownloadBytes.sql
```

```
--- Ch08TopIISDownloadBytes.sql ---
SELECT
    cs-uri-stem,
    Count(*) AS Hits,
    AVG(sc-bytes) AS Avg,
```

```
    Max(sc-bytes) AS Max,
    Min(sc-bytes) AS Min,
    Sum(sc-bytes) AS Total
FROM ex*.log
GROUP BY cs-uri-stem
ORDER BY cs-uri-stem
--- Ch08TopIISDownloadBytes.sql ---
```

DNS Name Cache

Many people do not realize that Windows keeps a cache of recently used DNS (Domain Name System) names. You can view this cache with the following command:

```
Ipconfig /displaydns
```

This is interesting because if the attacker resolved any DNS names, those names might still be in the cache, especially on a server that has little client traffic. The query Ch08DNSCache.sql lists all the unique DNS names in the DNS cache. Run this query with the following command:

```
ipconfig /displaydns | logparser.exe file:Ch08DNSCache.sql -
i:textline -rtp:-1
```

```
--- Ch08DNSCache.sql ---
SELECT DISTINCT
    SUBSTR(text,ADD(INDEX_OF(text,':'),2)) AS [DNS Name]
FROM stdin
WHERE text like '%record name%'
ORDER BY [DNS Name]
--- Ch08DNSCache.sql ---
```

Your results might look something like this:

```
DNS Name
---------------------------
1.0.0.127.in-addr.arpa.
m2.doubleclick.net
news.microsoft.com
ns1.msft.net
```

```
ns3.msft.net
ns5.msft.net
use1.akam.net
```

Using these results, you might be able to identify recent client DNS activity on the machine, possibly giving some indications of the attacker's motivations.

User Activity

Some attacks involve the attacker logging in with a new user account or using domain credentials to access a system. The first time any user logs in to a system interactively, Windows creates a profile for that user under the Documents and Settings directory. By looking at the creation time of those directories, you can know exactly when a user first logged in to a system.

The query Ch08NewUserProfiles.sql parses through these directories and displays them by date, starting with the most recently created directories. Run the query with this command:

```
logparser file:Ch08NewUserProfiles.sql -i:fs -recurse:0 -rtp:-1
```

```
--- Ch08NewUserProfiles.sql ---
SELECT
    Name,
    CreationTime
FROM '%SystemDrive%\Documents and Settings\*.*'
WHERE Name <> '.'
  AND Name <> '..'
ORDER BY CreationTime DESC
--- Ch08NewUserProfiles.sql ---
```

Your query output should look something like this:

```
Name               CreationTime
-----------------  ----------------------
m1.Burnett         2004-08-03 23:50:36.516
Administrator      2004-08-01 11:12:26.15
TSInternetUser     2004-07-23 19:47:05.951
LocalService       2004-07-23 19:43:05.875
NetworkService     2004-07-23 19:43:05.15
Default User       2004-07-23 09:03:52.46
All Users          2004-07-23 09:03:52.46
```

Note that in the previous query, the date for All Users is usually the Windows installation date and time. This query allows you to see when a user first logged in to a machine and potentially allows you to identify unauthorized users who have logged into a machine. Review this list to identify all users who have recently logged in to the system and pay special attention to user accounts such as TSInternetUser, which should not have a login profile if you do not use Terminal Services in application mode. Sometimes intruders use this and other accounts to gain access and avoid raising suspicion.

Notes from the Underground…

Reviewing the Event Log for Logins

If you wish to review the Event Log for logins from suspicious accounts, use the query Ch08SuspiciousAccountLogins.sql.

```
--- SuspiciousAccountLogins.sql ---
SELECT
    TimeGenerated,
    CASE Type
        WHEN '2'  THEN  'Interactive'
        WHEN '10' THEN 'RemoteInteractive'
      WHEN '11' THEN 'CachedInteractive'
      WHEN '12' THEN 'CachedRemoteInteractive'
```

Continued

```
        END AS [Login Type],
        EXTRACT_TOKEN(Strings,1,'|') AS Domain,
        EXTRACT_TOKEN(Strings,0,'|') AS User
    USING EXTRACT_TOKEN(Strings,3,'|') AS Type
    FROM Security
    WHERE EventID=528
        AND Type IN ('2'; '10'; '11'; '13')
        AND (
            User LIKE '%ASPNET%'
            OR User LIKE '%guest%'
            OR User LIKE 'helpassistant'
            OR User LIKE 'IUSR_%'
            OR User LIKE 'IWAM_%'
            OR User LIKE 'TSInternetUser'
            )
    ORDER BY TimeGenerated DESC
    --- Ch08SuspiciousAccountLogins.sql ---
```

Any logins returned from this query are suspicious and you should thoroughly investigate each one.

Managing local Administrator accounts on each machine on your network is a tedious and time-consuming task. You cannot disable these accounts, and managing these passwords is inconvenient. Consequently, many administrators use the same password or predictable passwords for these accounts. This, and the fact that these accounts provide full control over a machine, makes them an attractive target for hackers. The query Ch08LastAdminLogin.sql will report the last login time for all Administrator accounts on your network. Run the query with this command:

```
Logparser file:Ch08LastAdminLogin.sql?Domain=mydomain.net
```

```
--- Ch08LastAdminLogin.sql ---
SELECT
    ObjectPath AS Path,
    PropertyValue AS [Last Login]
FROM WINNT://%Domain%/
```

```
WHERE ObjectName='Administrator'
    AND PropertyName='LastLogin'
--- Ch08LastAdminLogin.sql ---
```

Due to the nature of Microsoft Active Directory Service Interfaces (ADSI) and the structure of this query, it will likely take several minutes to run, even more on a large network. Nevertheless, this information is extremely valuable in detecting abuse of local Administrator accounts.

Login Count

Sometimes Log Parser is useful in enhancing other tools. For example, Windows XP and 2003 come with a tool named wmic.exe for executing Windows Management Instrumentation (WMI) queries from the command line. Wmic.exe uses an SQL-like query language, but is not as robust as that provided with Log Parser. However, you can get the best of both worlds by piping the results of wmic.exe into Log Parser. The following is a command that accomplishes this:

```
Wmic.exe /locale:ms_409 netlogin GET Name, NumberOfLogons |
Logparser.exe "SELECT TO_INT(TRIM(NumberOfLogons)) AS Logins,
Name from StdIn where Logins IS NOT NULL ORDER BY Logins DESC "
-i:tsv -iSeparator:space -nSep:2 -fixedSep:off -nFields:2
```

This query takes the result of the wmic.exe command and pipes it into Log Parser. Log Parser then adds additional checking and sorting before displaying the results. Using the iSeparator, nSep and fixedSep parameters of the TSV input format, we can parse the variable output of wmic.exe into distinct fields. Log Parser reads the header line of the wmic.exe output and lets you refer to these fields by name (NumberOfLogons and Name).

This particular query displays a list of users on the system and shows how many times each user has logged in, starting with the most logins. This is useful in identifying unusual login activity from a particular account.

Services

When you re-create an attack, you do not always know the exact environment that existed at that time. For example, you might want to know which services are running to see if any of those services might have been used to compromise the system. But suppose that someone later turns off a service and there is no way to know if it was running at the time of an attack.

Although there is no way to know for sure what services were running at any point in time, we can determine if a service's startup mode changed since the time of an attack. The query Ch08ServiceStartChanged.sql searches through the services portion of the registry and lists the ten services with the most recently changed start modes.

Run this query with the following command:

```
Logparser.exe file:Ch08ServiceStartChanged.sql
```

```
--- Ch08ServiceStartChanged.sql ---
SELECT TOP 10
    KeyName,
    Startup,
    LastWriteTime
USING
    CASE Value
        WHEN '2'
        THEN 'Automatic'
        WHEN '3'
        THEN 'Manual'
        WHEN '4'
        THEN 'Disabled'
    END AS Startup
FROM HKLM\System\CurrentControlSet\Services\
WHERE ValueName='Start'
    AND Value<>'1'
ORDER BY LastWriteTime DESC
--- Ch08ServiceStartChanged.sql ---
```

Although the Registry Editor does not show dates, the registry records the last modified date for all keys. This information is extremely useful in this case because Windows stores the startup mode for each service in the registry. By checking the last write time for this value, we can determine when the startup mode for a service changed. Since this field contains a value from 1 through 4, we use the CASE statement to convert these values into readable text. Note that a value of 1 indicates that the service is a system driver, so we will disregard those in this query.

If a service is set to Disabled, but that value recently changed, we might assume that the service previously was enabled. Again, this isn't solid evidence, but it gives you a better picture of the server environment at the time of an attack.

Installed Programs

The last write time on registry keys is also useful for viewing the installation dates of recently installed applications. It is not uncommon for an intruder to install applications or tools on a target system. The query Ch08RecentSoftware.sql demonstrates how to gather this installation information. Run the query with the following command:

```
Logparser.exe file:Ch08RecentSoftware.sql
```

```
--- Ch08RecentSoftware.sql ---
SELECT TOP 10
    Value AS Product,
    LastWriteTime AS [Date Installed]
FROM
HKLM\SOFTWARE\Microsoft\Windows\CurrentVersion\Installer\UserDat
a
WHERE ValueName='DisplayName'
ORDER BY LastWriteTime DESC
--- Ch08RecentSoftware.sql ---
```

This query will list the same applications in the Add or Remove Programs Control Panel applet, but only shows the 10 most recent applications, sorted by the order in which they were installed, most recent first. Note that this query will not show programs that were installed then later uninstalled. However, some applications will leave files on the system even after uninstalling the application. In addition to the previous query, the query Ch08RecentProgramFiles.sql might also turn up programs installed by an intruder. Run the query with the following command:

```
Logparser.exe file:Ch08RecentProgramFiles.sql -i:fs -recurse:0

--- Ch08RecentProgramFiles.sql ---
SELECT
    TOP 10 Name,
    CreationTime
FROM 'C:\program files\*.*'
ORDER BY CreationTime DESC
--- Ch08RecentProgramFiles.sql ---
```

Related to installed programs is adding or removing Windows components. If you add or remove any Windows component, the Optional Components Manager goes through every component and generates an installation log, even if you did not change that particular component. Therefore, by running the query Ch08OptionalComponents.sql, we can determine precisely when a component was added or removed.

Run the query with this command:

```
Logparser.exe file:Ch08OptionalComponents.sql -i:fs -recurse:0

--- Ch08OptionalComponents.sql ---
SELECT
    Name,
    LastWriteTime
FROM c:\windows\*.*
WHERE name like '%oc%.log%'
--- Ch08OptionalComponents.sql ---
```

This query will produce results something like this:

```
Name          LastWriteTime
------------  ----------------------
medctroc.Log  2004-10-13 22:50:09.328
msgsocm.log   2004-10-13 22:50:09.203
netfxocm.log  2004-10-13 22:50:09.343
ocgen.log     2004-10-13 22:50:09.328
ocmsn.log     2004-10-13 22:50:09.984
tabletoc.log  2004-10-13 22:50:10.0
tsoc.log      2004-10-13 22:50:10.78
```

Notice how all dates and times are approximately the same, indicating that Windows updated all component logs, even if the component remained unmodified. This information further contributes to re-creating the environment at the time of the attack and recreating the intrusion.

Summary

Investigating an intrusion is a long and complex process, but by parsing through data and viewing this information from different angles, you gradually build a picture of what occurred. The key here is to summarize, sort, and slice your data enough times until key evidence emerges. As you gather information, use it to further refine your queries, but be careful to not let it blind you to other evidence that may be out there. Investigating intrusions is tedious work, but tools like Log Parser have put the odds of finding the intruder in our favor.

Solutions Fast Track

Locating Intrusions

☑ Your eyes, brains, and knowledge are the best tools for finding patterns in the chaos. Log Parser is a powerful tool you can use to help sift through the large amounts of data you've collected.

☑ Start with high-level queries that focus on unusual events. For instance, take a look at top 10 incoming or outgoing connection counts. Over time, you'll quickly know what's normal and be able to see unusual behavior.

☑ One very basic monitor you can set up is excessive failed logins on windows servers. This query is set up by filtering through EventCategory of types 2 and EventID of fewer than 541 where username is not blank.

☑ Pay special attention to any systems you have exposed to the Internet, especially if they offer any kind of remote console access. Set up queries to track logins to your terminal servers to track not only failed logins but also logins from unknown source IPs.

☑ Windows XP and 2003 will record the remote IP address of a connection to terminal service. Windows 2000, however, will not. On Windows 2000 you might find the log entry for a user disconnect or reconnect contains the IP of a remote system.

Monitoring IIS

☑ Almost every company doing business on the Internet will have a Web presence. Since you've obviously locked down your IIS server pretty well, you can set up some very quick and easy queries to monitor hostile activity against your Web servers. For example, look for newly created or recently modified files in your Web directories and

☑ Although Log Parser may not always allow you to query directly for the data you want, you might be able to use nested functions to re-order multiple fields into more useful reports.

☑ Search your IIS logs for the combination of return codes 200–304–200 from a single IP address. This method will allow you to find a malicious attacker testing his exploits against your server.

☑ When assessing the damage done by an intruder look at lists of Recently Used items that can be found stored in the Registry on a Windows system.

☑ Look at your IIS logs for large file transfers as evidence of an intruder moving data off your server.

☑ Use the Log Parser scripts provided to review information such as DNS cache, login counts, user directory creation, service modifications, and installed programs or Windows components.

Frequently Asked Questions

The following Frequently Asked Questions, answered by the authors of this book, are designed to both measure your understanding of the concepts presented in this chapter and to assist you with real-life implementation of these concepts. To have your questions about this chapter answered by the author, browse to **www.syngress.com/solutions** and click on the **"Ask the Author"** form.

Q: What sort of things should I be looking for?

A: As an admin, you've been living with your server for a while. Go with your gut feeling, and if you think anything seems wrong or out place, try to determine why. Even if it turns out to be a false positive, you will have learned more about your system and will know not to worry next time you see a similar issue or problem.

Q: What are other indicators of an intrusion?

A: Keep an eye out for mysterious files in your drive root, your System folder, or your program files folder. Review the event log using the scripts and look for inexplicable service changes, logins, or errors.

Q: Help! There are too many attacks against my server or too many errors to look at in the logs! What should I do?

A: Focus on the largest problems first. Figure out what event types are creating the most log entries and try to hit those. At the other end, look at the weird log entries that may appear only once or twice and investigate those next. The one-off events could lead to something bigger.

Q: Should I block an IP every time someone attacks my server?

A: This is up to your standards and practice. Can you really afford to manage a list of exceptions? On the other hand, if a remote site is slamming you and keeps connecting to your server, you might want to block the remote IP address on your router or firewall.

Managing Snort Alerts with Microsoft Log Parser

Solutions in this chapter:

- Gathering Snort Logs

- Building an Alerts Detail Report

- Building an Alerts Overview Report

- Managing Snort Rules

Introduction

Snort is an open source intrusion detection system (IDS) used in a wide variety of network environments. Snort is a lightweight, but extremely powerful tool for detecting malicious traffic on your network. With a flexible and robust rules definition language, Snort is capable of detecting nearly any threat that crosses your network.

However, if you use Snort, you already know that reporting is not its strength. On a busy network you might find that it records tens or hundreds of thousands of suspicious events every day. Fortunately, Log Parser is a perfect match for Snort for managing intrusion detection logs.

Building Snort IDS Reports

An intrusion detection system is only valuable if you review and act on the data it produces. Unfortunately, sometimes an IDS will produce overwhelming amounts of data that make it difficult to process. To aid in our interpretation of the data, we can use Log Parser to take snapshots of our IDS logs and present them in different easy-to-read reports. In this chapter, we will build an example IDS report using nothing more than the power of Log Parser.

Gathering Snort Logs

To process the alert data, we first need a consistent method for gathering the data. Log Parser is an excellent method for managing Snort logs because you can query the file while Snort still has the log open. Many administrators schedule scripts to regularly cycle the Snort logs, but this requires stopping the service to release the file so a script can move it. Using Log Parser, we can use checkpoints to read the most recent data from the file.

Although Snort supports several output formats that Log Parser could use, I have found the CSV format most flexible and consistent. To configure Snort to use the CSV output format, simply add the following line in the **snort.conf** file:

```
output alert_csv: alert.csv default
```

This configures Snort to create a CSV log file named alert.csv in the configured logs directory using the default output fields. By default the CSV output processor includes these fields:

- timestamp
- sig_generator
- sig_id
- sig_rev
- msg
- proto
- src
- srcport
- dst
- dstport
- ethsrc
- ethdst
- ethlen
- tcpfags
- tcpseq
- tcpack
- tcplen
- tcpwindow
- ttl
- tos
- id
- dgmlen
- iplen
- icmptype

- icmpcode

- icmpid

- icmpseq

Snort CSV logs do not include a header row, so we need a separate file to name each column. In the file download for this chapter, I have included the file AlertHeader.csv to use for this purpose. To read CSV Snort alerts, you would use a command like this:

```
logparser.exe file:alert.sql -i:csv -headerRow:off -
iHeaderFile:AlertHeader.csv -iTsFormat:mm/dd/yy-hh:mm:ss
```

Note that we specify the CSV input format, but instead of using the header row, we specify a header file using the **iHeaderFile** option. We also specify the timestamp format so Log Parser can interpret that field as an actual time stamp rather than a string.

NOTE

All of the queries in this chapter use the year in the timestamp date, which Snort does not log by default. To configure Snort to log the year, use the **–y** option when starting Snort. If your timestamps do not include the year, the queries in this chapter will return the error, "Semantic Error: argument of function TO_TIME must be a TIMESTAMP".

Building an Alerts Detail Report

In our IDS report we likely want to view summaries of the alert data such as:

- Most common alerts

- Most common source IP (Internet Protocol) addresses

- Most common target IP addresses

Using Log Parser's multiplex feature and template output format we can very easily create interactive HTML (Hypertext Markup Language) reports directly from the Snort logs.

Most Common Alerts

To begin our report, we will create HTML pages for the most common alerts. We will start with an index page showing the most common alert messages. Each line will have a link to a more detailed HTML page listing individual alerts with that message. The query for the index page is simple:

```
---Ch09Alerts-Index.sql---
SELECT DISTINCT
    sig_id,
    msg,
    Count(msg) as Alerts
INTO report\alerts.html
FROM alert.csv
GROUP BY msg, sig_id
ORDER BY Alerts DESC
---Ch09Alerts-Index.sql---
```

The key component here is the so much the query but the output template:

```
---Ch09Alerts-Index.tpl---
<LPHEADER>
    <html>
    <head>
        <meta http-equiv="Content-Type" content="text/html;
charset=windows-1252">
        <link rel="stylesheet" type="text/css" href="snort.css">
        <title>Snort Alert Messages</title>
    </head>
    <body>
    <p><h1>Snort Alerts Summary</h1><br/>
    <i>Created %SYSTEM_TIMESTAMP% </i></p>
        <table border="0" width="75%" cellspacing="2">
        <tr>
            <th><b>Signature</b></th>
            <th><b>Message</b></th>
```

```
                <th><b>Alerts</b></th>
            </tr>
</LPHEADER>
<LPBODY>
            <tr>
                <td><a href=http://www.snort.org/snort-
db/sid.html?sid=%sig_id%> %sig_id%</a></td>
                <td> %msg%</td>
                <td><a
href=alert\%sig_id%.html> %Alerts%</a></td>
            </tr>
</LPBODY>
<LPFOOTER>
        </table>
    </p>
    </body>
    </html>
</LPFOOTER>
---Ch09Alerts-Index.tpl---
```

You can run the query using the output template using this command:

```
logparser.exe file:Ch09Alerts-Index.sql -i:csv -
iHeaderFile:AlertHeader.csv -iTsFormat:mm/dd/yy-hh:mm:ss -
headerRow:off -o:tpl -tpl:Ch09Alerts-Index.tpl
```

Run this command and in a matter of seconds you should have a file named alerts.html that looks like the one shown in Figure 9.1. Note that the report lists the alerts in order, starting with the most common messages. If you click on the signature ID, it will jump to the reference page at www.snort.org. Note that the alert total is also a hyperlink, but we have not created that page yet. We now need to run another query to generate log details for each alert message.

Figure 9.1 Snort Alert Messages Summary

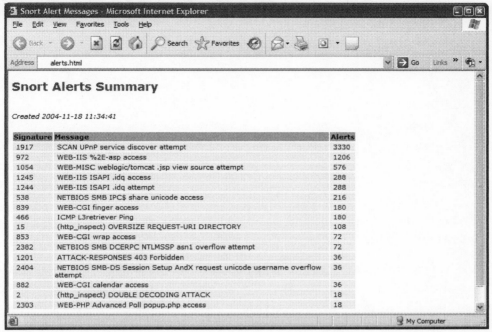

Creating a detail page for every individual message is surprisingly simple:

```
---Ch09Alerts-Detail.sql---
SELECT
    sig_id,
    TO_TIME(timestamp) AS Time,
    msg,
    proto,
    src,
    srcport,
    dst,
    dstport,
    ethsrc,
    ethdst,
    ethlen,
    tcpflags,
    tcpseq,
    tcpack,
```

```
      tcplen,
      tcpwindow,
      ttl,
      tos,
      id,
      dgmlen,
      iplen,
      icmptype,
      icmpcode,
      icmpid,
      icmpseq
INTO report\alert\*.html
FROM alert.csv
---Ch09Alerts-Detail.sql---
```

This query takes advantage of Log Parser's multiplex feature and creates a unique output file for each unique value of **sig_id**, the first field in the query. It uses this value in place of the asterisk (*) in the filename specified on the INTO clause. Since we use the signature ID in the output filename, it is easy for us to link to those files from the main alert.html page.

For the alert detail pages, I wanted use a title at the top of the page showing the particular alert message, as shown in Figure 9.2. However, you cannot use field placeholders in the LPHEADER portion of the template file. For example, if I placed **%msg%** in the LPHEADER, each page would simply have %msg% as the title.

Figure 9.2 Detailed Alert Messages

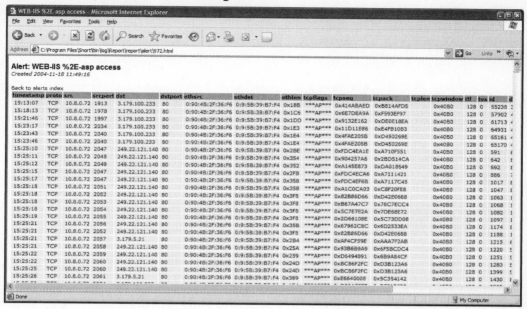

Nevertheless, sometimes a little creativity can make up for Log Parser's limitations. To write the individual titles, I actually run the query twice, once to write the headers and again to write the detail information. For the first pass I use this query and template file:

```
---Ch09Alerts-DetailHeader.sql---
SELECT DISTINCT
    sig_id,
    msg
INTO report\alert\*.html
FROM alert.csv
---Ch09Alerts-DetailHeader.sql---


---Ch09Alerts-DetailHeader.tlp---
<LPBODY>
    <html>
    <head>
    <meta http-equiv="Content-Type" content="text/html;
charset=windows-1252">
```

```
      <link rel="stylesheet" type="text/css"
href="..\snort.css">
      <title>%msg%</title>
      </head>
      <body>
      <p><b><font face="Arial" size="3">Alert:
%msg%</font></b><br/>
      <i>Created %SYSTEM_TIMESTAMP% </i></p>
      <a href=..\alerts.html>Back to alerts index</a>
</LPBODY>
---Ch09Alerts-DetailHeader.tlp---
```

Run the query with this command:

```
logparser.exe file:Ch09Alerts-DetailHeader.sql -i:csv -
iHeaderFile:AlertHeader.csv -iTsFormat:mm/dd/yy-hh:mm:ss -
headerRow:off -o:tpl -tpl:Ch09Alerts-DetailHeader.tpl
```

The query first pulls the **sig_id** and **msg** and creates a unique file for each **sig_id** and writes a header using **msg** in the LPBODY. At this point we have a set of files with nothing but a header. Next, we run another set of queries using Ch09Alerts–Detail.sql and this template:

```
---Ch09Alerts-Detail.tpl---
<LPHEADER>
                  <table border="0" width="100%"
cellspacing="2">
                  <tr>
                        <th><b>timestamp</b></th>
                        <th><b>proto</b></th>
                        <th><b>src</b></th>
                        <th><b>srcport</b></th>
                        <th><b>dst</b></th>
                        <th><b>dstport</b></th>
                        <th><b>ethsrc</b></th>
                        <th><b>ethdst</b></th>
                        <th><b>ethlen</b></th>
                        <th><b>tcpflags</b></th>
                        <th><b>tcpseq</b></th>
                        <th><b>tcpack</b></th>
```

```
                              <th><b>tcplen</b></th>
                              <th><b>tcpwindow</b></th>
                              <th><b>ttl</b></th>
                              <th><b>tos</b></th>
                              <th><b>id</b></th>
                              <th><b>dgmlen</b></th>
                              <th><b>iplen</b></th>
                              <th><b>icmptype</b></th>
                              <th><b>icmpcode</b></th>
                              <th><b>icmpid</b></th>
                              <th><b>icmpseq</b></th>
                    </tr>
</LPHEADER>
<LPBODY>

                    <tr>
                      <td> %time%</td>
                          <td> %proto%</td>
                          <td> <a
                          href=..\src\%src%.html>%src%</a></td>
                          <td> %srcport%</td>
                          <td> <a
                          href=..\dst\%dst%.html>%dst%</a></td>
                          <td> %dstport%</td>
                          <td> %ethsrc%</td>
                          <td> %ethdst%</td>
                          <td> %ethlen%</td>
                          <td> %tcpflags%</td>
                          <td> %tcpseq%</td>
                          <td> %tcpack%</td>
                          <td> %tcplen%</td>
                          <td> %tcpwindow%</td>
                          <td> %ttl%</td>
                          <td> %tos%</td>
                          <td> %id%</td>
                          <td> %dgmlen%</td>
                          <td> %iplen%</td>
                          <td> %icmptype%</td>
```

```
                    <td> %icmpcode%</td>
                    <td> %icmpid%</td>
                    <td> %icmpseq%</td>
                    </tr>
</LPBODY>
<LPFOOTER>

          </table>
     </p>
     </body>
     </html>
</LPFOOTER>
---Ch09Alerts-Detail.tp---
```

This time when we run the query, we use this command:

```
logparser.exe file:Ch09Alerts-Detail.sql -i:csv -
iHeaderFile:AlertHeader.csv -iTsFormat:mm/dd/yy-hh:mm:ss -
headerRow:off -o:tpl -tpl:Ch09Alerts-Detail.tpl -fileMode:0
```

Note that I used **–fileMode:0** in the command to instruct Log Parser to append to the files rather than overwrite them. In this pass, Log Parser will take the files already containing titles and append the alert details as shown above in Figure 9.2. The two-pass approach will obviously slow down report creation time with very large alert files, but it is still surprisingly effective for most purposes.

TIP

If you find that the two-pass approach is too slow, another option is to use Log Parser as a COM component in a script and process each output record individually.

Alerts by IP Address

Each IP address in the alerts report shown in Figure 9.2 is a clickable hyper-link that leads to a detail page showing all alerts for that IP address. Using a process similar to that used previously for the alert messages, I created a sum-mary page (Figure 9.3), and detail pages (Figure 9.4) using a two–pass approach. I repeated this process for both source and destination IP addresses to produce a fully interactive HTML IDS report. At this point, you can run the entire report with these Log Parser commands:

```
logparser.exe file:Ch09Alerts-Index.sql -i:csv -
iHeaderFile:AlertHeader.csv -iTsFormat:mm/dd/yy-hh:mm:ss -
headerRow:off -o:tpl -tpl:Ch09Alerts-Index.tpl

logparser.exe file:Ch09Alerts-DetailHeader.sql -i:csv -
iHeaderFile:AlertHeader.csv -iTsFormat:mm/dd/yy-hh:mm:ss -
headerRow:off -o:tpl -tpl:Ch09Alerts-DetailHeader.tpl

logparser.exe file:Ch09Alerts-Detail.sql -i:csv -
iHeaderFile:AlertHeader.csv -iTsFormat:mm/dd/yy-hh:mm:ss -
headerRow:off -o:tpl -tpl:Ch09Alerts-Detail.tpl -fileMode:0

logparser.exe file:Ch09SrcIP-Index.sql -i:csv -
iHeaderFile:AlertHeader.csv -iTsFormat:mm/dd/yy-hh:mm:ss -
headerRow:off -o:tpl -tpl:Ch09SrcIP-Index.tpl

logparser.exe file:Ch09SrcIP-DetailHeader.sql -i:csv -
iHeaderFile:AlertHeader.csv -iTsFormat:mm/dd/yy-hh:mm:ss -
headerRow:off -o:tpl -tpl:Ch09SrcIP-DetailHeader.tpl

logparser.exe file:Ch09SrcIP-Detail.sql -i:csv -
iHeaderFile:AlertHeader.csv -iTsFormat:mm/dd/yy-hh:mm:ss -
headerRow:off -o:tpl -tpl:Ch09SrcIP-Detail.tpl -fileMode:0

logparser.exe file:Ch09DstIP-Index.sql -i:csv -
iHeaderFile:AlertHeader.csv -iTsFormat:mm/dd/yy-hh:mm:ss -
headerRow:off -o:tpl -tpl:Ch09DstIP-Index.tpl

logparser.exe file:Ch09DstIP-DetailHeader.sql -i:csv -
iHeaderFile:AlertHeader.csv -iTsFormat:mm/dd/yy-hh:mm:ss -
headerRow:off -o:tpl -tpl:Ch09DstIP-DetailHeader.tpl

logparser.exe file:Ch09DstIP-Detail.sql -i:csv -
iHeaderFile:AlertHeader.csv -iTsFormat:mm/dd/yy-hh:mm:ss -
headerRow:off -o:tpl -tpl:Ch09DstIP-Detail.tpl -fileMode:0
```

Figure 9.3 Snort Alerts by Destination IP Address

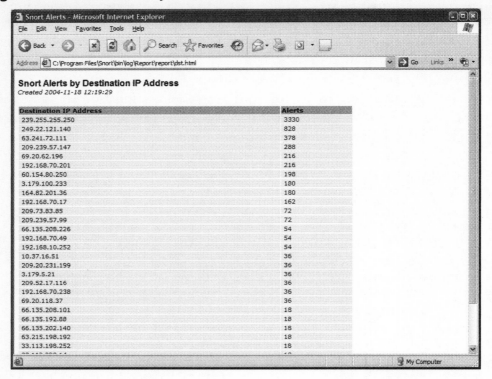

Figure 9.4 IP Address Details

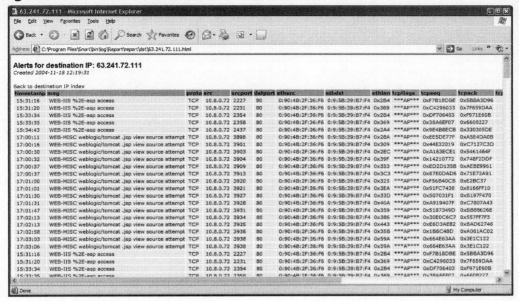

Building an Alerts Overview Report

Now that we have a detailed alerts report, we might want to build a summary index page. This page should include links to the detailed reports and also display graphs and short summaries of the data to get a quick overview of the network. Figure 9.5 shows the final report.

Figure 9.5 Snort Alerts Summary

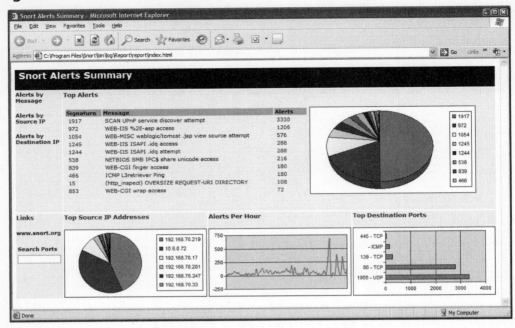

Since the summary report includes only one table of data with multiple graphs, I placed the entire HTML markup in a single template file, Ch09Summary-Index.tpl. This template creates the HTML for the report that includes references to the individual graphs. The query for the top alerts is similar to that used for the alerts index page, but only includes the top 10 records:

```
---Ch09Summary-Index.sql---
SELECT TOP 10
    sig_id,
    msg,
    Count(msg) as Alerts
INTO report\index.html
FROM alert.csv
GROUP BY msg, sig_id
ORDER BY Alerts DESC
---Ch09Summary-Index.sql---
```

The query for the pie graph is similar, but does not include the actual message and this time processes all records:

```
---Ch09Summary-GraphTopAlerts.sql---
SELECT
     sig_id,
     Count(msg) as Alerts
INTO report\AlertsTopAlerts.gif
FROM alert.csv
GROUP BY sig_id
ORDER BY Alerts DESC
---Ch09Summary-GraphTopAlerts.sql---
```

Finally, there are three queries for the remaining graphs:

```
---Ch09Summary-GraphTopSrcIPs.sql---
SELECT
     src,
     Count(msg) as Alerts
INTO report\AlertsTopSrcIPs.gif
FROM alert.csv
GROUP BY src
ORDER BY Alerts DESC
---Ch09Summary-GraphTopSrcIPs.sql---


---Ch09Summary-GraphAlertsPerHour.sql---
SELECt
     Count(*) as Alerts
USING QUANTIZE(timestamp,360) as Hour
INTO report\AlertsByHour.gif
FROM alert.csv
GROUP BY Hour
---Ch09Summary-GraphAlertsPerHour.sql---


---Ch09Summary-GraphTopDstPorts.sql---
SELECT TOP 5
     STRCAT(STRCAT(TO_STRING(dstport),' - '), proto) AS
Destination,
```

```
    Count(*) as Alerts
    USING dst as DestinationPort
INTO report\AlertsTopDstPorts.gif
FROM alert.csv
GROUP BY Destination
ORDER BY Alerts DESC
---Ch09Summary-GraphTopDstPorts.sql---
```

Finally, we can generate the entire index page with these commands:

```
logparser.exe file:Ch09Summary-Index.sql -i:csv -
iHeaderFile:AlertHeader.csv -iTsFormat:mm/dd/yy-hh:mm:ss -
headerRow:off -o:tpl -tpl:Ch09Summary-Index.tpl

logparser.exe file:Ch09Summary-GraphTopAlerts.sql -i:csv -
iHeaderFile:AlertHeader.csv -iTsFormat:mm/dd/yy-hh:mm:ss -
headerRow:off -o:chart -chartType:Pie3D -groupSize:350x190 -
values:OFF -chartTitle:"" -categories:OFF

logparser.exe file:Ch09Summary-GraphTopSrcIPs.sql -i:csv -
iHeaderFile:AlertHeader.csv -iTsFormat:mm/dd/yy-hh:mm:ss -
headerRow:off -o:chart -chartType:Pie -groupSize:300x150 -
values:OFF -chartTitle:"" -categories:OFF

logparser.exe file:Ch09Summary-GraphAlertsPerHour.sql -i:csv -
iHeaderFile:AlertHeader.csv -iTsFormat:mm/dd/yy-hh:mm:ss -
headerRow:off -o:chart -chartType:smoothline -groupSize:300x150
-values:OFF -chartTitle:"" -categories:OFF

logparser.exe file:Ch09Summary-GraphTopDstPorts.sql -i:csv -
iHeaderFile:AlertHeader.csv -iTsFormat:mm/dd/yy-hh:mm:ss -
headerRow:off -o:chart -chartType:BarStacked -groupSize:300x150
-values:OFF -chartTitle:""
```

The final result is a fully interactive IDS report using nothing more than Log Parser.

NOTE

You can create the entire report shown here using the CreateReport.cmd batch file included with the file download for this chapter.

Managing Snort Rules

Log Parser complements Snort with more than just reporting. Log Parser's powerful parsing features make it an ideal tool for managing and updating Snort rule definitions.

Snort's intrusion detection engine is nothing more than a network sniffer. The rule definitions are what give it the ability to identify attack patterns. For Snort to be most effective, you should customize the rules for your particular environment. You should also keep it up to date with the most recent rule definitions.

Snort uses dozens of rule files, each categorized by attack category. You might find it useful to combine these rules into a single file for easier management. Because Log Parser can easily read and parse all files in a directory, rule management is simple.

The following query reads all rule files in a directory and sorts them by the signature ID, removing any duplicate rules you might have:

```
---Ch09RulesBySID.sql---
SELECT DISTINCT
    TO_INT(EXTRACT_VALUE(Params, 'sid')) AS SID,
    Rule
USING
    Field1 AS Rule,
REPLACE_STR(REPLACE_CHR(SUBSTR(Rule,ADD(INDEX_OF(Rule,'('),1),LA
ST_INDEX_OF(Rule,')'))),':','='),'; ','&') AS Params,
INTO all.rules
FROM *.rules
ORDER BY SID
---Ch09RulesBySID.sql---


---Ch09RulesBySID.tpl---
<LPHEADER>
#-----------------------------------------------------------------
# Snort Rules sorted by SID
#     Generated %SYSTEM_TIMESTAMP%
# by %USERDOMAIN%\%USERNAME%
#-----------------------------------------------------------------
```

```
</LPHEADER>
<LPBODY>%Rule%
</LPBODY>
---Ch09RulesBySID.tpl---
```

Run this query with the following command:

```
logparser file:Ch09Rulesbysid.sql -i:tsv -headerRow:off -
lineFilter:-# -o:tpl -tpl:Ch09RulesBySID.tpl
```

Note in the query that I did not use SUBSTR and INDEX_OF to extract the **sid** value, but rather used the replace functions to make the parameters look like a URL (Uniform Resource Locator) query string. This allows me to use the EXTRCT_VALUE functions to easily grab any value I want from the rule. Note also that I used a template file rather than outputting directly to a file. This is so I can include a comment header but also because I want to sort by SID, but not include the value in the output. You cannot sort by a field specified in the USING clause.

Using this same technique, you might find it useful to create a rules reference page. This query reads all rule definitions and generates the HTML reference page shown in Figure 9.6:

```
---Ch09RulesRef.sql---
SELECT DISTINCT
    TO_INT(EXTRACT_VALUE(Params, 'sid')) AS SID,
        EXTRACT_VALUE(Params, 'classtype') AS Category,
        REPLACE_CHR(EXTRACT_VALUE(Params, 'msg'),'"','') AS
Message,
        Rule
USING
        Field1 AS Rule,

REPLACE_STR(REPLACE_CHR(SUBSTR(Rule,ADD(INDEX_OF(Rule,'('),1),LA
ST_INDEX_OF(Rule,')')),':','='),'; ','&') AS Params
INTO Rules.htm
FROM *.rules
ORDER BY SID
---Ch09RulesRef.sql---


---Ch09RulesRef.tpl---
```

```
<LPHEADER>
      <html>
      <head>
            <meta http-equiv="Content-Type" content="text/html;
charset=windows-1252">
            <title>Snort Rules Reference</title>
            <style>
<!--
H1 {
      font : bold 14pt Verdana, Geneva, Arial, Helvetica, sans-
serif;
      color : #4A4322;
      }
TD {
      COLOR: Black; FONT: 11px Verdana, arial, geneva,
helvetica, sans-serif;
                  border : 0px solid #EBE7D3;
                  vertical-align : top;
                  background-color : #EBE7D3;
                  }
TH {
      COLOR: Black; FONT: 11px  Verdana, arial, geneva,
helvetica, sans-serif;
      background-color : #9F9B64;
      text-align : left;
}
-->
</style>
      </head>
      <body>
      <h1>Snort Rules Reference</h1><br/>
                  <table border="0" width="75%" cellspacing="2">
                  <tr>
                        <th><b>Signature</b></th>
                        <th><b>Message</b></th>
                        <th><b>Category</b></th>
                  </tr>
```

```
</LPHEADER>
<LPBODY>
                   <tr>
                        <td><a href=http://www.snort.org/snort-
db/sid.html?sid=%SID%> %SID%</a></td>
                     <td> %Message%</td>
                     <td>%Category%</td>
                   </tr>
</LPBODY>
<LPFOOTER>
        </table>
     </p>
     </body>
     </html>
</LPFOOTER>
---Ch09RulesRef.tpl---
```

Run this query with the following command:

```
logparser file:Ch09RulesRef.sql -i:tsv -headerRow:off -
lineFilter:-# -o:tpl -tpl:Ch09RulesRef.tpl
```

Figure 9.6 Snort Rules Reference

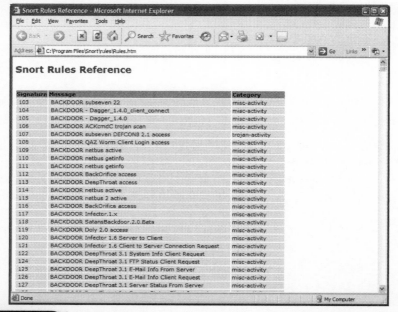

Log Parser has a powerful feature that allows you to parse files directly from a URL. You can use this feature to download new Snort rule definitions. The following command downloads the newest Bleeding Snort rules from www.bleedingsnort.com.

```
logparser "SELECT Field1 INTO bleeding.rules FROM
http://www.bleedingsnort.com/bleeding-all.rules" -i:tsv -
headerRow:off -o:tsv -headers:off
```

Of course, once you download the rules, you can merge and sort them as shown previously in this chapter.

Summary

As you can see, Log Parser is a powerful addition to Snort, both for reporting and for rules management. In very little time and using nothing more than Log Parser itself, you can create elaborate interactive HTML reports to view and drill down through thousands of IDS alerts. With Log Parser's charting features, you can view the data from different angles to help identify high priority alerts.

Index

Numbers

"5 9's," downtime and, 40
5 Ws, 145
404 status codes, 151

A

access control, 197
access rules, business partners and, 135
accountability, 197
Administrator accounts, last login time for, 297
alarms, 4
alerts, managing via Log Parser, 305–328
  alerts overview reports and, 319–322
  detailed reports and, 308–319
allowed connections, logging, 135
Apache, Web log settings and, 146
Application event logs, 146
application-level protocols, logging/capturing, 65–73, 109, 179
Arcsight, 30
argus (component of Argus), 44
Argus, session logging and, 44–52, 108
attack information, 148–152
attackers, tracking top, 160
audit standards, log file archiving and, 263
authentication, 197
availability, 197
awstats tool, 156–161

B

bandwidth monitoring, Snort and, 57–64, 108
Barnyard, 41
BASE/ACID graphics, 9
best practices, ESM deployments and, 230
blackholing traffic, 90–101, 110
Bleedingsnort.org, 91
blended threats, 12–16, 34
BPF filters, 179
Bro, 109, 178
  application-level protocols logging/capturing and, 65–73
  DNS data gathering and, 79–90
  e-mail senders/receivers, identifying via, 101–106
  memory leaking and, 74
  tracking users' Web activities and, 74–79
  traffic, blackholing to malware-infested domains, 90–101
Bro logs, creating reports from, 178–189, 190
browsers, detecting, 71–73
BSD, 178
business partners, 135, 141

C

centralized repository reporting, for ESM, 222–224
CIRT counts, 15
CIRTs (Computer Incident Response Teams), 5
code solutions
  reporting for management, 16–20
  status pages and, 20–29
commercial solutions, 30
Computer Incident Response Teams (CIRTs), 5
confidentiality, 101, 116, 197
configuring systems/devices, 198
connections
  logging allowed, 135
  Web, backdoor Snort sessions and, 43
CreateReport.cmd, 322
.csv files, 59–62, 64, 245
  configuring Snort for, 306–308
Cygwin, 142

D

daily reports, 11, 33
daily_proto.txt, 54
data integrity, 116
database servers, firewall logging and, 140
database tables, 125
databases
  Argus logging and, 45, 46–52
  firewall event data and, 118
  malware reporting and, 96
DDoS/DoS attacks, 53–57, 108
deny-by-default policies, 114

Syngress: *The Definition of a Serious Security Library*

Syn·gress (sin–gres): *noun, sing.* Freedom from risk or danger; safety. See *security*.